Managing The One-Person Business

Managing The One-Person Business

Mary Jean Parson

Dodd, Mead & Company
New York

Library of Congress Cataloging-in-Publication Data

Parson, Mary Jean.
    Managing the one-person business.

    Bibliography: p.
    Includes index.
    1. Self-employed.   I. Title.
HD8036.P37   1988   658′.022   87-20069
ISBN 0-396-08943-7
ISBN 0-396-09149-0 {PBK.}

For Liz, Garry, Harry, Pat, Chris, Priss, Alix, Muriel, Arlene, Kirk, Frances, Bob, Pat, Tharon, Irene, and Susan—all of whom run one-person businesses and all of whom shared a lot of their experiences with me to help me write this book.

Contents

Acknowledgments

This book contains a bibliography of the considerable amount of material used and adapted for the purpose of writing about the one-person business. While few, if, any of those authors focus on the one-person business, their expertise has been invaluable in the preparation of this book. I urge you to read their work. It is a giant step in the "sharing" process that we all need.

I wish to thank the one-person business owners listed on the dedication page who shared generously of their experiences and feelings regarding this most special kind of business. They are a few of the millions of us who are embarked on this adventure.

As always, I thank Bob Markel for his dedication and hard work on my behalf; and it has truly been a growing experience to work with a real professional, my editor, Cynthia Vartan.

There is one "without whom the book could not have been written"; that is, within the time limits we set ourselves. His name is Evan Sanders, a business administration major at Birmingham-Southern College who "interned" with me for a month and served as my researcher, collector, and organizer of half the chapters. He is intelligent, thorough, organized, and good-humored—all qualities that will help him as an entrepreneur, which is his goal.

All these people helped to assemble this material, which I hope you will find useful in the years to come.

Introduction

Six hundred thousand new businesses are formed in America every year, and a great number of those companies are "sole proprietorships" or "one-person businesses."

The sad truth is that nearly 90 percent of those new businesses will fail within five years (according to *Venture* magazine) from an assortment of errors: the lack of a business plan, inadequate financing, and the inability of the principal to make a "go" of the business alone, to name a few.

Looking at the bright side, however, we can assume that 10 percent, or sixty thousand new businesses succeed every year, and that is a heartening success story. Many of those businesses grow; they move out of the garage into a small shop with several more "principals" and a number of employees. Some of them move to the "big board" and become publicly held companies. The saga of Apple Computer is an example. Although statistics are hard to come by, it is safe to assume, however, that a great majority of those sixty thousand businesses remain one-person businesses.

What kind of businesses are we talking about? Doctors, lawyers, and accountants spring immediately to mind because so many of them choose to practice their profession alone. The range is as great as the imagination of the entrepreneur: writers, word processor owners, craftspeople, computer software writers, agents and representatives, truckers, suppliers of goods to vending machines, carpenters, painters, electricians, plumbers, landscape and gardening people, actors, musicians . . . the list goes on and on. As we review it and add to it, we realize that it represents the very fabric and texture of American life. In 1986 there were approximately twelve million small businesses (those employing under twenty people) and about twenty-five million Americans worked for such companies.

However, just because there are a lot of small businesses and one-person businesses does not mean that it is easy. Running such a business represents some of the greatest professional challenges simply because the person *is* alone. The idea and concept are developed alone (often "bouncing ideas" off a partner would be a welcome change); the money is raised alone; the work is done alone more often than not; the risks are taken alone and cannot be spread around; the tedious drill of office procedures are done alone and can take valuable time away from more productive activity; the blame for failure cannot be shared, and then, neither is the praise!

It seems obvious that what the risk-taking entrepreneur needs is someone to talk to. Where do you turn when you need specific advice, counsel, information? Maybe a friend will lend an ear or your lawyer will talk with you "off the clock" or your family is sympathetic most of the time to your concerns. However, unless you have a mentor or someone who has "been there," more often than not, you have to dig in several places before you find the information you need.

This book is intended to fill a lot of that gap. This can truly be your "office and home companion," because it is filled with information (gathered from many people and many sources) that the one-person business needs at some point in its development. While no book can be "all things to all people," this book can cut down on a lot of your phone calls, trips to the bookstore and library, and general frustration.

From the development of a business plan, raising the money, buying services, and information on the various forms needed, to tips on whether to incorporate, merge, or sell out, this book can save you time and energy better spent in developing your business.

Some businesses, whether start-up or ongoing, are run by one person, and some businesses will and should always be run by one person; adding more employees, expanding space, going public, taking on a partner will not necessarily enhance the business or make the founder happier. While owners of one-person businesses must be expert in *all* phases of a business and, obviously, that can be difficult, if not impossible, the right resources, the right planning, the right allocation of time and energies can make an owner successful and America richer in the process.

This book is not about cost cutting (although it will be discussed) or about time planning (although it is crucial, as you will see.) It is about satisfaction. One-person business owners may be sole proprietorships or corporations; they may be local or national in service and scope; they may work at home, in an airplane, or in a luxurious office; and they may be known or unknown by the public or media. To be successful they must create their *own* criteria for success, plan their ventures, and execute them with expediency and efficiency. Unlike the "other" world, where success is measured by tenure and salary, their satisfaction is measured by happiness, control, and profit.

It is fashionable to speak of space today as the last frontier to be explored. I disagree. I think entrepreneurship is the great frontier of twentieth and twenty-first century America. Why? Because it is limited only by the imagination of each individual, which is to say, there *are* no limits; because it offers the greatest challenge any person can ever experience: it tests your imagination, your courage, your flexibility, your endurance . . . and it tests you *alone*.

So, here's to the one-person business—the great pioneers of America's future!

Chapter 1

To Plan or Not to Plan

Congratulations. You've decided to run your own business, and you've decided to run it by yourself. You are now a "one-person business." You have lots of company, but you want to be unique. You want to be one of the *successful* 10 percent of start-up businesses.

On the other hand, you may already be running a one-person business and you just want to do better. You want to increase your personal income, improve your life-style (that condo on the coast is very appealing), be more visible in your community, build something that your child will enjoy taking over someday . . . whatever. You are doing okay, but okay is not enough. You want to be really successful . . . on your own terms. Working smarter, not harder, is what this is all about. Right? Right!

If that is the case, why are we beginning this book with a chapter about writing a plan? The answer is: to take out the surprises, for you, for your customers, for your creditors (if any), and to smooth out the bumps that occur in an always-surprising future.

A business plan helps you coordinate your company's activities. The *process* of planning is, in many ways, more important than the plan itself. It requires you to define what your company is and what it wants to be. The plan becomes a tool for managing your company's business. It becomes the guideline, the framework, against which all your business decisions will be made. It is the tool by which you will monitor your activities and measure your company's performance. Typically, you compare today to yesterday or this time last year. Successful managers measure today against the plan for today. Finally, the plan becomes a tool for communicating your company's products, services, benefits, images, goals to those interested parties with whom you must communicate. If you know who you are and what you are in business to do, others will also understand.

You write a business plan every year for yourself, not for financial

1

partners. A business plan is your tool for efficient management. It is particularly important for the one-person business because, as a sole proprietor, you have no or few other persons to help you monitor the activities of your business. The plan is your road map, your warning signal, your monitoring tool to keep you on the path of achieving your goals.

Why write a plan? The following are five good reasons:

1. *Time has become a competitor.* If your idea has competition, the time needed to cope with that competition runs out quickly. You need to have hard facts and data to make yourself competitive in the world—not as it was and not as you might like it to be, but as it is now.

2. *Technological change has speeded up so significantly in the past twenty years that "business as usual" is business doomed to failure.* Whether your venture is service oriented or a manufacturing idea, a cottage industry or an information resource, *technology* is something you must consider. Is a particular technological innovation competitive with what you do, or can you utilize it in your business? What is on the horizon that is an asset or a liability to your dream? Serious research and current knowledge of the technology that is "out there" can make a difference in the way you work and, possibly, in the way you prosper.

3. *Understanding the complexities of our environment can be the key to success or failure of the one-person business.* It can drown you or it can offer myriad opportunities for thriving businesses. Those complexities involve the political, economic, demographic, and cultural needs/aspirations of a segment of the population you wish to reach. "Gut feelings" are important and many studies show that instinct and inspiration are significant in the start-up of the one-person business. However, facts, research, statistics, interviews, on-site inspections can make the difference between success and failure. Most one-person businesses will serve a specific, targeted market. Identifying, analyzing, knowing that market and serving it with integrity can make the difference.

4. *Writing the plan helps you with your financial planning.* The financial plan is the last thing you write. Your banker, accountant, and lawyer may think this is heresy, but it is true. Only

when you have gone through the whole process of writing your plan should you commit yourself to numbers. The reasons are multifold: the analysis will alter/dictate the numbers; the exercise may lead you in other directions; the exercise may lead you to abandon your first idea and go on to another; the analysis will prepare you to answer any questions an investor may have; the analysis will make you the expert in the venture you are running and, therefore, give you a sense of confidence not easily found in other, less rigorous exercises.

5. *By writing, we remember better.* Although science cannot tell us why, we have a firmer commitment to things that are written than to things that are thought or spoken. There is something about the kinetic activity between the brain, the eye, and the hand that presses those written words more firmly in our memory than simply thinking about them or talking about them. Writing a plan seems to make it more real and to make it more a part of our persona and commitment.

What Is Your Business?

One exercise I use in my planning seminars is to ask each manager to write in three sentences—no more than 150 words—the following: "What is your business and what does it do?" It sounds like a simple assignment, but it is the most important 150 words you will ever write. (The fact that it will become the material that will go on your IRS forms, your marketing letters, your advertisements, etc., is not irrelevant, but in order to write a valid business plan, which is our concern here, the first requirement is that you know who you are and what you do.)

Test Your Assumptions

Our very existence is based on assumptions we make on a daily basis. The same is true in business. We assume something is so because we have not tested it against hard questions, new information, fresh analysis. In the four major planning phases we must ask some specific, preliminary questions.

The Planning Process:

- What business am I in?
- What business do I want to be in?

Marketing:

- Why do my customers come to me?
- Are they leaving? Do they go elsewhere?
- Who is my competition?
- What is my risk exposure. If I take an action, will it be risky?

Organization and Finance:

- Should I grow? And if so, how?
- How fast should I grow?

Long-Range Planning:

- What am I doing right? Wrong?
- Who do I listen to?

It is particularly important that a one-person business owner write the answers to these questions. The reasons are obvious: (1) You do not have other principals with whom to discuss your business (although we will speak in Chapter 9 about using other advisors in a number of ways); (2) The assumptions that you write can be tested against researched facts, which are covered in the rest of this chapter.

Quantitative and Qualitative Standards

As in all businesses, it is necessary for you to set standards by which to work as a one-person business. While a changing environment and the evolving nature of your business may compel you to readjust your quantitative standards from time to time, it is my belief that one's qualitative standards should remain fixed, to set the tone and nature of the venture.

Write them down, let them rest, then go back and review them. If you are already in business, a review of these standards every year or two is a valuable exercise. It helps you confirm what you are and who you want to be.

The exercises that follow should be done *before* you begin to write your plan. They provide the solid ground on which the structure of your business will be built. They also allow you to be honest with yourself from the very beginning; and, although it may not fit popular myths and adages, it is my belief that honesty, integrity, and credibility are the foundations upon which long-term, successful businesses are built. As a one-person business, those will be cherished designations for you in a highly competitive world.

Quantitative Standards

It is important that you address at least the following quantitative issues.

Budgets:

- Will you have one operating budget or will you plan your expenditures on the basis of individual personal budget, fixed costs, operating budget, marketing budget, cost-center/product-line/service-line budgets, variable costs such as consultants/services, etc?

Revenues:

- Will your income derive from one product or service or several?
- Is it seasonal?
- Will you start one product or service and plan to phase in others at later dates?
- Shouldn't you plan those revenues on a weekly or monthly calendar?

Customers:

- Have you identified them?
- Do you have a base already?
- Do you wish to change your customer base?
- Must you seek them out by defining and targeting them?
- Can you identify your customers by product or service, by calendar projection, by size and depth?
- Can you prove it?
- Do you have primary and secondary data or letters of commitment that assure you and others that there *are* customers?

Profits:

- Do you plan to make a living or make a profit? Both?
- Is the business to be a sole proprietorship or a corporation? The structure of your organization can determine your life-style, your taxes, your viability to investors, your investment program, your future growth.

5

Assets:

- Are they real or intangible?
- Is cash flow more important than things?
- Can ideas, reputation, productivity be quantified?

Liabilities:

- How much debt can you manage? Do not underestimate time and the unexpected.

Return On Investment (ROI):

- What is acceptable to you and your creditors?
- Can you manage life-style, advertising, production, profits within the planned ROI? (In other words, if you set say, a 20 percent ROI—pay-out in five years—will it strap your business growth, inhibit your life-style, drain your resources?)

Qualitative Standards

This exercise helps you answer the question, "Who am I?" and, more importantly, "Who or what is my company?" It will help you confirm/reconfirm that very first exercise: 150 words describing what your company *is* and what it *does*.

Image:

- How do you wish to be perceived? By your customers? By your competitors? By your suppliers? By your investors? By civic and community organizations?
- These questions go to the heart of such things as where you work, how you dress, the design and placement of your marketing, the look of your stationery, your involvement in public affairs.

Management:

- Are you perceived as a "doer" or an "airhead"?
- Are you efficient or in a harassed state?
- Do you complete work on time or offer many excuses?
- Do your customers compliment you in public and by letter?

Talent:

- Are you a leader or a follower?
- Do you innovate or capitalize on accepted ideas?
- Do you tailor your efforts for each client?
- Please understand that one perception is not necessarily better than

the others. The important thing is for *you* to define what you wish to be and then to do it as well or better than anyone else.

Community Contribution:

- Do you give to your community, in time, expertise, money, contacts, experience?
- Do you expect a return?
- Do you need community involvement for your business to grow and prosper and, if so, is it possible to participate without taking away from valuable business time?

Political/Social Influence:

- Are there things happening in the political and social environments that can affect your business?
- Are you aware and involved? Should you be?
- Are you a leader or a follower?

Planning: A Basic Function of Management

A plan that is written and filed away is not a plan. A plan is an organic tool of management, growing and changing as the environment, circumstances, and business change. It may be a road map to where you want to go; but you can miss the road if you do not monitor on a regular basis, where you are, how you got there, whether or not you are where you want to be, and where you want to go from there. Planning should become a habit, as familiar as brushing your teeth every morning.

The following pages are offered for your use, whether you are just starting out or have been in business for years. While there is no universally correct way to write a plan, each plan should be *written*, and, while each business will have its own peculiar nuances and particular emphases, *all* businesses should deal with at least the elements given here.

If you have spent several days or weeks or months working on the material from the preceding pages, you are very familiar with what your business is or what you want it to be. That work has been for your eyes only. A good portion of the following material is also for you alone. However, it will also be useful to your banker/investors, your accountant/financial analyst, your advertising/public relations agency. Moreover, it becomes the source for monitoring your progress.

There is no shortcut in planning, and there is a tedium at first, which discourages the impatient. There is no magic either. It is simply plain, hard work. However, when it becomes ingrained as a habit, when it is a generic part of your management style, you will wonder what you ever did without it.

Keep in mind that you should use simple declarative sentences. The plan should not tell too little; neither should it tell too much. Although portions of it may be used as "selling pieces," it should not be promotional fluff. It should be practical and achievable.

It is a good idea to put changes and modifications on your computer (if you have one). Monitoring and updating are easier that way.

New or Experienced Businesses

Now a word about the new business versus the ongoing business.

If you are just starting out, it is crucial that you work your way through all of the exercises in the following pages, even though not every item on every page will be relevant to your business.

I did an exercise in writing this chapter that confirmed once again that the *process* is important. I assumed I was starting several new one-person businesses: a lawn care/maintenance business, a word processing business, a telephone answering service, a public relations service, and sales of computer business software for doctors. Every item, every question on the forms made me think more deeply and more creatively about the business. In some places I wrote "N/A" (not applicable), but only after I thought about it. The thinking was valuable, because it assured me that nothing was "slipping through the cracks." I am reassured again that the process—in its entirety—is important to anyone starting a new one-person business. (Remember, you are alone, so you are talking to yourself. Talk to yourself thoroughly!)

I "bothered" some friends of mine who have been running their own one-person businesses for a while. One is an interior designer, one a computer software consultant, one a media researcher. Two operate from home, one from an office. All get out and sell themselves as well as take care of the office details. I had them go through the planning forms to see if they were useful to an ongoing business. They all said that they were.

Two things were apparent from their answers: They knew a great deal about their own businesses and the competitive environment, and the question dictated by the forms made each manager think carefully of current activity and future possibilities. They gave "N/A" as the answer to many questions, but only after they had thought about it.

Again I was assured that the process worked. Considering *all* points on a regular and ongoing basis can make a good manager a better manager and assure him or her that the business is going in a profitable direction.

New or experienced, managers need a written business plan. Let's begin.

The Business Plan

Following is a *sample* of the form your business plan will take. Some items will be longer, some shorter. The key is to use the following material as a checklist of all items you should consider.

Business Plan

Business Name: _____

Address:

Principal:

Business Definition:

Mission (What the business is):

Function (What the business does):

Economic Assumptions for 19—— (These are increase/decrease assumptions on which the following plan is based.)

Inflation Rate:

Cost of Living Increase:

Cost of Goods Increase:

Rent Increases:

Telephone:

Travel and Entertainment:

Prime Interest Rate:

Other:

OVERVIEW:

Environmental Considerations:

Economic/Trends and Business Cycles:

Cultural/Social/Changing Tastes and Markets:

Political/Regulatory and Legal Considerations:

Demographic/Age and Income Trends:

Technological Influences:

Sources of Material Supply:

Artistic/Development Potential:

Special Market Appeal/Positioning:

Other Uncontrollable Factors:

Business Considerations:

Critical Success Factors (What is critical to success or failure?):

Competitive Position (Is there competition? Where will you rank?):

Industry Trends and Developments (What is happening in your particular business?):

Your Strengths:

Your Weaknesses:

Major Opportunities:

Major Threats:

Land Required:

Building/Plant/Space Required:

Equipment Required:

BUSINESS DESCRIPTION:

Description of Product or Service:

What human need is it designed to satisfy?

Is the demand elastic or inelastic?

Is it repeatedly purchased?

Is it a "big-ticket item" or an inexpensive one?

Is it a specialty offered by none or few others?

What are the fixed costs associated with providing it?

What special training or skill is necessary to provide it?

How capital intensive is the business?

Is its success solely dependent on you?

BUSINESS STATISTICS:

Image (How do you wish to be perceived?):

Management Qualifications (Supply your qualifications to run this business):

Business History:

Date of Organization/Incorporation _____

State in Which Incorporated/Operating _____

Capitalization
   Number of Shares Authorized _____

   Number of Shares of Stock Outstanding _____

   Par Value of Stock _____

Owner(s)	Number of Shares	% of Stock Owned	Date Acquired	Capital Contribution

Capitalization Information if Sole Proprietorship:

Operating Plan (Calendar Year): Part I

Goals (Be specific. *What* do you wish to accomplish?):

Produce revenues of $_____

Produce net income of $_____

Receive $_____ in annual compensation

Develop _____ customers/clients

in _____ categories

_____

_____

_____

Secure market share of _____% in _____ categories

_____

_____

Other:

Strategies: (Identify how your goals will be achieved, by broad categories):

Product/Service (What is special, unique? Specify):

Marketing (Do you plan to use one or several methods? Specify):

Management (Are there special skills, techniques you will employ? Specify):

Finance (How will the money work as hard as you do? Specify):

Long-Range Plans (What will ensure a viable future for your business? Specify):

Some Explanations

The Action Plans form that follows will provide you with the monitoring tools you need to help you stay on your plan and achieve the goals you set for yourself on the first page of your Operating Plan.

Let's use an example.

Under Product/Service on the Operating Plan form, suppose that you wrote that your lawn care service would "provide inexpensive, personalized service to select clients on a weekly basis."

You also wrote at the top of the Operating Plan form that you would "develop twenty clients in three categories" as follows:

individual home owners	15
apartment complexes	3
commercial complexes	2

On the Action Plans form, you would write under Product/Services:

Service	Date	Objective	Budget*	Completion Date	Status**
1. Inexpensive/ Personalized	3/1	15 home owners	$_____	(Expected length of	

2. Inexpensive/ 3/1   3 apt $_____ contract)
    Personalized   complexes
3. Inexpensive/ 3/1   2 commercial $_____
    Personalized   complexes

*Cost of doing the job
**On a weekly basis you will note how many of these contracts you have consummated.

In each of the categories (Product/Service, Marketing, Management, Finance, Long-Range) you will refer to the Operating Plan and write down the strategies you have identified, the objective (goal) that should be accomplished, the budget (specific cost) associated with each strategy, and the date by which you plan to achieve the goal.

The last column (Status) on the Action Plans form should be used on a weekly basis to monitor your progress and to help you identify the work accomplished and the work yet to be done.

Your Action Plan is probably the most important form in your plan. Make a number of copies of it (leaving the Status section blank), put it in a ring binder, and use it as your monitoring tool. Every Saturday morning or every Sunday night or some time on a regular weekly basis, review it, bring it up to date, and check your progress.

Action Plans

Be specific. How will each strategy be accomplished?

Activities:	Date Assigned:	Objective to Fulfill:	Budget:	Completion Date:	Status:
1.					
2.					
3.					

4.

Marketing:

1.

2.

3.

4.

Management:

1.

2.

3.

4.

Finance:

1.

2.

3.

4.

Long-Range:

1.

2.

3.

4.

The second part of your Operating Plan is your "cue sheet." This is where you write candidly, for your eyes only. If your bank, your accountant, your creditors need to know what you plan to do if the unexpected occurs, you have thought it out. For example, if a drought were to occur and your lawn care customers canceled contracts, what would happen to your operation and what would be the financial impact? What are your alternate plans? Would you go into the replanting business? Extend contracts for extra months? What would you do?

Operating Plan: Part II

Critical Factors* (What can go wrong? Would it alter your business/plans?)

Factors	Operational Impact	Financial Impact

Alternate Plans (Can you compensate for critical change?)

Factors	Operational Change	Financial Change

*These are factors that will inhibit activities that are absolutely essential to your business.

Marketing Plan

Selling a product or service is what marketing is all about. The first priority is a good product or service (value received for value given), and what you know about your customer/client (market research) is the most important piece of information in a good marketing plan. Marketing is the way you move your products and services to your consumers.

Marketing Plan

Customer Definition:
Nature of customer (A consumer, manufacturer, distributor, wholesaler, retailer, professional, organization, participant, observor?):

How many are there? (In a region you define by area and by demographics?):

Do they favor a particular seller now? Who?:

Why do/should the customers purchase your products/services? (Unique features, performance, reliability, speed, price, contacts, etc.):

Segment of customers you identify as targets:

Competitors:

Name	Location	% Share of Market	Estimated Sales	Your Targeted Penetration

Selling

The following forms compel you to identify *how* you are going to sell your product or service.

Let's say you plan to start a word processing service in a city that has a university and many shopping areas. You have done all the preliminary study and research required in the preceding pages. You have targeted your market, located a place, calculated your operating costs and cost of equipment, evaluated your competition, and projected your revenues. On the following pages you will identify your marketing strategies for achieving your goals. The page might look like this:

Sales:	Strategies:	Budget:
#Student/faculty papers	Adv., PR, Merchandising	$_____
#Commercial flyers	Adv., Publicity	$_____

#Walk-ins	Adv.	$_____
#Professional papers	Adv., PR	$_____

Market Penetration:
Student/faculty papers (20%) —
Commercial flyers (40%) —
Walk-ins (unknown) —
Professional papers (25%) —

Market Share:

Growth:
Professional papers (Concentrate on advertising agencies) Adv. $_____

Diversification:
Use of PC desktop printing Adv., PR, Publicity, Merchandising $_____

Profit:
1 unit (price less fixed costs and product costs) $_____

10–100 units (price less fixed costs and product costs) $_____

Flyers (price less fixed costs and product costs) $_____

Marketing Objectives:	Marketing Strategies:	Budget:
(These should agree with and support your original operational planning goals.)	(This can be advertising, public relations, promotions, merchandising, publicity. Name one or more.)	$_____

Sales (Dollar volume, units, product/service lines, etc.):

Market Penetration (Saturation of market combined with competitors, etc.):

Market Share (Where you
stand among your com-
petitors):

Growth (Through new cus-
tomers or new products/
services):

Diversification (Ideas for
new or modified products/
services):

Profit (By unit or total):

Strategies/Activities

On the following four forms you will assemble very specific things
you will do to market your product or service. You will identify what
vehicle you plan to use (name of radio station or magazine or organization you will deal with); the *purpose* of the activity (to promote
sale or market penetration or whatever), *when* you will do it (all year
in the phone book or one time only in the Kiwanis annual dinner
program); and how much each activity will cost.

Remember, your *time* is money. So, if you plan to give speeches
to an organization or write a column for the local weekly paper, indicate the number of hours in the Cost column on the Public Relations form and place a value on them. Even though you cannot bill
for those hours, they should have a value so you can determine if
they are worth the time. If they improve your image, build contacts,
increase sales, then they are worth it. If they do not help your business, then consider dropping them.

Now for some definitions:

Marketing is the all-inclusive term, the umbrella, that covers all the activities you will use to sell a product or service. *Selling* is what marketing is all about.

Advertising is *news* about your product or service. You pay for it and, in doing so, control *what* is said, *where* it appears, how *often* and *who* it reaches. The Advertising Strategies form identifies at least nine places where you can advertise. There are others, but these will get you to start thinking of the most cost-effective ways for you.

Public Relations is the business of inducing the public to have an understanding of and goodwill toward a person, service, company, or product. It develops a good image and is hard to measure, but the Public Relations Strategies form will give you some ideas of the things you can do to be known and respected in your community.

Publicity is an act designed to attract public interest. More than money, it requires creative ideas, good writing, good "drum beating." *Placement* is the key. The media will cover you if your event "fits" their need and market. The Publicity Strategies form can stimulate your imagination.

Merchandising is a sales promotion activity that can cost you money, either in its design and execution or in the cost of discounting. However, it is especially effective for a new company or a new line of products or services. You may wish to use one or two ideas from the Merchandising Strategies form, not *all*.

Advertising Strategies/Activities:

Type (Be specific):	Purpose (Sales, Market Penetration, etc.):	Duration:	Cost:

1. Magazines:

2. Newspapers:

3. Telephone Directory:

4. Direct Mail:

5. Radio:

6. Television:

7. Posters/Billboards:

8. Store/Office Signage:

9. Organization Printed
   Programs:

10. Other:

Public Relations Strategies/Activities:

Type (Be specific):	Purpose (Sales, Market Penetration, etc.):	Duration:	Cost:

1. Special Events:

2. Joint Ventures:

3. Speeches:

4. Column/Comment
   Placement:

5. Interviews:

6. Teaching:

7. Lectures:

8. Contributions:

9. Other:

Publicity Strategies/Activities:

Type (Be specific):	Purpose (Sales, Market Penetration, etc.):	Duration:	Cost:

1. Press Releases:

2. Photographs:

3. Industry Statements:

4. Travel:

5. Entertainment:

6. Contests/Awards:

7. Joint Tie-ins:

8. Other:

Merchandising Strategies/Activities:

Type (Be specific):	Purpose (Sales, Market Penetration, etc.):	Duration:	Cost:

1. Novelties:

2. Discounts:

3. Couponing:

4. Two-fers:

5. Special Store
   Displays:

6. Convention/
   Meeting Displays:

7. Other:

Market Research

It is foolhardy to run a business without *some* marketing research, whether you do it yourself or hire it done. The Marketing Research Strategies form indicates some of the options you have in obtaining data that can help you define the marketplace, target your specific market, and plan where to spend your marketing dollars.

Secondary data is that information you garner from *other* sources: census data, Chamber of Commerce statistics, newspaper and broadcast sales information, City Hall buy/sell records, published surveys, etc. You can learn about specific products/services, neighborhoods, trends, etc. from material compiled by others. You can research it yourself or hire it done, but it is material you can use in verifying your market potential and should be obtained on a regular basis.

Focus groups are research exercises done by professional marketing researchers and are particularly helpful in testing image, ad copy, and product name. People representing a cross section of the potential market are assembled in a room and questioned by a professional, shown ad copy or product, and allowed to express their opinion. The owner/manager and the chief researcher watch through one-way glass, "reading" face and body language during the exercise. The final written analysis plus the experience of watching gives the owner/manager a significant amount of knowledge regarding perception of image and advertising. It is expensive, but valuable.

Interviews (personal/telephone/mail) are another research option. With the help of a professional researcher, questionnaires can be designed to answer a wide range of questions that the owner/manager may need answered. Depending on the length of the questionnaire and the extent of the sample (number of people interviewed), this research can be modest or expensive in cost. In highly competitive fields or in professions saturated by other practitioners, this form of research can be invaluable in avoiding financial risk.

Observation is a good way to do some kinds of research: counting cars at the competing drive-in; counting garbage cans at the competing restaurant; counting walk-ins at the competing copy center; counting special events staged by a competing PR person; counting yards not well done by a competing lawn care service are a few examples. Nothing beats "seeing it for yourself." Numbers on a page can never tell you everything you need to know about managing your business.

Coupon attachments/warranties are ways of assembling marketing data when you produce a product. On a discount coupon or a warranty you can attach a survey card. To file the warranty or to claim the coupon rebate or premium, the consumer must fill out certain demographic data, such as age, sex, income, etc. This helps to build a useful data base of your consumers' "profile."

Publication solicitation is a way of using advertising to get responses, which can then be surveyed by mail or telephone to obtain further information on possible customers. "Giveaways" are a good example: an ad solicits people interested in "free" information or a product. They send for it and you send it; but you also compile the names on a mailing list to use for a similar or related product or service. It is also a way to have your product sampled and to build a mailing list for future use or for sale.

Market research is research conducted to establish the extent and location of a market for your product or service. It determines whether or not your concept is viable and whether or not the dollars you plan to put into it will have a suitable return. It is the gathering of factual information regarding consumer or user preferences. It is an ongoing activity.

Market Research Strategies/Activities:

Type:	Purpose (Sales, Market Penetration, etc.):	Type:	Cost:
1. Secondary Data (Self-Compiled):			
2. Secondary Data (Hire Compiler):			
3. Focus Groups:			
4. Personal Interviews:			
5. Telephone Interviews:			
6. Mailed Interviews:			
7. Observation:			
8. Coupon Attachments/ Warranties:			
9. Publication Solicitation:			
10. Other:			

Marketing Flowchart

After you have completed the extensive planning exercises on the marketing forms, you are ready to transfer the information to at least two flowcharts.

Take two large sheets of paper and write the twelve months across the top. On the left side of the first sheet, you will write all the *Media Advertising* that you have planned, listing it by specific paper, radio station, posters, flyers, mailed announcements, or whatever you have planned to do during the course of the year. Then, under each month, write in the *Dollar Amounts* you plan to spend on each effort in each month. When you total up the monthly columns, you will know what you plan to spend on advertising in each of the coming months, and, when you run a total from left to right, you will know how much you plan to spend on advertising by category and for the year.

There are two other exercises that you can now do with these numbers. You can divide each month's totals by the total yearly expenditure and find out the *percentage* of advertising you will spend each month. More important, you can divide the amount of monthly advertising expenditures by the amount of *revenues* you take in each month, to determine how effective your advertising is. This kind of analysis can help you fine-tune your advertising over time and use that which gets the best result in a particular month or quarter.

On the second chart, you will repeat the exercise of putting the months of the year across the top and the list of advertising media on the left side. On this chart, you draw *arrows* from the name of the medium across the months in which you plan to buy it. This will give you a quick, graphic way of looking at your advertising campaigns and knowing when you plan to do them, where they overlap, how they support each other, and which is the most effective in a given month.

As the results come in, you can analyze the most effective advertising and, through monitoring, make changes during the year to maximize its effectiveness. These charts can help you do that in a rapid way.

Ledger Items For Business Expenses

Following are the minimum categories for which you should set up ledger pages to keep track of your expenses. Please check with your accountant to set up the expenses by Cost of Sales/Production, Marketing Costs, Prorated Expenses, and Administrative Costs. Those broad categories will help you *manage* your company better, not just keep track of expenses.

Business Expenses

Advertising:

Auto Rental:

Assets Purchased:

Bank Service Charges:

Business Expenses (typing, copying, safe deposit, personal appearance, skilled services, etc.):

Car License, Registration, AAA:

Dues and Memberships:

Employee Benefits (Insurance)*:

Entertainment:

Fares (plane, train, bus):

Freight/Shipping/Delivery:

Gifts (not over $25 each):

Gas, Oil, Lube:

Insurance (car/vehicle):

Insurance (home, office, work place):

Interest:

Legal and Professional Services:

Materials (for products):

Meals and Lodging out of Town:

Publications and Subscriptions:

Office Supplies and Postage:

Office Expenses (gas, electric, cleaning, repairs/maintenance, percent of mortgage interest and taxes if home/office):

Parking Fees and Tolls:

Paid to Consultants, Subcontractors, Temporary Employees, etc.:

Repairs and Maintenance (vehicles):

Repairs and Maintenance (office equipment):

Telephone:

*Medical, Dental, and Life allowable as expenses only if you are a corporation.

Financial Plan

After you have completed all the exercises we have discussed, you are ready to do your Financial Plan. If you are uncomfortable with the challenge, please refer to the books listed in the Bibliography or confer with your accountant to prepare the material. If you are going out for capitalization through bankers or investors, the Financial Plan will be a crucial part of your presentation.

There are a *minimum* number of reports you will need to prepare:

Income Statement is a Profit and Loss statement of projected revenues and expenses, done usually on a monthly basis, resulting in a profit and/or loss projection for the period covered.

Balance Sheet lists your assets, liabilities, loans and mortgages, stockholders' equity (if any), and the total "balance" of the net worth of your venture.

Cash Flow Analysis, sometimes called a "Uses of Funds Statement," projects your income and expenses on a monthly basis, in order to calculate the cash on hand at the beginning and end of each month.

Long-term Debt Statement, is a statement of loans, principal outstanding, maturity dates, terms of repayment, interest rates, lenders and collateral used for each loan.

Key Indicators Chart consists of those items that are particular to your business, including such items as contracts in hand by month and amount, fixed and controllable costs, ratio of advertising to revenue, particular market shares already obtained, etc.; that is, those items that distinguish *your* business from others.

Personal Balance Sheet should be included if your own net worth is important to the function of the business.

Lines of credit, letters of credit, credit references are necessary to assure investors of your personal viability.

Chapter 2

Do You Have the Personality to Work Alone?

All one-person business owners are entrepreneurs, although all entrepreneurs may not have one-person businesses. Webster defines the entrepreneur as: "one who organizes a business undertaking, assuming the risk for the sake of the profit."

A one-person business owner will inevitably possess the traits, desires, and characteristics common to successful entrepreneurs. In addition, they have other traits and needs that are uniquely their own. It is no wonder that the one-person business is so singular a phenomenon.

While anyone starting a business will ask the question, "Can I do it?" as a one-person business owner you must ask the harder question, "Can I do it, alone?" Moreover, do you *want* to? That drive must be perceived as something more positive and exciting than just the challenge of starting something new and succeeding in it. ("*Just the challenge*"!—as if that were a minor drive!) History's great visionaries—Magellan, Joan of Arc, Columbus, Susan B. Anthony, the astronauts—set out on singular quests, but their success was accomplished with the help of others. *Your* quest is ultimately to be made alone. Politicians refer to the desire to win as a "fire in the belly." Though a rather primitive description, it aptly describes the singular drive of an individual to succeed.

This chapter will probably provide few answers, but I hope it provides you with some definitions and some questions. I have searched a lot of current literature to discover definitions of the traits and drives that motivate successful one-person business owners. I have found none. Although we represent millions of businesses in America, there is no literature that defines our characteristics, analyzes our motivations, or specifies our values.

We must start with the common denominators—those traits we share with our brothers and sisters who are called "entrepreneurs."

Several organizations and publications deal with the needs, traits, values, and relationships of start-up business owners. They can be valuable references for advice, information, training seminars, interaction with other entrepreneurs.

American Entrepreneurs Association, 2311 Poniius Ave., Los Angeles, California 90064.

This organization has a magazine of new businesses and their success factors, extensive publications on the fundamentals of starting and running businesses, and a personality testing service for entrepreneurs.

International Center for Entrepreneurs, Inc.

The center is run by William McCrea and Gail Henrie in Indianapolis, Indiana. It offers seminars throughout the country for entrepreneurs, so that they can learn from one another by trading their dos and dont's, their successes and failures, their correct decisions and mistakes.

Venture Magazine, 805 Third Ave., New York, NY 10022.

Sponsor of the Association of Venture Founders (AVF), this magazine and organization concentrate on the successful entrepreneur (net worth of $1 million or more).

Center for Entrepreneurial Management, Inc., 29 Greene Street, New York, NY 10013.

Provides training and seminars as well as access to books on the subject.

The National Association for Female Executives, 1041 Third Ave., New York, NY 10021.

This organization has an extensive and effective network association throughout the USA, as well as a number of written and taped materials for use by the success-oriented individual. It publishes *Executive Female* magazine.

INC. Magazine, P.O. Box 51534, Boulder, Colorado 80321-1534.

While not oriented to the one-person business, this magazine has excellent material for start-up successes and a large library of specific materials of value to the small business owner.

What are the Traits of a Successful Entrepreneur?

Several magazines, associations, and universities have tested the characteristics of the successful start-up owner/manager and there is a remarkable consensus in their findings. Following is a summation of those findings; they define, at least, a *part* of the drive that motivates a one-person business owner.

1. *Goal Setting and Perserverance*. Successful persons have the ability to set clear goals and objectives that are high and challenging, while, at the same time, realistic and attainable. Concurrently, there is a commitment to long-term future projects and to working toward goals that might be quite distant in the future. Essential to success is a strong determination to get the job done at almost any cost in terms of personal sacrifice.
2. *Human Relations Ability*. Successful owners can sell. This means they have the ability to convince others to move in specific directions. This cannot be done if they do not have good relations with others. Characteristics such as cheerfulness, cooperation, and tact are all important.
3. *Communications Ability*. Verbal communications, verbal and written comprehension, and written communications abilities are strong. The ability to communicate ideas to others is vital in every business, but imperative in the small business.
4. *Competing Against Self-Imposed Standards*. Successful owners have the desire and tendency to set self-imposed standards that are high, yet realistic, and then to compete with themselves and their former achievements (not the goals and achievements of others). Since the goals of the business are set and met by the owner, the small business relies on the individual who can do both tasks. There is no one to blame for failure in a small business other than the person who wears all the hats.
5. *Dealing With Failure*. Since things rarely go right the first time in a small business, successful persons use failure as a means of gaining a better understanding of how to prevent the same thing from happening again.
6. *Self-Confidence and Belief in Self-Determination*. Successful owners have a firm belief in their ability to achieve goals that are self-determined. They also believe that success or failure is

within their personal control, rather than being determined by luck.

7. *Moderate Risk-Taking*. There is risk involved in every business enterprise. Successful owners have a predisposition to taking moderate, calculated risks that provide a challenging, reasonable chance for success.

8. *Taking Initiative and Seeking Personal Responsibilities*. There is no one in back of an entrepreneur making important decisions or determining what comes next. An important ingredient to success is to be able to fill a leadership vacuum when one exists. In addition, successful owners like situations in which their impact on problems can be measured.

9. *Drive and Energy Level*. Running one's own business is hard work. Successful owners have the ability to work long hours with less than normal sleep. Vigor, good health, and persistence are typical traits.

10. *Tolerance for Ambiguity*. Every small business has many crises that can be solved only by the owner. Successful owners have the ability to live with modest-to-high levels of uncertainty concerning job and career security and are able to work on a number of different tasks simultaneously.

11. *Thinking Ability*. Successful independent business persons have the ability for original thinking, creativity, and critical analysis of situations. Problem-solving ability is of prime importance, particularly if it can be done well under pressure.

12. *Use of Outside Resource Persons*. Successful owners have the demonstrated capacity to seek and use the opinions of others in order to take corrective action and to improve the quality of business decisions. This is an orientation that seeks to obtain expertise and assistance in the accomplishment of goals.

13. *Technical Knowledge*. It is dangerous for a person to go into a business that is unknown territory. If the person does not have the requisite knowledge, then it will be obtained through a self-study program, by working as an employee in a similar business, by obtaining a franchise, by taking in a partner or hiring an experienced consultant, contract worker, or employee. Some of the latter options are not attractive, as they put the owner at the mercy of others.

14. *Number Sense*. Business success is evaluated through a series of accounting reports. A person does not have to be an expert in

understanding these reports, but "numbers" do not frighten successful persons. Sooner or later, important decisions are based on the "numbers." The better the person is able to understand these figures, the better the decision will be.

15. *Money Sense*. Successful persons recognize that money is an important factor in running a business. They gain an early respect for money and learn how to use it.

16. *Age*. There is no "magic age" to the success of the small business owner. Generally, the successful owner is old enough to have had life experiences without having the stuffing completely knocked out. Ages thirty to thirty-five seem to be a time in life when people are willing to strike out on their own. Another significant age bracket is fifty to fifty-five when things are settled financially and a person can look around at new opportunities.

17. *Family Background*. Successful owners seem to have a family background that shows evidence of entrepreneurial endeavor on the part of the father, mother, or close family relatives.

18. *Ethnic Background*. Immigrants and children of immigrants have a higher incidence of going into business for themselves than do native-born Americans.

19. *Employment History*. People who really want to go into business for themselves have a hard time working for others. Most bosses are not as smart as they are, and the jobs seem to get dull very quickly. Paper routes or other independent work history as a child help create the self-employment spirit in people.

20. *Educational Background*. A great deal of education tends to drive the self-employment spirit underground, particularly in business schools. Education in America, except possibly in the arts, is geared to developing employees, not employers.

Are any of these traits more important than any others? All are important in the summaries and testing done by *Venture* Magazine, the American Entrepreneur Association, and others. However, the International Center for Entrepreneurs has taken these traits to create a profile of successful entrepreneurs, which may make the personality more vivid:

They work long hours and days without normal sleep. They believe they are masters of their own fate. They are builders, who are willing to put in years to develop a business. For them money is not an end unto itself. However, they realize that money in the form of profit is both a necessity and a barometer of achievement.

They are goal oriented. They know where they want to go and how to get there. They hate to waste time or to be late. They are risk takers, but not gamblers or impulsive fortune seekers. They prefer moderate and challenging risks. To them their business is not a casino.

They are not afraid of failing. Failure to them is a learning experience. They recognize when they need help and advice. They become realistic about their own shortcomings. They compete with themselves. They want to better their last performance. They do not believe that success or failure depends on fortune or luck. They believe that they control their own lives and businesses. They can live with uncertainty, confident that it won't last forever. They will straighten things out.

They capitalize on the talents of people and know how to motivate people. They are receptive to change, yet believe in "stick-to-it-iveness." They do not give up easily, but they also know when to walk away from an unproductive activity or decision. Above all, they realize that honesty is their best policy. A reputation of dishonesty or unreliability leads to disaster. Mistakes have to be admitted and dealt with openly.

What About the One-Person Business?

None of us would have any argument with any of the above designations. We know that all of them apply, in varying degrees, to the one-person business owner. While it is unlikely that *any* small business owner would possess *all* of the traits identified, it is likely that the successful entrepreneur or one-person business owner would possess a majority of these traits.

What are the elements that compel a person to embrace and utilize all of the above traits and compulsions and add to them the desire to make a successful go of it *alone?*

In an effort to discover some of that answer, I sent out a survey to over fifty one-person businesses—all of them thriving, all content to remain one-person businesses. The owners live in small and large cities; they work all over the country; they are of a variety of ages;

and they have all been in business five years or more (some of them over twenty-five years). They conduct a variety of businesses and work in a variety of ways: some at home, some at offices; some financed themselves, some sought financing; most started small and grew with their businesses. The question that interested me most, however, was: "What was the hardest problem, if any, of working alone?"

All of the answers were interesting, but the following summarize the tone of the responses:

Artist: Cash flow!!

Researcher: Inspiration; motivation usually created by group dynamics.

Craftsman: Self-discipline.

Interior Designer: Trying to do ten things at one time with a flair!!

Psychologist: Discipline; keeping up morale.

Computer Consultant: There's always too much work.

Research Consultant: Marketing myself.

Photographer: You are responsible for your life. You can't blame anyone else for screwing up. I made a choice long ago to keep this a one-person business. I like that freedom. Although one is severely limited in how much you can do and how much money you may make. My business is very personal. I like dealing on that level.

PR Consultant: To remember to seek advice when needed. For now, I prefer to manage my work, not workers.

Music Writer and Teacher: Never enough time to pursue both careers adequately.

There are themes running through these very honest replies:

- The need to be in charge
- Self-discipline
- Use of time
- Maximizing marketing dollars and time
- Personal goals and satisfaction
- Setting meaningful and productive interchange with others
- Value of personal satisfaction

While none of these themes are unknown to the entrepreneur who starts a business and is responsible for it, they are solved, more often than not, by additional staff. One-person business owners do not have that luxury (or that burden, depending on your point of view). How do you keep those "problems" under control—alone?

41

Of the seven themes, it appears that some of them are inherent traits in the individual, and some are learned skills. The inherent traits are:

- The need to be in charge
- Personal goals and satisfaction
- Value of personal satisfaction

The learned skills are:

- Self-discipline
- Use of time
- Maximizing marketing dollars and time
- Setting meaningful and productive interchange with other people

If you possess both these inherent traits and learned skills, it is likely that you have the personal and external support systems to provide the encouragement and high morale, which are so important to any entrepreneur, but doubly so for the one-person business owner.

Do You Have the Personality to Work Alone?

Only you can answer this. There are "tests" we've mentioned created to assess your own traits against those of successful entrepreneurs. You could take those, if you wish, to determine how you "stack up."

As to the demands of working alone, it seems to me that the best test is an *honest* appraisal of the traits and skills listed above as they compare with your own. Do you honestly have an inherent need to be in charge? Are your personal goals more important to you than the goals of anyone else, including family, friends, colleagues? Is your personal satisfaction, the joy of what you are doing, more important to you than money? The opinion of others? The need for constant reinforcement? If the answers are "yes," then you are probably well on your way to success, alone.

Are you willing to spend the time, energy, and money to acquire the skills and characteristics that will put you "in the lead"? (You are reading this book, so you *must* have some commitment to improvement already!) If you are willing to utilize the knowledge and abilities of others, as needed, you extend your abilities past personal boundaries; the sum, in effect, becomes much stronger than the parts.

Ultimately, your strength and success will come from within. The principal trait characterizing the typical one-person business owner is a sense of uniqueness: "one and only; sole; without like or equal; very unusual." If you know, deep in your heart, that Webster's definition of uniqueness applies to *you*, then you have already taken the giant step necessary to being the one-person business owner. Perhaps the photographer said it best: "You are responsible for your life . . . My business is very personal. I like dealing on that level."

Chapter 3

A Sole Proprietorship, Partnership, or Corporation?

What do you want to be when you grow up? Assuming that, unlike Peter Pan, you *do* want to grow up, the likely answer to the above question is, "Successful!" One of the heartiest laughs I have ever had came when one of my clients (successful in one business and about to start her second) earnestly said to me, "I only worry about two things: money and success."

After we stopped laughing, she explained to me exactly what she meant. She had her personal priorities pretty much under control; she had a good relationship with her family; she knew how to relax and have fun (everything from near professional tennis to museum visits); she was building personal equity and net worth; her professional reputation was sound. We were working together on a business plan for her new venture, trying to develop the best way to structure it. Her "worries" were quite valid and more succinctly phrased than I have ever heard them!

We decided, by the way, on a corporation, although her other business was a partnership. The decision was based on sound, hard-nosed analyses of what she planned to do, how she planned to do it, how she hoped to capitalize it, and what sort of profits she wanted to take home each month.

In this chapter we will embark on the same trip of exploration, to help you decide what you want your company to be when you reach that very heady and adult state of going into business for yourself.

You have a number of alternatives. You can be a sole proprietorship, a partnership, a corporation (either "S" or "C"). Each has advantages and disadvantages, and we will explore them in broad terms. However, this is *not* a legal book or a tax book. This chapter, properly used, should allow you to ask some tough questions of your lawyer and accountant, so that they will work together to help you form the business entity that is right for *you*.

Remember also that *nothing* is permanent. You may do business as one or more of these structures during the life of your venture.

Analyze Your Intent

As you commence the planning of your venture, as outlined in Chapter 1, you will ask hundreds and hundreds of questions regarding its potential, its internal and external strengths and weaknesses, and the precise means by which you plan to conduct your business. All of these questions should be answered to the best of your ability *before* you begin preparing budgets and financial statements, and they should be answered before you decide absolutely on the kind of structure you plan to form.

1. Do you plan to operate totally alone without any assistance from services, independent contractors, part-time or temporary help? Do you plan to hire services to do certain functions? Do you plan to engage individuals or groups to do specialized or mass work?
2. Do you have any liabilities to the public? Can you be hurt or can you hurt someone in your business? Can someone who is helping you be hurt? Can your product or service damage someone or something? Is there a possibility of a negligence claim?
3. Are you a landlord to yourself or other people?
4. Do you plan to capitalize your business yourself? Will you need loans? Investors? Venture capital? Financial credit or assistance from others? Do you need flexibility for assuring adequate cash flow?
5. Would it be helpful to be able to employ members of your family? Share the work and proceeds of the business with them? Protect them from the business now? Allow them to share in the business in the future? Allow them to prosper as the business prospers?
6. Is your business a "stand alone" venture? Are you selling only your time and expertise? Do you need tools or equipment? Must you accumulate goods in order to provide your product or service?

7. Will your income be sufficient to allow you to pay for your medical and insurance benefits, pension planning, and long-term disability out of *after* tax dollars, or do you intend that your company should carry these expenses for you?

8. Is your business to be your sole occupation or do you plan to run it *in addition* to other work? If the latter, just for a while? Always?

9. Do you have personal income that you wish to pass through into a business venture without substantial tax implications? Do you wish to loan it? Give it? Buy stock?

10. Do you want to create a situation whereby other people can join you in the business later? As partners? Working? Silent? Investors? Do you wish to run a business on someone else's money, allowing them to share in its profitability?

11. Do you plan to put up personal assets in order to start your business? Do other people plan to "stand good" for your debts with notes or assets?

12. Do you plan to perform your business duties personally or do you plan to "hire yourself" through an entity that can also hire others?

All of these questions and many more should be asked and answered thoughtfully and in detail. I suggest that you write the questions and your answers, so that you will be prepared to tell your tax and legal advisors of your wishes and intent. It is likely that you will be unable to answer all the questions immediately, but they should be asked, and you should be prepared to answer the "what ifs?". What do you want now? What do you want short-term? What opportunities would you like to allow for the future?

Categorize Your Answers

Once you have answered the above questions (and those that will be posed by your lawyer and accountant) you will have a better view of what sort of business entity you should be.

Sole Proprietorship

This is the easiest business to begin and run. You decide what you are going to do and how you are going to do it (by writing a business plan), and then you set up shop to begin. You need a name and address for the company, and you register with your state as "doing business" under that name and address. The state will send you forms to fill out, which will help you decide whether or not you have to charge sales tax, and the federal government will send you periodic forms to fill out in case you have employees.

You will buy a ledger to start your bookkeeping (your accountant will help you set up the specific details for your particular business, if it is complicated), and you will open a bank account under the name of the business; all income and expenses will flow through one account, assuring you of good records of your business transactions.

You will file your individual income tax return (1040) as well as a "Profit (or Loss) from Business or Profession (Sole Proprietorship) Schedule C 1040.

That's about it. You are in business. You have a number of advantages. Your start-up costs were minimal, and maintaining the business side of your company will be relatively inexpensive, as you have little need for legal documents, etc.; your bookkeeping is the normal minimum required in good business practice; and your income tax returns should be relatively modest (and inexpensive) to produce. You probably have no employees and will pay for services, which are deductible as business expenses, as needed.

If you operate from a room or rooms of your home, you have additional deductions as business expense up to the amount of your "net income": a portion of your rent (or mortgage interest), taxes, utilities, maintenance, repairs, cleaning, and security. If you rent a place to run your sole proprietorship, all those costs are business expenses against your income.

There are some disadvantages to the sole proprietorship. Following are some of the costs you may *not* deduct as business expenses against the income from your business: medical and dental insurance (75 percent), life insurance, long-term disability insurance, IRA, pension plan, or Simplified Employee Pension Plans (SEPs), Defined Benefits or Defined Contribution Plans. Further, you are vulnerable to negligence or liability claims to the full extent of your *own* net worth. In a sole proprietorship, you *are* your business, and any claims against your business dealings can go straight through to your personal net worth.

Does this mean that you should not be a sole proprietorship? Of course not. If you have written a careful Business Plan and know that a simple work mode is right for you, then that is the way you should run your business. Simply because you can not count the above costs as business expenses does not mean that you ignore them; you simply recognize that they must be bought with *after* tax dollars, the money you have (after you have paid your business expenses and the profit has passed through to you as earned income, on which you pay income taxes). You *know* you must have insurance, and you buy it: medical, dental (if you can get a good policy), life, disability, and any negligence or liability insurance required or available in your profession. This can be horrendously expensive, but it is a necessity in this litigious society with its high medical costs. You will also continue to contribute to your IRA.

Subchapter S Corporation

It is at this point that your lawyer will probably urge you to be a subchapter S corporation, which we will discuss in a moment. Under the new income tax laws, it is worth considering. Your lawyer will tell you that corporate taxes are now more than individual taxes, but, because an "S" corporation is treated as an individual for tax purposes, it is worth incorporating to take advantage of the best of both worlds.

Well, that is partly right. Let's explore the particulars so that *you* can make the business decisions necessary for your own security and well-being.

A subchapter S corporation is a small business corporation having no more than thirty-five shareholders and one class of stock. For income tax purposes, "S" corporations are permitted to be taxed like partnerships: corporate income or losses are credited or debited to the shareholders in proportion to their share holdings. By treating the shareholders like partners and the corporation like a partnership for tax purposes, any losses your "S" corporation incurs can immediately flow through to you, as an individual taxpayer; on a corporation return, they are carried forward, year to year, until they are finally offset by corporate profits. With the "S" corporation, you have the protection of a corporate structure for liability purposes, but the benefits of individual tax rates. You have the ability to offset personal income (from other sources) with corporate losses from your "S" corporation.

However, if the "S" corporation is intended to be your *principal* business (with the implication that you plan to make a profit!) there are other facts you need to know. As in the sole proprietorship, you *cannot* deduct as corporate business expenses, medical and dental insurance (75 percent), accident or life insurance, IRA or pension contributions, disability insurance, death benefits for other shareholders (your family, for instance), and certain meals and lodging expenses that are expensed in the C corporation.

In other words, the "S" corporation protects you from certain liabilities and negligence claims (which is not to be sneezed at) and allows you to take deductions against other *earned* income. If those things are important to you, then it is worth considering. However, it will cost you $400 to $500 to incorporate. (Do not pay more, and read the Bibliography for some "do it yourself" suggestions.) Furthermore, the bookkeeping is more detailed, thereby raising your accounting costs on an annual basis. If you are still interested, let's talk about those "tax advantages" that your lawyer (or accountant) will mention.

In 1987 the individual tax rates are as follows:

Rates	Joint Returns	Heads of Households	Singles
11%	0–$3,000	0–$2,500	0–$1,800
15%	3,000–28,000	2,500–23,000	1,800–16,800
28%	28,000–45,000	23,000–38,000	16,800–27,000
35%	45,000–90,000	38,000–80,000	27,000–54,000
38.5%	Above 90,000	Above 80,000	Above 54,000

The Corporate rate, as of July 1, 1987, is:

Taxable Income	Tax Rate
Not over $50,000	15%
$50,001–$75,000	25%
$75,001–$100,000	34%
Over $100,000	34%*

*An additional tax of 5 percent up to $11,750 is imposed on corporate taxable income over $100,000, up to $335,000. Thus, corporations with taxable income of at least $335,000 will pay a flat rate of 34 percent.

In 1988, the individual tax rate will be:

Tax Rates	Joint Returns	Heads of Household	Singles
15%	Up to $29,750	Up to $23,900	Up to $17,850
28%	Over $29,750	Over $23,900	Over $17,850
33%	Between $71,900 and $149,250	Between $61,650 and $123,790	Between $43,150 and $89,560

What do all these numbers mean when you talk to your accountant or lawyer about forming a Subchapter S corporation? They mean that it really may not be such a good idea. Remember, the losses *and* profits are passed through the "S" on a year-end basis to you as an individual, and you pay taxes as an individual. In 1987, if you made over $28,000 (on joint returns), over $23,000 (as a head of household), or over $16,800 (as a single), you would pay 28 percent in taxes of the amount in excess of those numbers. If you were an "S" corporation, that is what you would pay. If you were a "C" corporation (we will discuss that later), you would pay 15 percent in taxes up to *$50,000 taxable income* (read that "profit.") You are not much better off in 1988 and beyond. The limits on individually taxed income are $29,750, $23,900 and $17,850 respectively. It does not take a Ph.D. in mathematics to figure out that you would be just as well off as a sole proprietorship or partnership (coming up!), as far as taxes are concerned. Your advantages as an "S" corporation are the liability protections (which may be important) and the losses against other income (which may not be). Put another way, you can make up to $50,000 as a "C" corporation (with a lot more benefits, which we will discuss) and pay only 15 percent in corporate income taxes; whereas, as an "S" corporation, you will pay at the individual tax rates, which are higher, for a *lower* amount of income.

"S" corporations have the greatest advantage in the following ventures:

- Syndications and other money-raising ventures.
- Tax-shelter arrangements.
- As a tax-cutting tool for personal investments.

The income, deductions, and tax credits of the firm flow directly to the shareholders, in proportion to their stock holdings, to be claimed on their personal tax returns.

For example, business losses can be used to cut the tax on shareholder salaries, but, at the same time, shareholders have personal protection from corporate liabilities (such as lawsuits and unsecured debts).

An "S" corporation can receive most of its income from passive investments in the form of rents, dividends, and interest. This is an instance whereby an "S" corporation creates certain advantages. The tax benefits flow through to investors in much the same way as they do in a partnership, and the same shelter advantages result. However, in addition, the corporation protects all the investors from personal liability; since shareholders can be executives and managers of the firm, they can control how their money is spent; shares of stock may be much easier to sell or transfer if the investor wants to get out.

Because most businesses incur tax losses during their start-up phase, entrepreneurs can attract investors by starting up a new business in the "S" corporation form. The flow-through of losses will cut the after-tax cost of the investment. The amount of losses a shareholder can claim is generally limited to the amount paid for the stock plus the amount of any loans he or she has made to the company. Excess loans can be carried forward and deducted from the company's future income. A company that expects to lose money can elect "S" corporation status to pass its losses through to its owners. It can then return/turn to "C" corporation status when it returns/gains profitability. There are restrictions to electing "C" to "S" or "S" to "C," and, as in all these broad guidelines, you should consult with legal and tax experts for the best move for you.

Partnership

It may seem peculiar to discuss partnerships in a book about one-person businesses. Isn't that a contradiction in terms? Well, no. There are partnerships in which one person *is* the business, and that is what we will talk about. Briefly, the advantages of a partnership are that they take very little legal work to be formed; they require a nonelaborate accounting system, a modest amount of tax filing, and, if the partnership papers are drawn well, can be dissolved without a great deal of cost and fanfare.

The disadvantages are that each partner is liable for the promises and debts of the other, as they relate to the company; there are severe limitations on the "benefits" that you can count as company expenses, and your profits will be taxed at your individual tax rates (which we have seen may be higher than corporate rates).

Should you consider a partnership? Of course. What kind?

The most obvious situation is where one partner supplies the money and the other supplies the expertise. This could be 50/50, 80/20 or any other variation. The guideline is to have *everything* worked out in advance and written up in the partnership papers, which you should at least review with a lawyer even if you choose to do the detail work yourself. Those papers specify the names, duties, obligations, and shares of the partners, thereby allowing you to be very specific about the intentions of the business.

Perhaps you want to go into the lawn maintenance business. There is certain equipment you will need, and there are operating expenses, such as office/shop space, advertising, telephones, contract laborers, supplies, and operating money for the first six months. Mom has some money and believes in you. She can give you the money (up to $10,000 tax free), she can lend you the money (at the rate comparable to the bank's), or she can go into business with you as a silent partner, sharing in the profits in an agreed-upon fashion. Perhaps she puts up $10,000 as her partner's share and you put up your time, skill, and labor. (This will be spelled out in your Partnership Agreement.) Your Business Plan will identify capital costs and operating costs. (Your plan might even be an attachment to the partnership papers.) You do the work, run the business, pay the expenses. At regular periods, (monthly, quarterly) you pay out profits, retaining some funds in the partnership account for operating costs. You may split the profits 50/50 or in some other combination. If you work hard and your one-person operation is a success, both you and your partner will make money on the value each of you has invested.

Perhaps you have made a nice income on other transactions: the sale of your residence, the sale of stock, whatever. You want to start a business with that profit and want to pass it through (without a high-tax implication). You form a partnership with your spouse, who will perform certain limited duties (bookkeeping, office organization and maintenance, supervising the advertising, for example). You *loan* the partnership the profit you made in the other transaction, and you begin your business. All normal business expenses are paid out of the partnership income and you retain some money in the account for future operating costs. Your spouse has also invested in the partnership (say, 5 percent) and, at periodic times, you pay a management fee to each of you of, say, 95/5. You have set aside high capital gains tax and started your own business; your spouse has made a modest investment of money and time; and you both can enjoy the fruits of *your* labor.

Perhaps you know someone who has invented a new product or holds a patent or has "concepted" a new service. You know it has all the makings of a success, but the creator/inventor has neither the time nor the expertise to make it work. You form a partnership. Your partner contributes the idea and you contribute the work. Perhaps you both contribute money in agreed-upon proportions. Perhaps you loan the business money. Perhaps you raise it in other ways. (See Chapter 4.) Your Partnership Agreement delineates what you *give*, what you *do*, and how you *profit*.

These examples should serve to make clear that a one-person business *can* be a partnership. To repeat, you need detailed partnership papers (do not pay more than $300 to 400 if you use a lawyer) filed in your state, as well as the usual "doing business" papers. You need good accounting records (an accountant could help you set it up for $200 to $400 with no more than a $50 monthly fee, including tax filings) and you will file two tax returns: the individual income tax return (1040) and Form 1065.

As long as you realize that you will have to buy all of your "benefits" (insurance, pensions, etc.) with *after*-tax dollars (the partnership cannot pay for them) and that your liabilities (should something go wrong with the product/service as relates to customers, creditors, etc.) are not protected by the so-called "corporate shield," then the partnership form is a relatively inexpensive way to run your business.

The "C" Corporation

The so-called "C" corporation is the standard corporation entity used by thousands of companies. It can have unlimited numbers of shareholders, must have a board of directors, files a number of complex state and federal tax returns, and exists as a total legal entity.

If this writer has a bias, it is for the "C" corporation, particularly if you wish to protect your personal worth from corporate liabilities *and* if you wish your insurance and benefits to be paid out of pretax (corporate expense) dollars. The list of advantages is well-known:

- Limited liability
- Ease in doing business from one corporation to another
- Lower taxes (if your corporate profit is under $50,000 annually)
- Tax-free (or nearly) dividends
- Deferred compensation
- Pension benefits (better than a $2,000 IRA)
- Medical and insurance fringe benefits

The *disadvantages,* which will be detailed by your legal and tax advisors, are more paper work, a more expensive formation cost (between $500 and $1,000), and more expensive accounting costs because of the requirement of more filing forms.

If you are operating on a shoestring, have no fears of any liabilities. If you are willing to buy your insurance and benefits with after-tax dollars, then you may be willing to forego some of the advantages to save money.

However, when you have concluded the planning process, the marketing analysis, and the capitalization exercises in this book, you will be well aware of whether or not a $1,000+ legal cost and an accounting charge of $500 to $1,500 a year compensate for the other financial advantages that a "C" corporation may offer you. We will do some comparative exercises later in this chapter that will allow you to evaluate the pros and cons of the several forms that you may choose. In the meantime, let's identify some of the details, such as the Board of Directors and board meetings, which you will wish to discuss with your advisors.

Board Meetings and Minutes

Don't neglect all the formalities of board meetings, even though they seem to be useless ceremonies, especially when the company is owned by a few people (who may be your investors) who see each other regularly. It is possible to keep the formalities to a minimum, but they should not be eliminated entirely.

If the corporation does not "act like one," creditors could claim that it is really a partnership in disguise, and push to hold the owners personally liable for the debts of the corporation. Directors could be personally liable for unpaid wages in certain cases and for failure to withhold taxes and could pay them to the IRS. There could be personal liabilities under OSHA and the Employee Retirement Income Security Act.

Know the laws of your state! In some states, board meetings can be conducted by telephone, if the directors can hear and talk to each other. In some states a "close corporation" may dispense with boards and board meetings and the stockholders may manage the business directly. Even here, careful records must be kept to preserve the protection that is afforded by the corporate entity.

Have a formal stockholder meeting at least once a year, with proper notice (or waiver of notice) to elect directors. Have the proper documentation of meeting notice or a waiver, minutes, and (if necessary) proxies. Stockholders can also act by majority written consent in some states. Again, the action should be documented.

The board should meet regularly with the proper notice or waiver, probably at least four times a year. At one meeting, have directors formally nominate and elect officers of the company.

Keep the minutes of board meetings. Record time and place, who was present, noting a quorum. Be aware that directors cannot use proxies, and usually cannot vote or be counted for quorum, unless physically present.

The minutes should briefly state that there was a discussion of the business of the corporation and results of the last quarter of the operation were reviewed. This indicates that the directors know what the officers are doing. Be sure to mention major happenings, fires, strikes, lawsuits, etc. Avoid forecasts in the minutes.

The Board of Directors

As the chief executive and major owner of the company, you will wish to retain title as Chairman of the Board and/or President. Your other major investors will expect to be on the Board, and some of them may wish to be officers. President, Vice-President, Secretary-Treasurer are the usual minimum number of officers. It is not necessary to make a board member an officer, but it is unusual to have an "outsider" (a nonemployee or a nonstockholder) as an officer. Your bylaws can make provision for whatever you think is best for your company. (With a small ownership, you may wish to make your accountant your treasurer and your lawyer your secretary, but *know* what kind of opinions and personalities you are "buying into" before you invite them to be on the Board! Perhaps sell or award them shares in the company to make them eligible.)

Keep the Board in odd numbers: three, five, seven; do not make it large and unwieldy. Use the Board as an opportunity to get good advisors and supporters from outside: your financial advisor, a good marketing cohort, etc. Outside Board members (nonemployees, nonstockholders) reassure bankers, investors, and customers that broad interests are being addressed. A good rule of thumb is to keep outsiders to one-third the total makeup of the Board. You can opt to pay a board fee and/or travel allowance for board meetings, if it will assure the participation and interest of those present. Obviously, putting family members on your board is also a way of assuring that your family knows what is going on and takes an active interest (financial and otherwise) in your venture. If they are shareholders also, they share in the profits (by board fee, dividends, or as fee or salary for consultants or as employees).

Whether you give them the stock (the gift limitation is $10,000 annually, tax-free) or they buy into the company, there are two good reasons why it may be desirable for family members to acquire their stock directly from the corporation as soon as the corporation is set up:

1. The stock will be cheaper at that time than later, assuming that the company succeeds.
2. The rules governing corporate redemptions (sales of shares) are less restrictive when the stock is acquired directly from the corporation, rather than by a transfer from the family head or other family member.

The Corporation as Tax Shelter

The ability of family members to buy stock at par value in the early life of your corporation allows you to include them in the company you are building and to share in its profitability (at their lower tax rates, presumably). You and your spouse *can* file separate tax returns, if there is a financial advantage, and your children (over age 14) will be taxed on unearned income at their own rate. Consult with your tax advisor for details and nuances.

Leasing assets to your corportion is another way to shelter certain income. The assets may be owned by: (1) an individual shareholder or some member of his or her family; (2) a partnership, limited or general, in which family members participate; or (3) a trust for the benefit of family members. Again, consult your legal advisor.

In addition to the medical insurance that your corporation will carry on you, you can also count as business expense the cost of medical expenses *not* covered by the insurance. (If you ever have full time employees, you would need to provide them with the same coverage. As long as you are a one-person business, the advantage is all yours.)

Your corporation is allowed to accumulate earnings of $150,000 if its principal function, according to the IRS, is "services in the field of law, health, engineering, architecture, accounting, actuarial science, performing arts, or consulting"; earnings of $250,000 if it escapes that "service corporation" classification. Over these amounts, if you do not conform to IRS guidelines, you may receive punitive taxes for cash held "greatly in excess of its reasonable business needs." What does this mean?

It means that with careful planning, you can receive *dividends almost tax free*. It means that the "retained earnings" of your corporation (held within reasonable limits, please) can be invested in stocks, bonds, and other investment instruments, so that they *earn* money while you retain them for the future welfare of your company. Eighty percent of the dividends you receive from such investment is excluded from taxation, as long as the amount does not exceed 80 percent of your corporation's taxable income (computed with certain modifications). The law is a bit more complex than this may seem, but the principal is clear. A corporation can earn dividends from its investments in other corporations at considerably less taxation than you as an individual would pay for the same investment.

While the following list is by no means to be construed as an absolute definition of the guidelines for retained earnings, it offers some insights (and some questions you should ask of your tax advisor) as to how much and why you should retain some of your profits for the future:

- To provide for bona fide expansion of business or replacement of plant.
- To acquire another business enterprise through purchasing stock or assets.

- To provide for the retirement of bona fide indebtedness created in connection with the trade or business (such as the establishment of a sinking fund for the purpose of retiring bonds issued by the corporation in accordance with contract obligations incurred on issue.
- To provide necesary working capital for the business, such as for the procurement of inventories.
- To provide for investments or loans to suppliers or customers, if necessary to maintain the business of the corporation.

There are stringent rules prohibiting the unreasonable accumulation of earnings and profits, which you can read about in some of the books recommended in the Bibliography. The point is that you can *keep* a reasonable amount of your profit (income not distributed as salaries and dividends), invest it in high-yielding instruments, pay the corporate tax rate on it (15 percent if it is under $50,000 annually), and keep 80 percent of the profit on your investment if the total kept is no more than 80 percent of your total net profit. That is a pretty good deal for a small corporation, and one that tells us that the tax system favors our labors.

Controlling Taxation—Yours and Your Corporation's

Remember, you as an individual pay taxes on your salary, your bonus, and your dividends from your corporation. Your corporation can receive a write-off for your salary and your bonus, but not your dividends. Therefore, you stand to benefit from both tax considerations if you consistently pay yourself a modest salary, say $40,000 or so, and give yourself a bonus, if your corporation has been particularly successful in a given year. Bonuses need not be consistent from year to year, as your profitability is not necessarily consistent. *You* pay your individual tax rate for the salary and bonus, but both are corporate expense write-offs with your corporation, reducing (with planning) your corporate taxes for the year, and thereby reducing your total tax bill.

One further note: Be sure that your corporate pension and profit-sharing plans use total compensation, which is salary + bonus, as a base, rather than straight salary, so that you can further reduce your corporate tax liability by your pension contribution from the corporation; this, of course, while building your own retirement funds.

Now a word about those pension plans that you can pay for with corporate funds:

1. *Defined Benefit Plan.* Be sure you use a good lawyer with good actuarial tables. You must state when you want to retire and how much money you need to retire with, and you need to work out a formula that will allow you to allocate that amount of money each year from your corporate earnings to invest (shelter) in your retirement fund.
2. *Defined Contribution Plan.* In your original pension plan documents you may specify the minimum contribution you plan to make each year. The amount can vary from year to year, depending on how good business is, as long as it does not go below the minimum. Have your lawyer help you set it up when you prepare your incorporation papers.
3. *Simplified Employee Pension Plan (SEP).* These are very easy to establish. You can do it with your lawyer and a brokerage house, or a mutual fund, for that matter, with no fees and transfer costs. The new tax rules sound complicated, but they have a relatively simple definition, if you remember the phase-out rules. (Phased-out pro rata between $25,000 and $35,000 of adjusted gross income for a single taxpayer, between $40,000 and $50,000 of adjusted gross income for married taxpayers filing a joint return, and between zero and $10,000 of adjusted gross income for a married taxpayer filing a separate return.) As an employee of your corporation, you may make contributions to a SEP based on the above rules to a total of $30,000; up to $7,000 of that may be considered "elective contributions," which you will count as a part of your personal income and pay individual taxes on accordingly), and up to $23,000 can be contributed by your corporation and can be deducted from your corporation's income as a business expense. Obviously, this is worth looking into with your tax advisor as a way to prepare for your future, if your corporation is extremely successful or if you are over forty-five and planning your retirement seriously.
4. *IRA.* Under the new rules, an *employee* may make deductible IRA (Individual Retirement Account) contributions to a SEP in addition to what the employer may contribute (or to a separate IRA with its $2,000 a year limitation), subject to the phase-out

rules listed above. As your own employer, this means you can have both an IRA and a SEP, as long as your elective contributions do not exceed $7,000 and the phase-out guidelines. However, for all practical purposes, there is probably no need for you to have both. If your corporate profits are not such that the SEP is a viable instrument for you in a given year, you are urged to continue your contributions to your IRA; that way, you shelter your *personal* income with a $2,000 deduction and have the advantage of tax-free earnings until the age of 59½ (or beyond).

Benefits Planning

As a one-person business, you will find the cost of insurance extremely high, because, for reasons which will become less justifiable in the coming years, insurance carriers base their rates on "group" coverage, rather than on the individual, even though the individual may be a better risk. It is of little comfort to you to know that the cost is deductible as a business expense, thereby reducing your corporate tax liability; you have paid out the money and it is more than it would be if you worked in a large company. For the time being, your only solution is to try to join organizations and associations that offer group rates.

Fortunately, groups such as AARP (American Association of Retired Persons) have some clout in automobile, household, and hospital coverage, but you must search out associations that can command reduced rates in other required areas. I belong to a professional organization that has acquired group rates for long-term disability, which is one of the benefits that is most important for the one-person business; an insurance agent was able to enroll me in a semiprofessional society that commands group rates for major medical and dental insurance, which is another deductible if you are a corporation; AAA (Automobile Association of America) provided very good automobile insurance because of my driving record; and I shopped for liability, life insurance, and office equipment coverage.

It's a bore. The insurance world is not attuned to the one-person business . . . yet. We must be covered, so we must pay the piper. However, we have to shop for the best piper.

Now a word about life insurance. Buy it from an agent or broker who can sell from a number of companies, not just one or two, and be sure that you get three or four competing bids for the same coverage before you buy. Agents make money based on the type and how much insurance they sell. Their objectives are not the same as yours. Protect your own.

Ask these questions:

1. Who am I buying insurance for? My family? My children under age 21? My stockholders? Investors?
2. How much insurance do I really need? Do I need to pay for a million dollar policy? Could I add on later without penalty?
3. What period of time do I wish to insure? Can I buy increments? Will my age or health or location greatly affect additional cost at a later time?

As a general rule, it is better to buy *pure* insurance, rather than use insurance policies as a part of your financial planning. The exception would be if you wished to build cash value on which to borrow later. But, remember. That is a lengthy process, with cash values accumulating in the later years of a policy's life. Also, *you* can generally get a higher yield on your money than is possible in a cash-value-accumulating life insurance policy. You should consider "term insurance" instead of "whole life." It is cheaper, and it is pure insurance. Also, it allows you to add on coverage, usually more easily.

Whether you are a sole proprietorship, a partnership, or a corporation, you must analyze whom you wish to protect with life insurance.

If you have loans outstanding, (mortgages, lines of credit, etc.), you will want to carry enough life insurance to pay off those debts and indicate so in your will. Your family or cosigners should not be left with debts in case of your sudden death.

If you *are* your business, with no investors, partners, or stockholders, then you will want to protect your clients, customers, heirs, and estate from the loss of your presence and services. The amount of insurance you carry should cover your contribution to your family's welfare for a specified number of years and the reasonable costs of winding down your affairs, including any outstanding obligations to clients/customers and to suppliers.

If you are a corporation, there are two ways of looking at your company in case of your death: (1) Do you and your shareholders intend that your family or a member of your family will take over

61

the company in the event of your death? or (2) Do your shareholders want to make your family "whole" and hire management to run the company when you die?

If the first option is your intent, then your will should leave your shares, presumably a majority, to the person or persons who will assume control, and you should consider some life insurance (so-called "key man") going to the corporation to cover the reasonable costs of a transition at your death.

If you want the second scenario, the preplanning is a little different. Your attorney will help you work out a "buy-sell" agreement with your shareholders, whereby you *predetermine* the formula for evaluating your business in the event of your death. You can agree to have the business appraised by two appraisers, with arbitration setting the final figure; you can agree on a set sum in advance; you can agree on a price that will rise or fall with the Consumer Price Index, some arbitrary percentage, or an amount proportionate to net asset value, value of in-house contracts, or some other criteria. The point is that you decide *in advance* and have the agreement drawn early. Then you may agree to buy insurance to cover that amount, the coverage fluctuating year to year, based on a regular appraisal of your agreement, so that your heirs are the beneficiaries of the insurance and your shareholders acquire your stock in proportion to their ownership.

If it sounds complicated, it need not be. Remember, it will be a lot more complicated if you don't decide what will happen. Nobody needs or appreciates that kind of unnecessary problem.

The need for disability insurance should be obvious. You lose income and your company loses your services. There are some helpful ways in reducing the high cost of such insurance.

An option is for your company to buy a disability policy, with the benefits payable to the company itself for loss of services if you, the executive, are unable to work. Then the company pays the benefits to you. The premiums are not deductible; thus, the insurance payments received by the company are not taxable income, but the benefits paid to you, the executive, are a deductible expense by your company.

On an individual disability income policy, as opposed to a group policy, consider the following guidelines:

- Take the longest waiting period (before payments start) to get the lowest premium, maximum protection per dollar.
- Be sure the policy is guaranteed renewable to age sixty-five.
- Look for a provision to buy additional protection without another physical exam, if necessary for inflation protection.
- Remember that insurance payments are tax free. Buy only enough insurance to match *after*-tax income.
- Check the fine print as to what happens if disability is partial or if you are able to do some work but not in your present field of activity. The policy should waive premiums during disability.

Closely Held Corporation as a Tax Trap

If a closely held corporation (one to six persons) receives 60 percent or more of its income from nonoperating sources, such as investment, personal service income (e.g., personal consulting fees), or rent, any undistributed income may be subjected to the 50 percent holding company tax. This applies if, at any time in the last half of its taxable year, more than 50 percent of the stock is directly or indirectly owned by or for five or less individuals.

If it is likely that your company's income would be scrutinized as a personal holding company (the above guidelines), then keep your ownership at six individuals. If a shareholder dies, make sure that some of his or her shares are purchased by some unrelated party; increase the number of shareholders from five promptly; or, increase your operating income to above 40 percent.

Annuities

Tax-sheltered annuities are investments you can make with your pension or retirement-planning money. The Tax Reform Act of 1986 tightened the rules for employer contributions plans to the degree that such plans must not discriminate in favor of highly compensated employees or for a more than 50 percent shareholder-employee. Since you will be your major shareholder and your only employee (at least for the foreseeable future), the rules will not affect you, until you decide to change and enlarge your business by hiring other employees.

Annuities may be purchased by individuals as well as by corporations for their employees; so, whether you are a sole proprietorship, a partnership, or a "C" or "S" corporation, you should investigate them as a part of your tax sheltering and retirement planning.

Annuities are generally sponsored by insurance companies and come in two varieties: "fixed" and "variable." Usually, you make a lump sum payment of ($5,000 to $10,000) and the money draws interest for a specified time (generally not less than seven years or at some predetermined retirement age).

The fixed annuity draws a guaranteed rate of interest for a period of months and sometimes up to five years. Then the rate can change, either up or down, but never below a contract rate, which is usually 3.5 percent.

Variable annuities are more like mutual funds, where you can switch your investment between stocks, bonds, and money market securities. While they are riskier, they have also performed well over the last few years. The interest accrues on a tax-free basis and no tax is due until withdrawals equal the full original investment. If the investment is well handled by the carrier, the interest accumulated can equal or exceed the amount drawn down in current monthly payments, postponing tax payments for a long time.

Some annuities allow you to make periodic payments (monthly or yearly), which is why they are attractive considerations for your retirement planning.

Comparison of Business Organizations

Let's run a modest comparison of some of the things we have discussed regarding the advantages and disadvantages of the sole proprietorship, the partnership, and the "S" and "C" corporation.

Suppose that you run a small PR consulting business by yourself. You rent a small office and you have no employees. You are married, file a joint return on your income taxes, and have one child. With exemptions, mortgage interest, contributions, and other deductible items, you have $11,000 worth of deductions on your personal income tax. Following are the expenses for running your business:

Operating Expenses

Rent $ 4,800

Utilities	1,500
Telephone	1,500
Office/Business Expenses	900
Postage/Freight	1,200
Office Supplies	2,700
Legal and Accounting	1,500
Contract Labor	5,200
Auto Ins., Regis., AAA	350
Auto Repairs, Maint.	800
Parking, Tolls	750
Travel & Entertainment (80%)	3,600
Meals & Lodging (out of town)	2,000
Dues and Publications	650
Advertising	2,100
Gifts	450
Bank Service Charges	250
Insurance—Office	375
Equip. Maint. & Repair	175
Depreciation	1,100
City/State Licenses	100
	$ 32,000

Personal

Salary	40,000
FICA, Unemply. Taxes	5,000
	$ 45,000

Benefits

Life Insurance	1,400
Long-Term Disability	850
Major Medical/Dental	1,400
Car lease	3,120
	$ 6,770

Pension

You want a SEP or Keogh	10,000

Year-End

Sole Proprietorship/S Corp		C Corporation	
Company Income	$100,000	Company Income	$100,000
Operating Costs	(32,000)	Operating Costs	(32,000)

Salary & Taxes	(45,000)	Salary & Taxes	(45,000)
Profit (passed Through)	23,000	SEP (sheltered)	(10,000)
		Benefits	(6,770)
		Corporate Profit	6,230
		Income Tax @ 15%	(935)
Personal Income (40 + 23)	63,000	Earnings/Dividends	5,295
Less Personal Deductions	(11,000)	Personal Income	
		(salary & dividends)	45,295
Less Keogh @ 10% Income	(10,000)	Taxable Income	34,295
Taxable Income	42,000	Personal Income Tax	(5,736)
Personal Income Tax	(7,893)		
Summary		Summary	
Income	63,000	Income	45,295
Keogh (sheltered)	(10,000)	Corporate Taxes	(935)
Remaining Income	53,000	Personal Taxes	(5,736)
Taxes	(7,893)	Net Income	38,624*
Benefits	(6,770)		
		*Includes sheltered	$10,000
Net Income	38,337		

You can ask, "What's the big deal? I end up with 38 percent profit on my income and I shelter $10,000 for my retirement? Why do I have to choose?"

Good questions. In a small company such as this, without the need for the "corporate shield" against liability claims, the dollar differences are miniscule.

However, it is easy to do the math for a company that grows and has more income than this. If you continue to take a modest salary ($40,000 to $50,000), increase your operating costs (inevitably, if the business grows), increase the amount you will shelter in your pension, and continue to pay your benefits out of corporate dollars, you will still reduce the corporate tax liability (you pay only 15 percent up to $50,000 earnings), retain money for the continued life and expansion of your company, and pay a modest dividend. Your corporate tax remains low and your personal tax remains relatively static. (You can control this with the amount of dividends you choose to pay yourself.)

In the sole proprietorship or "S" corporation all profits would pass through to you as ordinary income, and you would pay 28 percent tax on the amount over $29,750. If your company is a success, your tax liability rises.

Your tax advisor will tell you that the "S" corporation offers other advantages that a "C" corporation cannot deliver on a small business ($100,000 or thereabouts). You will be told that you can also pass through *losses* to offset your other income for tax purposes, particularly in the first year(s) of a new company. And that's right . . . as far as it goes. However, under the new tax law, it can only offset *earned* income, *not* "passive" income, such as interest, dividends, rents from properties. If you are earning other income from, say, another job or another company in which you have management responsibility, such a loss would be helpful on your tax return. If you have other income from investments, such as stocks, bonds, mutual funds, rentals, the loss is not applicable and is simply a loss. Investigate *all* the ramifications, remembering our earlier caveat: you are not stuck with one business form forever; you can change as your business and personal circumstances dictate.

Independent Contractor

In Chapter 7 we discuss independent contractors and how you may hire them to help you with your business. It should also be mentioned that you can *be* an independent contractor, especially if you are a "C" corporation. Your company contracts clients for your services and then turns around and hires you on an independent contractor basis to perform the jobs. Your company does not pay you a salary or your employment taxes; it pays you a flat fee. You, in turn, report your fees as personal income *less* the many expenses you have for doing business (check with your accountant for the latest list under the 1986 Tax Act.) Your corporation pays 15 percent income taxes on profits earned up to $50,000 and you pay personal income taxes at the 15 and 28 percent rate on your adjusted income.

Be very careful to consult your lawyer and accountant for assistance before you embark on this course. The IRS has very stringent rules for independent contractors, and all the provisions must be met in order for you to escape penalty for trying to avoid taxes. Some of the criteria you must satisfy:

- Do you require close instruction to do the work, or are you relatively independent in your work?
- Do you require special training or are you already prepared?
- Does your work integrate closely with others in the company or is it special?
- Do you render your services personally?
- Do you have authority to hire, supervise, and pay assistants?
- Do you have continuing relationships with your clients or is it irregular?
- Do you set your own work hours?
- Is full time required or do you service other clients?
- Do you work on your employer's premises? (This is the hardest to satisfy many times. You don't *want* to work at your employer's place of doing business.)
- Do you set the order of sequence of your work?
- Do you give oral or written reports on your work?
- Are you paid by the hour/week/month or by the job?
- Do you receive payment of business and/or traveling expenses or do you pay them yourself?
- Do you furnish your own tools and materials?
- Do you have a significant investment in the operation of your business?
- Do you realize and declare a profit or loss in this business?
- Do you work for more than one firm at a time?
- Do you make your services available to a general public and not just to one client?
- Do you have the right to discharge your assistants?
- Do you have the right to terminate your agreements?

This is an opportunity to net more of your income, if you meet the criteria. But check it out carefully before you take the plunge.

References

The Bibliography at the back of the book lists a few of the references that have been used in the preparation of this chapter. You should also check the Appendix for other information regarding the setting up and management of your company. Annually, Simon & Schuster in New York City publishes a series* of workbooks that contains all the legal forms necessary to do business in each state. Check your library for the latest. Also check your library for *Best's Insurance Reports,* which can supply you with invaluable information on your insurance coverage, from annuities to medical.

Use this chapter and the questions it poses to exhaust your own inquiries of your attorney, your accountant, your financial advisor, your insurance brokers, and your family. It is *your* business. Do what is right for *you.*

*(state) Business Kit For Starting and Existing Business.

Chapter 4

Where Do You Get the Money?

There is no set way of financing a business. Take whatever financial approach is necessary, within reason, of course, and within the limits of your company's ability to repay it.

Evidence indicates that, second to lack of planning, more businesses fail from insufficient financing than from any other reason. The two are, of course, interrelated. With proper planning, you will *know* how much money you need to get started, to operate from six months to a year with no profit or losses, and what you will need as a cushion against the catastrophically unexpected.

All investments involve the making of projections about future events. While the future is not predictable, it need not be clouded in mist. Using the research and analysis tools recommended in Chapters 1 and 6, you will have a better understanding of what you can expect. And that is what investors are interested in: reasonable projections based on hard facts and sound principles. There are other things they will look for, and we will discuss them, but *your* confidence in your projections goes a long way toward making *them* confident.

Before you can talk about raising money to fund your company, you need to analyze the prospects of your business in a way that bankers and financially oriented people can understand.

- Profit potential
- Start-up costs
- Operating costs
- Hidden costs

If the business is new to you, allow at least a 20 percent margin on all your estimates; it is your cushion against things you do not know or cannot find out.

Begin your financial planning long before you try to set up the business. That may seem like the most obvious advice in the world, but it is amazing how many people think they can *start* a business and *plan* a business at the same time. While planning is an ongoing process throughout the life of the company, it should be done before you start the business. The very nature of the business, its structure, financing, and marketing, are based on the results of that initial analysis and planning.

Learn the language of finance and keep up with the current financial events. Why? Because you need to be able to converse about business in a businesslike way. You need to know what's going on that may affect your business. The Appendix includes some terms that might be of use to you.

As a note, if your only motivation for going into business is to be "rich and famous" then you are unlikely to make it. Those may be your personal dreams, but they are not the specific, step-by-step, realistic goals that make a good business plan or an appealing business investment. We all hope that success (however you interpret it) will be yours, anyway. But, remember. An investor is always going to ask, "What's in it for *me*?"

The crucial element of your plan, then, will be the Financial Plan. The Financial Plan is a coordinated set of data that evaluates your current financial condition, articulates your goals and potential, and provides a strategy for achieving them over a specified period of time. It should include at least the following:

- Operating budget
- Cash flow analysis (sources and uses of funds)
- Balance sheet
- Income statement
- Break-even analysis
- Financial ratios

Before you go shopping for capital, from any source, you should have the answers to these questions:

- What will the money be used for?
- How much do I need?
- When will I need it?

- How long will I need it?
- If I borrow it, how can I repay it?

Sources of Financing

If you are financing through *internal* resources, this means that you get the money *yourself,* because you want to retain full and complete ownership of your company. The following are some internal resource possibilities:

- Cash saved
- Portfolio, real estate
- Early retirement/profit sharing
- Mortgages and lines of credit
- Bank loans
- Other loans
- Small Business Administration
- Credit cards
- A combination of some of the above

Financing through *external* sources means you are willing to go outside your own resources and share part of the business with someone else.
Possibilities are:

- Family/friends
- Working partners
- Venture capitalists

Internal Resources

You can finance your own business. There are safe ways of doing it; it just takes planning. Following are some suggestions.

Cash Saved

Saving money is the most fundamental and most neglected element of good fiscal management. You should develop a savings plan as early in your life as possible to develop the funds necessary for a number of personal goals: education, travel, retirement, unexpected illness and, of course, starting your own business. The best way to save and to plan a business by saving is to build savings (and investments) into your budget. You probably have a personal budget, some loose list of monthly expenditures, and, if you are like most people, you rarely keep it up to date and you always spend more than you think you are going to (or that is in the budget). A good personal budget is the *key* to good fiscal management. There is one included in the Appendix and you will note that an important part of the budget is "Savings/Investments." In my view, this is one of the three items (along with housing and utilities) that you should pay *first* out of your income. That sort of discipline is sometimes hard, but, if you have a set of important goals, it becomes easier and eventually more exciting as you see the amount build.

Obviously, this concept will work if you *plan* to start your own business several years in advance and target the amount you wish to accumulate. If you are employed elsewhere and wish to shelter those savings/investments, Series EE savings bonds and tax-free bond funds are good (and safe) instruments to consider.

As in all things, there is a contrary view to financing your business yourself. Some poeple call using your own savings "the last resort" in business financing, and they have a point. If the savings is also the only nest egg you have, if you lose your job, get ill (what about disability insurance?) or retire early, using it for your business could be very risky. The answer to that is to *proportion* your savings/investments: some for retirement, some for living expenses should you become unemployed, some for catastrophe, some for starting your business. It is cheaper than paying interest on loans or giving away a piece of your business to someone else.

Savings is a habit that is taught—as early as the days you sold Girl Scout cookies or had a paper route—but you are never too old to learn! The secret is a goal that you believe in.

Portfolio/Real Estate

Money works harder when you know how to use it. Whether you are investing your savings in order to capitalize your own business in the future of whether you are investing the profits from the company you are currently running, your money should work harder than you do. If you got a 10 percent raise at your job last year, your savings/investment portfolio should have increased by 20 percent. Make it work! Doubling your own capacity is a reasonable target. Now that increase can include what you targeted for additional investment, but in fairness, the dividends and interest alone should approach that 20 percent mark. If you got a 5 percent raise, your portfolio should have increased at least 10 percent. Is that arbitrary? Yes. Is it achieveable? Yes.

Keep track of your investments. Monitoring them at least once a month is a minimal effort you should expend. The IRS will want the records at the end of the year, but *you* want them much more often so you can switch from the nonperformers to high achievers.

You can force yourself to "grow in wealth" by budgeting an amount each month to put in a money market fund or an investment account (as little as $50 or $100 can make a big difference in a short period of time). Should you take risks? Reasonable ones, yes. Instead of "safe" bank money market funds, high-growth stock funds can grow in a bull market; CDs and money market funds preserve capital and grow in a bear market.

When investing, sometimes turning to a brokerage firm for guidance is a good idea, but be sure to know your broker on a personal basis. To get real value out of this important relationship observe the following:

- Know your own goals.
- Don't be swayed by the investment goals and strategies of others.
- Collect the basic facts about your financial situation.
- Discuss your financial situation honestly with your financial consultant.
- Make sure you and your financial consultant have the same investment orientation.
- Remember that brokers make money on how much they *sell*, not on how much you *make*.
- Be wary of "special situations" that they are pushing.

There are three different categories of financial advisors to be aware of: (1) financial "supermarkets," which offer all kinds of services; (2) bank trust departments, which may be more conservative than you need; (3) certified financial planners, especially those who are not connected to a particular brokerage house or insurance carrier and who, therefore, do not make money by selling you something.

Remember that, if you have a portfolio of stocks and bonds with a brokerage firm, you can borrow on it—usually up to 50 percent of the value of your stocks and 70 percent of the value of your bonds. The rates should be comparable or better than those at banks, and they can be negotiated on a short-term basis. The ongoing value of your portfolio will influence the pay-back time and rate of interest.

Use of real estate is another way to finance your new business. We are not talking about mortgaging your home; that is dealt with later. This is real estate as an investment.

It is possible to put down a small amount of cash as a down payment and acquire a property (either a house, apartment, or small commercial building) that you can then rent. With careful analysis, you can acquire a property that will produce a positive cash flow (the rents exceed the cost of your mortgage, interest, taxes, maintenance), particularly with the use of depreciation on a rental property. If the property has been carefully bought, that is, bought in a neighborhood that is improving, not declining, it will also appreciate in value over a few years. The other important point in your long-range planning is that the purchase of such real estate builds your net worth (the estimated value of the house/property less the amount of the mortgage). This can become important when you go to get funds for your new venture. Your personal balance sheet is something that will be looked at very carefully, and most lenders/investors still look with approval on real property.

Another use of real estate is to buy a home, live in it (usually five to seven years), sell it, and use the money to finance your business. "What is so good about that?" you ask. "Where am I supposed to live after I sell?"

Let's do an exercise. Suppose that you buy a house for $50,000 and make improvements of $15,000 over the years. You sell it eight years later for $125,000 and pay off your $30,000 mortgage. Your $125,000, less the $65,000 you had in the house, less the $10,000 closing costs and moving costs nets you a $50,000 profit. In real cash, you had $125,000, less your $30,000 mortgage, less your $10,000 closing and moving costs, or $85,000 in cash. You buy another residence for $100,000 (thereby canceling any capital gains, because it costs more than your $50,000 profit), with a $25,000 down payment and a $75,000 mortgage. You form a company (sole proprietorship, partnership, or corporation), you personally *loan* the company $60,000, which is what's left over from your house sale, and you start your business. You pay interest on the loan as a company, which is deductible as a business expense and taxable as income to you personally, but the repayment of *principal* is not taxable to you personally—it was a loan. *It* is also deductible from your company income, because it is a business expense.

Real estate of a variety of kinds can help you finance your company without going outside and involving others; and, since your loan to your company will probably be on a "demand note" (payable on demand), you can pay it off as your company prospers, not when times are tough.

Early Retirement/Profit Sharing

It is obvious that if you have worked for a company that has a profit-sharing plan for its employees, instead of the typical pension plan, you can build a tidy nest egg for yourself to use before you reach the usual retirement age of sixty-two or sixty-five. If your company allows you to contribute to that plan (the so-called 401 k plan), you should do so. It shelters both income and interest from income taxes and helps that fund to grow larger, faster. Then, when you are ready to start that second (or third) career, you can look to a substantial capital fund without help from outsiders.

You should be aware of the tax consequences when you take out the money. Again, consult with your tax advisor *before* you do so, in order to arrange the timing and the use of funds to your best advantage. In broad terms, the money is taxable as ordinary income when you take it out, and that can mean some big taxes the year you take it. In addition to putting you into the 28 percent tax bracket (probably), there is an additional tax on money taken out that exceeds $112,500. Your advisor may recommend that you roll over some of the money (with sixty days of receipt) into your IRA, avoiding taxes on it at that time and taking the remainder as taxable income. Preplanning is very important and will allow you to put aside that which you need for your new business, preserving the rest for your retirement planning or unforeseeen emergencies. You should also investigate forward-averaging when you take out the money, to see if it is helpful in your own tax situation.

The key word, as always, is *planning*.

Mortgages and Lines of Credit

Sooner or later, you may have to go to the bank for money, and there is something you must understand: bankers just do not understand us. By "us," I mean those of us who run our own businesses, the "self-employed." Even though they place great stock in your net worth (your personal balance sheet) and on your business plan, they are also concerned with your ability to pay back the money. When they see the words "self employed," they immediately conclude that your long-term income prospects are "iffy" at best, even though you may be a lot more secure than they are. They could be fired tomorrow! You can't. It is not logical, but it is a fact of life, and you should be aware of it and be prepared for it. Obviously, a folder full of contracts or customer commitments would go a long way toward assuring them that there *is* going to be income and that they are going to be paid back in an orderly way.

With the Tax Reform Act of 1986 and its phase-out rules of interest deductions on your income tax, just about the only viable loan available to most Americans right now is the mortgage loan (first or second) on your residence (house, condominium, or cooperative) or an equity line of credit on that residence. The only substantial difference in the two is that, with a mortgage, you usually draw out the loan amount immediately and start to pay it off with a predetermined principal and interest payment. With an equity line of credit, you can use checks to pay for things and the interest (which can fluctuate with the bank's arrangement with you) does not "kick in" until you actually use the money.

Two words of advice: If you have *lots* of equity in your residence, low monthly mortgage payments, and plan to be there for quite a while longer, it is justifiable to consider it as an asset for starting your own business, just as you would with your stock portfolio or your profit sharing plan. However, if your payments are high, you may not stay there too much longer, and you have other resources, remember that your home is probably the most expensive thing you will ever own. Do not risk losing it if you have other resources with which to run your business.

So . . . if you have decided to go forward and approach the bank, be prepared for the following issues the bank will raise and be prepared for the kind of answers the bank expects.

1. *Stability*. The bank looks for people who have lived and have been employed in the same community for a long time. Note that they say "employed." For newcomers to a community, it is crucial that you supply them with good references in your previous place of residence.

2. *Financial Responsibility*. The bank wants to know if you pay your bills on time. They will ask you for credit references, including previous mortgage holders, sources of previous loans, credit cards, etc. Do not try to fool them; they will contact the credit bureau and find out. *You* can contact the credit bureau, too, by the way, and *should*, to see what is on your record and whether or not it is accurate. That argument over the light bill may still be on the record.

3. *Disposable Income*. The bank wants to know your ability to repay a loan by considering your income and expenses, as well as your potential for *increasing* your income during the life of the loan. This is where some of the problems with self-employed people can begin. They ask that you verify your income, which is difficult if you are just starting out, and they ask what your income is going to be, which can usually be substantiated only by your business plan, not by a pile of W-4 forms from an employer. Further, in my experience, they never ask for your budget (personal, that is). You and I both know that "disposable income" is the difference between what you take in, what you must pay out each month, and what is left over. There is no place on any loan application I have ever seen for your budget (your expenditures) either for your personal life-style or for the operation of your business, so, unless they happen to glance at that page in your business plan, they won't see it. Educating bankers may be one of the tasks of the one-person business in the future; there is a need to show them what you earn, but to also show them how you *manage* what you earn. They don't have a grasp of "disposable income," even though they ask for it; and their "formulae" do not work for most small businesses.

4. *"What is the purpose of the loan?"* Most bank officers can understand it if you need to send your daughter to college, buy an automobile, improve your house. They *do not* understand that you need to start your own business. Why can't you work for an employer, like they do, like everyone else? You are not making

their job any easier. This is where your business plan is crucial. However, in my experience with the people I've consulted, *getting* a banker to read a business plan is just about as easy as getting them to levitate at dawn. They would rather follow the formula and move you through the system, and the evidence still abounds that they would give credit to a golfing buddy who is up to his bowtie in debt before they would to a woman, minority, or a young person with a good business plan and a passion for the business. What to do? *Persist*. Go to a smaller bank that may need you or know you. (We will talk about that later.)

5. *"What will be the term of the loan?"* Be prepared for this question. Show them how you plan to pay off the loan as you operate your business. That loan repayment is a crucial part of your financial statements.

6. *"How long have you worked at your present job?"* Don't you love it? This is where you must assemble a dossier of testimonials from previous employers, creditors, business associates. You cannot rely on a company's reputation any more; you must rely on your own. Since your own is undoubtedly splendid, don't be shy about flaunting it.

7. *"What credit references do you have?"* It is a perverse commentary on our financial system that you can borrow *more* money if you *owe* money than if you do not. When you are looking for a loan, the bank prefers that you have some sort of established credit, preferably credit cards, other loans, and charge accounts at department stores. People who own their houses and cars outright, and who pay their bills promptly or with cash, have a terrible time justifying their credit existence. It is to be hoped that, under the interest revisions in the Tax Act of 1986 and the continuing ridiculous credit card interest rates, people will begin to come to their senses and get out of the credit interest trap. However, bankers will never get out of it; that is how they make their money: by charging interest. *Interest* is a beautiful word to them.

You *have* to establish and maintain good credit. If you have a mortgage payment each month, that is a good beginning. Keep a couple of credit cards and pay them promptly and in full each month. Use gasoline credit cards, paying promptly each month. Pay your insurance premiums once a year in a lump sum, borrowing the money to do so from a bank or savings institution to establish credit. Then pay it back monthly. I know, it will cost you interest. But if you need a credit rating, it is a place to begin.

8. *"What are your monthly payments?"* Here again, the intention is good, but the question does not address all the elements that prove the viability of your business and your life-style. The "payments" referred to are car payments, credit card payments, loan payments, but they don't necessarily encompass the rest of your personal money management, as well as the tax planning and shelters that you may well have as a part of your use of funds. Don't be satisfied to answer the questions in writing and let the piece of paper waft through the system unattended. Mark the area for "attachments" or insist on an interview to discuss your personal money management and your business plan. (If your bank or banker does not have time to listen to your explanations and read your plan, then it is obvious you need another banker. Fortunately, banking is becoming competitive; you do not necessarily have to take boredom or a closed mind for an answer.)

9. *"What accounts do you have at our bank?"* Whoopee. The implication is that you would be better off if you did do business with that bank, and, of course, that is true in most business relationships. However, it should be *quid pro quo*. If you don't get help from a bank, don't give them your business. I know a woman who wanted to start an office services complex and went to the bank she had been with for years. Only when her husband, who was an employee at a local company, cosigned the loan, did she get the money. She was very successful with the first complex of about fifteen offices and opened a second complex of about twenty offices in another area with her own earnings. It, too, prospered. She decided to open a third complex in yet another thriving area; she went back to the bank for the seed money—her bank—and was turned down. Needless to say, she moved her account, and the third complex is doing very nicely, thank you. While banks are not in business to take risks (although most of them do; how much money is loaned to Mexico and other countries?), they *are* in the business to serve their customers, their community, and their stockholders. It is a fine

line to walk, but the burden, ultimately, rests on the bank. All loans are not for cars. All businesses are not USX. Education is the answer, and we in the one-person business world must begin. "Take a banker to lunch," take a friend or friends to lunch, particularly if they run their own one-person businesses; build a network of strong people who can initiate this education process.

10. *"What is your debt-to-income ratio?"* This is easy to figure out. Take all your total monthly installment debts, excluding your home mortgage payment, and divide the total by your net income per month. If the total is more than 25 percent, you are going to have trouble; that is the limit most banks find acceptable, because they figure your home mortgage at a 25 to 30 percent portion of your net income also. How do you cope? By showing your real net-after-taxes income. As a one-person business, with the extensive personal money management you will employ, it is unlikely that your net after taxes will be the same as the employed person who has all kinds of taxes taken out each week. Again, we are talking about educating the loan officer to the "real facts" (as a country lawyer friend of mine used to say).

If all this sound like a diatribe against bankers, it is not. Some of my best friends are in the banking business! But they are not accustomed to the one-person business, as their forms and questions show. However, we are America's past and the hope of the future. If they plan to prosper with us, they will have to come around to understanding us and the particular nature of our businesses. It is up to us to start that education process.

When all is said and done, your ability to get a loan from a bank to start a business or to run your business will depend upon:

- *Your credibility:* whether or not you are the right person to run the business.
- *The project potential:* whether or not your company will grow and make a profit, so that you will be able to pay back the debt.
- *Collateralization:* whether or not you have any assets, unencumbered, which can serve to protect the lender in case your business does not succeed.

Bankers have a different view of business than we business people do. We have been taught to believe that most businesses fail because they are poorly financed, or undercapitalized. Bankers believe that few businesses go under simply for lack of cash. They believe that is usually a symptom, not a disease. Most are appalled at how poorly owners *plan*. That is why we emphasize planning throughout this book; not because it will appeal to the bankers, but because it is the *core* of good management. Seat-of-the-pants improvisation may work, if your name (and face) is Paul Newman and you are selling salad dressing, but few of us are Paul Newman. (It's very good salad dressing, too, by the way!)

To get yourself organized before you go to the bank, you need:

1. Personal financial statements, including personal balance sheet, income statements (including the last two income tax returns, if they verify your retained earnings), credit letters of reference from your current location (if you are new to the area), credit letters of reference or referral addresses (if you have relocated), and a yearly personal operating budget perhaps verified with bank statements.
2. Your complete business plan, which you are prepared to leave with the banker, with particular emphasis on the financial statements that we have identified earlier as well as any contracts, customer orders, or promises that are relevant.
3. Your biography and some record of your achievements.
4. A complete statement of sources and uses of funds. Do not expect the bank to put up *all* the money. It could happen, but it is unlikely. They will want to see that you have made a commitment to the business, and it would help if there were other sources of finance also.

Here are some tips from several one-person businesses:

1. Don't assume a bigger bank will be a better prospect for your loan. Stay with a bank that already knows you, and if you are known, sometimes a smaller bank is better.
2. Don't delude yourself. A bank's favorite type of loan is not for new businesses, and especially not for one-person businesses. You don't fit into their formulae and guidelines. It will be hard slogging, no matter how good your plan is and no matter how good your presentation is.
3. Dress in a manner your banker can relate to. It is distressing to talk about "dressing for success" and "power colors" and all the attendant hokum that has become an industry unto itself. Unfortunately, the book is still judged by its cover, and, as Harold Hill

says in *The Music Man,* "you gotta know the territory." Do it. Make your banker feel comfortable by dressing in the style that he or she expects. You will get further.

4. Talk the banker's language. You should know the terms so that you are in charge of the discussion and can present your best case. One banker I interviewed said, "We're looking for secondary sources of repayment—stocks, property, and savings—and projected statement of income. If the applicant doesn't know what 'projected statements' means, I know I am wasting my time."

5. Don't be intimidated by your loan officer. Most owners of small companies would rather spend a day at the dentist than forty-five minutes negotiating a loan with a banker. The secret is planning and preparation. If you truly know what you are talking about and really believe in your venture, then your knowledge and enthusiasm will show through. *You* will control, and enjoy, the conversation.

6. If your loan is rejected, don't give up! There are other banks, other lending institutions, other sources. Your belief and good preparation are the important elements. One banker's rejection should not dissuade you.

Other Loans

There are other kinds of loans you can take to help start up a business. Although your business plan—e.g., *what* you are going to do to repay the money—is important to the lender, there are other elements which add credibility to your request.

Cosigners are probably the oldest way to get a loan. A friend, relative, or colleague will cosign a loan on your behalf, knowing that, if you default, he or she is responsible. It is perfectly legitimate and it is done all the time. Frankly, such an arrangement is usually made because the cosigner has better credit, net worth, or disposable income than the person seeking the loan, and the lender knows that the money can be recovered from one or the other. I consider it the method of last resort, particularly in funding a new company. Should a disaster happen and the cosigner has to pay, you can be sure of losing a friendship, and, if the person is the talkative type, probably your reputation, too. Consider it *very* carefully before you do it.

Asset loans means financing what you own and using your assets as collateral. These will probably be such items as your land and building or your equipment and machinery. The lender will keep tabs on your assets and set certain operating restrictions. If you are already in business and need a little "bump" in capital, you will probably investigate an asset loan. Your ability to raise capital this way depends primarily on the quality of your collateral and not so much on the soundness of your plans for using the borrowed funds.

Short-term loans are very useful. They tend to be granted by banks without too much concern for collateral, since these loans are usually self-liquidating from sales made in the ordinary course of business operations. If you have a track record of business, these are the loans that may "tide you over" until accounts receivable are in or the new "season" for your product is in full swing. They are generally for a year or less; the interest rates tend to be a little high, but are still tied to the prime rate in effect at the time.

Trade credit loans represent a major source of funds. This is financing what you buy and using inventory as collateral. Lenders look for these qualities in inventory: perishability, ease of valuation, resale value, salability. If your business is one of products, this offers a means for regenerating capital (you can probably borrow from a bank for considerably less than you would resell the product). Furthermore, you have one other psychological fact working on your behalf: the bank does not *want* the inventory; they want you to sell it and succeed. Whether they intend to or not, they become partners in your desire for success.

Small Business Administration

Most cities have an SBA office. Visit yours and get to know the people, even if you don't need them right now. They each have priorities for a given region. See if you fit in. If you don't, see if you can help change their minds. Throughout his term, President Reagan has tried to abolish the SBA; but those efforts have only made it stronger. Recent meetings of small business owners in Washington have strengthened the image and determination of the agency to stay in business in this "age of the entrepreneur." It has made mistakes in the past, and there are administrators throughout the country who have closed minds to certain kinds of business. However, *if* it prevails it will inevitably mature and change with the needs of the small or one-person business.

At this writing, the interest rate on an SBA loan is 12 percent for guaranteed loans and 11 percent for participation loans. The maximum term for an SBA loan is ten years. These rates will, of course, change as the prime changes, but not as often and not as precipitously. In all instances, the loans are competitive with the best rates in the commercial marketplace, and the criteria for acceptance are skewed to favor the small business person, as per the charter of the administration.

Credit Cards

During the writing of this book, I became acutely aware of the mail deliveries that brought me "free" credit cards, even though I had not applied for them. Within nine months I received at least twelve credit cards from banks and companies all over the country! All I had to do was sign them and start charging!

It is obvious that you could start up a business with credit cards. They pour into your mailbox with the same regularity as investment and charitable contribution solicitations, and they offer wonderful enticements such as: "$5,000 credit with just your signature!"

What they neglect to mention is that the interest rate is from 18 to 20 percent, and we have a tendency to lose control in the "plastic world."

If getting a friend to cosign a loan is the "last option" you should consider in starting a business, then using credit cards to start or run your business should be the "next-to-last" idea. In Chapter 7 we discuss the recommended way to use credit cards in your business, but the idea of capitalizing your business with that kind of interest is very distressing, partricularly as it is not even deductible as a business expense.

Please, don't do it. It is truly a last resort, and only then for "small ticket" items.

Combination of Courses

When all is said and done, you will use a variety of sources to start up your business and to continue it through its "down" times and fallow periods.

Leeann Chin started a small restaurant business that has grown and grossed $5 million in five years. The SBA gave her a $165,000 loan; friends invested $125,000, and she used her personal savings of $15,000. She had a good plan, lots of enthusiasm, and a reputation for hard work. It has paid off for everyone.

It is not an unusual combination. You can get loans, if you don't go to one place for all of the money, and you have to exhibit some confidence in your venture by putting in a substantial portion of the money yourself. If *you* don't believe in it, why should anyone else?

The smart way is to plan *whose* money will be spent *how*. Will your money be spent for current expenses, preparation, and start-up costs in promotion, advertising, supplies? Will you go to a lending institution for capital costs, such as office renovation and equipment? (Something they can call "collateral.") Will you go to friends for the down payment on lease, utilities, telephone? (This is "I believe in you" money.) Will you go to the SBA for a year's operation money, with a good plan and good references? ("I can *do* this, if I'm given the chance!") Divide up your needs and spread them around at different rates and different time frames. You do not want your debt to be your greatest expense, so *plan* it, like you do everything else.

The loveliest idea I have heard is about a woman who wanted to operate a very special kind of agency. She decided to write a "best seller" book to capitalize it. She wrote the book and it *was* a best seller. She now has the agency. Now *there's* a capital idea for capitalization!

External Resources

Now we will talk about those outside resources that can help you launch your business, refinance your business for particular needs, or that can become an ongoing source of funding at regular times, such as at inventory buy-up or for renovations.

They fall under three broad categories: (1) family and friends; (2) working or silent partners; (3) venture capitalists.

Family and Friends

More often than not, you can find friends or members of your family who believe in your undertaking more than your banker. That is not hard to understand; they *know* you better than your banker. As we have discussed in the earlier section, they are good sources for *lending* you the money (at a rational interest rate, of course) and sometimes, like the mom who helped her son start the landscape business, they are willing to be "silent partners" in your venture, putting up the money, while you put up the hard work and expertise. For that, they expect a reasonable return when you pay consulting fees or dividends.

Sometimes they are not content to be "silent" when some of their money is in play. They might be shareholders who expect to have their opinions listened to, and their votes counted, when you are making business decisions, or, if they are limited partners they might expect to have substantial input. You don't want to cool their enthusiasm, or their interest in further investing, but you may not welcome the contribution they make.

A few items of advice are in order:

1. *If friends or relatives buy a piece of your company or a piece of something you control or are developing (a piece of commercial real estate, for instance), be sure that the responsibilities and authority are spelled out in advance.* Don't wait for a disagreement or something to go wrong to arrive at a settlement. Have it in writing as a part of the initial papers. Just having talked about such potential problems will many times help avoid them in the future.

2. *When a friend or relative buys into your business, protect yourself by arranging, and signing, a buy-out or buy-back agreement, with predetermined terms.* The contract should make it worthwhile for them to invest in you and your dreams. At the same time, it should protect *you* in case you are enormously successful and want to get control back.

3. *When you are selling stock in your company's future, remember that there is the amount of stock "authorized" (1,000 shares @ $1 par value or 100,000 shares at $1 par value, or any amount you and your attorney agree is feasible), and then there is the amount of stock that is "issued" or sold.* (This can be a considerably smaller number than the amount your company is authorized to issue or sell.)

There is a reason for this, as long as your stock is never traded as a public stock; *you* can set the value you place on the stock. As long as you retain the majority of stock issued, you will always have control of your company. Shareholders vote the number of stocks they hold, not the amount of money they put in. It is possible that early investors might pay $1, $5, $10 for your stock on the assumption that they believe in you and your ideas. As you grow successful, however, you might be able to raise more money for expansion, etc., by selling shares for $50 or $100 each. Even in an "S" corporation (thirty-five shareholders or less) or a closely held corporation, it is possible to raise a considerable amount of money from a small group of people who know you and believe in your concept. Be sure that you have written into your Incorporation Papers and the Buy/Sell Agreement that the shareholders cannot sell their stock to outsiders without first offering them to the corporation and then to the other shareholders, and set an appraisal system for such a transfer. In this way, you can always control who your shareholders will be. If you want to "keep it among friends," these provisions are important.

Working Partners

Earlier we discussed partners who put in money or time to help, but who, with regard to the running of the business, remain "silent." They are content to take their profit share or lend their moral support and let the operation—glory and mistakes alike—rest with you and your "one-person" business.

There may be occasions in the life of your company, however, when you need a partner to put up a lot or most of the money he or she is not content to remain silent. This does not mean that they necessarily become a full-time working partner, thus changing the nature of your business. Indeed, they may keep their own full-time profession. They do become active, however, in the managerial and operational decisions of your business. These are sometimes the hardest business relationships to be reckoned with.

Most people form partnerships because: (1) they want to expand the business; (2) they are insecure about making decisions alone. In all honesty, however, a partnership should probably be your last resort; far more of them fail than work.

The worst possible partnerships are the ones between friends. There is a distinct possibility that the partnership will fail and that the friendship will go with it.

Partners generally agree that they have been successful when each has *complementary* skills and character traits. Partners don't need to be alike (except perhaps in their shared values, ethics, and objectives); they need to be *complementary* in skills that are necessary for the business, in work habits, and in personalities. We have all heard of the partners who are "good cop, bad cop"; "the inside person, the outside person"; "the people person, the numbers person." They are phrases that describe balance, filling in to "complete." This seems to be the essence of a good partnership; this kind of balance provides the chemistry to make it work.

Conversely, when that delicate balance is missing, a partnership can be a disastrous venture. When the partners are too much alike, the business never seems to take off; when they are violently opposites in character or personality or values, the disagreements can blow them apart. This is truly a situation where knowing the person who is becoming involved in your business and its conduct can make or break that business.

There are usually two kinds of partnership formations: (1) One individual, unable to raise the requisite capital alone, is forced to seek an association with another whose wealth fulfills the need of the enterprise; or (2) One prospective partner may have money to invest, but not sufficient experience to make a go of the venture; the other prospective partner possesses experience, but lacks capital.

A major advantage in taking a partner is, of course, that the partner may be bringing money you need to the venture. However, remember that this also means there will be less money for you. Other advantages, as we have stated elsewhere, are that a partnership is less formally organized than a corporation; the burdens of taxation and the filing of returns and statements are much lighter.

There are certain legal disadvantages to a partnership, which you should remember. A partner is subject to personal liability for the obligations of the partnership, and you are also subject to liability for any loss due to the incompetence or fraud of your partner.

Some people enter partnerships with their competition, even stores that are next to or close to them. If it is worked out carefully in advance, this can pool resources, consolidate inventory and/or staff, and multiply the customers by combining them. Here again, values and objectives must be similar, while personalities and skills should be complementary.

The simplest and most common partnership is between family members—parent and child, husband and wife—when two or more parties pool their assets and funds in order to build a larger account and manage their growth in a joint account. Obviously, mutually shared values and objectives are just as important in this simple arrangement as in any other kind of partnership.

Venture Capitalists

Sooner or later, all of us may have to go to strangers to get capital for our dreams. By strangers, I mean people who are willing to put money into your care, for a piece of the business. They are not really in business to collect interest; they are in business to make a profit on their money through your hard work.

There is nothing wrong with it. They worked to make their money; now they want *you* to work to make *their* money, which is in your keeping, make *more* money.

It is the hardest sell you will ever make. The best book on the subject is written by Arthur Lipper III (see Bibliography). In his book Lipper includes his company's statement of policy and procedure regarding risking capital to new ventures. I suggest that you read it, along with the rest of the book. One paragraph gives the flavor of the tone and objectives of a serious—and successful—venture capitalist:

> Finally, we believe that entrepreneurs should 'rent' money from financers, such as ourselves, rather than initially be given it in the form of equity. Therefore, our favorite medium of funding is through the provision of commercial bank guarantees. Such guarantees require the recipient of the loan to ultimately repay the loan as well as to pay interest on a current basis. Our inducement to provide guarantees frequently takes the form of revenue participation in the guaranteed entity. We may also require other forms of guarantee fee payment, all dependent upon our assessment of the individual situation. We are not inflexible as to format, but do believe strongly that the investor's funds should, at least initially, enjoy a preference to the interests of those not at the same level of financial risk. We try to be fair and to respect (and reward) the entrepreneur. We require, however, that our capital be respected. We have worked long and hard to earn it.

Venture capitalists are, at best, risk takers. They are interested in making money, but they are driven by something else; they are intent on changing the status quo. Probably because they are the ultimate entrepreneurs, they understand the drive, the dreams, the single-mindedness that go into launching a business on your own. They will be your best—and your worst—audience. Unlike that banker or your wife's brother, who wonder why you can't keep a good job like everyone else, they will know what drives you and will subconsciously share your hopes and ambitions. They will also scrutinize your plans and data with a microscope. When you exceed your projections, based on facts and "worst case" scenarios, they will reward you; and when you fail in your projections, they will take a larger share of the business than they had before.

They will be your "partners" in every sense of the word, participating in your decision making and holding your feet to the fire of hard work and adhering to the plan. They will also be your biggest cheering section, when you do a good job.

This is not written to discourage you from seeking capital from the people who invest it for a living. Quite the contrary. There is a lot of money out there. Read the Sunday sections of almost any major newspaper and the *Wall Street Journal*. There is money chasing new ideas every day. Some are more honest than others; some take more of your business than others; some are tougher than others. Do not be afraid to ask for references and check them out.

Don't be afraid to approach them! Just know that you have to be *really* prepared before you do it, and be prepared also to give up part of your business—usually permanently—in the process.

Ad Astra

Good luck! Reach for the stars. There are many problems in running a one-person business, but getting money should not be one of them. There are many sources, and sometimes it is best to go to several of them, to spread the liability and keep the control. The keys are simple: a good idea, a good plan, a firm belief in what you are doing, and the dedication and hard work necessary to make it a reality. That kind of professionalism is attractive to many investors.

Chapter 5

Where Will You Work?

Where to conduct your one-person business is many times as important a decision as the kind of business to run, how to do the marketing and what structure to create.

The obvious reason is financial. There are advantages and disadvantages to each kind of location, and we will explore some of them shortly.

The other reason is more subtle, more intangible. It is best described by that often-overused word, ambience. Where you are and the decor of the place in which you conduct your business has a subconscious effect on you *and* on your clients and customers. Designers will tell you that a place makes a "statement." Just as the design of your stationery and your choice of words in a marketing letter tell something about you, so does your working environment.

I am not suggesting that you necessarily need to hire an architect and designer and spend $75 per square foot to decorate a place to work (although that may be a necessary capital expenditure if your business is design and your competition is fiercely committed to high style). There are wonderfully successful work spaces that are rebuilt warehouse lofts, and a cabin on the river may be the best place for you to create the wooden sculpture that you sell. I am suggesting that the location and "look" of the place you choose to work in should be suitable for your own particular emotional and psychological needs, your physical needs in the actual conduct of business, and the comfort and assurance your clients will feel when they come to you. You should *plan* your location as carefully as you plan your financial papers.

Your marketing research will help you determine the best location, if your business requires that people come to you or if you must be able to get to your basic clients quickly. When Willie Sutton, the famous bank robber, was finally arrested, a reporter asked him, "Willie, why did you rob banks?" He replied, "Because that's where the money is!" Obviously, *you* want to locate your business "where the money is," if it requires that people can get to you easily, conveniently, and safely.

If *you* go to them, the choice of location can be based on good financial reasons supported by your own personal needs. (What kind of surroundings depress you? make you cheerful? make you proud?)

Having decided on location, you can turn your attention to size, design, rental vs. ownership, costs (capital and ongoing), and ease of access (for you and others).

Unless you have super taste and have some experience in office layout, design, and furniture/equipment costs, it is worth your while to engage an interior designer to work with you. For a small office, you can probably get someone to work with you several hours on a purely consulting basis, helping to clarify your thinking and giving you information and direction that you can then follow up on yourself. You might even be able to arrange a *quid pro quo,* where you swap service for service. Remember, it is worth the time and money in the long run to engage a professional. After all, you are going to work in this place, by yourself, for a long time, and you want it to be a pleasant and productive environment.

Our work spaces take many forms: the shop/studio where we create items, do repairs/service, remodel/refinish, store equipment and take orders; an office environment where we create and work alone or where others visit us for counsel or service; vans and trucks in which we travel to our customers to service their needs. Obviously, a successful, one-person business can be limited only by the limits of our imagination. I read a wonderful story of an accountant who has her office, including computer and software, in a van, which she drives all over the territory, serving her clients on a weekly or monthly basis! The van, by the way, was handsome, well-painted, and well-maintained.

Working at Home—Renting or Owning

Whether your rent or own your residence, there are advantages and disadvantages to conducting your business from there. Your first considerations must be space and location. Don't conduct your business from your home just because is is "easy." Remember the admonitions earlier in this chapter to locate your business where the business should be. And a lack of necessary *space* for the business can inhibit its growth and ultimate prosperity.

If the location is suitable (I can write anywhere, for instance and that accountant can park her van anywhere) and the space is adequate for your needs, there are other considerations you should weigh in making your decision.

Here are the pros to working at home:

- Based on strict IRS guidelines, you can deduct a *portion* of your housing/office costs in proportion to the amount of space occupied by your business. If your house or apartment is fifteen-hundred square feet and you occupy one room of two-hundred square feet, then you can reasonably deduct 13.3 percent of your rent (or mortgage interest and real estate taxes, if you own it), utilities, cleaning, maintenance, security (and depreciation, if you own it) for a business expense. Check out the IRS guidelines in your annual tax report, but be certain that the space is used *only* for the conduct of your business and not as the family dining room after 6 P.M.
- If you work at home, you have flexible hours. You can work around your own personal time clock, around other demands on your time, or around-the-clock when necessary, without having to worry about coming and going at all hours of the day or night.
- You don't pay additional space cost for your business. In fact, you have an advantage, because you can *deduct* certain costs, thereby increasing your total cash flow.
- If your home phone is not tied up by a popular teenager or a lonesome senior citizen (or your bridge club!), you can save a lot of money by using one phone line for both business and personal calls. We will discuss phones later, but *how* you conduct yourself on the phone during business hours is crucial to the image you are trying to create.
- If it is important for you to be home with family, working at home can be a real boon to the one-person business. You can "go to work" without leaving loved ones alone.
- Since you are familiar with the neighborhood in which you live (and, presumably, like it, or you wouldn't live there!), you have the advantage of not having to accustom yourself to another neighborhood.
- As your business grows, you can expand outside your residence as

needed. However, if your business remains static or contracts suddenly, you don't have a lease to contend with, which could take away money you would really rather pour into the business.

- Frankly, you can save wear and tear on your car, your clothes, and your nerves by working at home. However, we are assuming that you dress and "go to work" in the proper manner every day; working in your bathrobe with the sports network or soap operas on is not what we mean by working at home!

Here are the cons:

- Depending on your business, working at home may be totally inappropriate. Unless your home office/shop is *specifically* a workplace, preferably with a separate entrance, it can be uncomfortable for clients to come to you. Carefully consider this before you decide to work at home. The last thing you need is to be considered a dilettante or amateur.
- To repeat, the IRS has very strict rules for the deduction of a place of business in your residence. Be sure you know them and comply with them, before you make the arrangements.
- It is possible that you might have to get city rezoning to run your business in your home. Check it out in advance to avoid problems, difficulties, and expense.
- No matter how much you love your family, you may not need to work near them. Your privacy, your clients, your creativity, your hours—a wide variety of circumstances—may make it necessary that you work *away* from home and the interference of your family members.
- With few exceptions, there is a need to mingle with other people, exchange ideas, commune, take a break, refresh with a different environment. All those social contacts that enrich our ability to "keep up" with changing tastes and trends are hard to do all alone. Sometimes they become the most compelling reasons to work *outside* the home.

Renting a Workplace Outside the Home

Should you choose to rent a work space outside your home, you have several choices within the rental mode. You can rent your shop or office "as is," in the location of your choice, and finish it off to suit you. Try to obtain "improvements" from the landlord, either in dollars per square foot (from $5 to 40, depending on your city, the building location, and condition, or in total dollars for work to be done (walls, carpeting or flooring, heating and air-conditioning ducts, lighting drops and/or fixtures, electrical outlets, security buzzers, window treatments—as much as you can get!) Sometimes you will get the money and can hire your own contractors; sometimes the landlord will give you an allowance and do the work with his or her own crews. Whatever the case, try to negotiate for as much as possible, so that your remaining responsibility will be decor—paint, wallpaper, finishes, window treatments, furnishings, and the like. As a negotiating point, you may be able to persuade the landlord to do a little more work than usual because, with the new depreciation tax rules, the depreciation is of more value to him or her than it is to you, with a lease of three, five, seven years. *You* will compensate by paying a bit more rent monthly, which is deductible to you as a business expense.

As another option, you can place your one-person business in a sublet in someone else's office or shop. Many times a company has a one-room office that is not occupied and that they are happy to sublet. It is unlikely that you can negotiate many changes in the decor, but that may be a money saver for you, if the ambience is satisfactory already. You *may* be able to negotiate receptionist, typing, or telephone-answering service, utilizing the staff already in place. (Be sure *your* name is on the front door, too!) It is not the ideal way to establish a business, but it is a perfectly honorable and feasible way to acquire good working space with a modest outlay of capital dollars. Artists will share studio space; shops will share bench space; dealers will share table space at auctions, flea markets, and antique shows. The cooperative movement is alive and well in America. Don't be afraid to get in on it—or start one!

The latest advantage for the one-person business is the burgeoning office service center and the "incubator" sponsored by state governments and universities. These are complexes that offer office space (and sometimes shop space) with other services, such as receptionist, telephone and answering, photocopying, stenographic, mail processing and pickup, bookkeeping and accounting, travel arrangements, and word processing. You buy more than the space you occupy, but the opportunity to do business in a "full service" office, without the hassle of finding your own services or hiring and supervising employees, is worth investigating. In my experience the best of these are not run as real estate ventures, but rather as *service* ventures; the landlords take pride in the ambience and quality of service they offer. As usual, shop for the right place, a good price, and get references before you sign up.

Regardless of the mode of rental, there are, of course, advantages and disadvantages to renting the place in which you do business. Here are the pros:

- All costs associated with renting your work space are deductible as business expenses.
- You are confident that you are doing business in a professional setting.
- You surround yourself with other professionals, some of whom, inevitably, will work with you, share with you, and have professional interchange with you.
- You keep your home life and your work life separate.

The cons are:

- The situation may be more expensive than your business can afford.
- You may be subject to lease restrictions (three to five years) that could limit your expansion or burden you financially.
- Your professional "neighbors" may change for the worse.
- You may not have a good landlord; you may be frustrated by someone else's incompetence or lack of professionalism.
- You may not be able to expand or break your lease when needed.

Owning Your Own Workplace

All things considered, owning your own real estate is still the best investment in America. "A little place of my own," is still the achievable dream of most Americans—brand new or sixth generation. With mortgate interest rates at a reasonable level for some time now and for the foreseeable future, the trend toward cooperative and condominium ownership for the "new families," the desire to restore and rehabilitate older buildings (with the continuing support of low government interest rates and alternate minimum tax), and the focus of the Tax Reform Act of 1986 on deductible interest for residencies, vacation homes, and rental property, the climate is cheerful for the ownership of real property.

This bodes well for the one-person business on several fronts.

There is substantial security in the investment in real property, either as a home (with the possibility of office or work space included or attached), as a vacation home for rental (with personal usage for fourteen days or 10 percent of the time rented), as an investment on rental property (either apartment, residential, or commercial), or as a property to be owned for your own work.

Owning your own work place offers a number of advantages. This can take a number of forms, as is obvious from the above paragraph. You can either own the home which your office or shop is located in or attached. You can own a building in which you do business and also serve as a landlord to other tenants. You can own a building in which your company is the only tenant. You can own a condominium. (The new trend in offices and shops are complexes with a number of businesses owned individually as condominiums.)

There are tax advantages to owning the property as an individual or as a partnership and then renting it to your company. You take the tax deductions of mortgage interest, taxes, depreciation, and your company takes the business expense for rental.

There are advantages to your company owning the property, with the attendant deductions, and renting out parts of it to other businesses, thereby generating both "passive income" and "passive losses," which have a tendency to offset each other on tax returns.

There is also the possibility of your company owning a property that it partially occupies (your office) and renting the rest of the property to you as a residence (your home). This offers some opportunities to transfer deductions and income/expenses between the two tax returns, which could be beneficial.

As always, you should analyze your position and your best interests in conference with your tax advisor and decide what is best for your own situation. The key, under the new tax act, is to decide where you need "passive income" (from rentals, dividends, interest) and where you need "passive losses" (from depreciation, maintenance, interest payments, and taxes).

There are a few more advantages and disadvantages you should consider when buying real estate for your company.

The pros are:

- Many of the expenses of owning property are deductible on your tax return, including mortgage interest, real estate taxes, mainte-

nance and repairs, security, cleaning, and depreciation. This comes in handy at tax time.
- You have no landlord to worry about, and you can manage your own property and work style.

The cons are:

- It may be hard to sell or rent the property when you want to. You lose some flexibility as an owner.
- You may not like being a landlord for other people. It is not the easiest career in the world, especially if it is not your *real* job.
- If you are in a condominium situation, you may find yourself disagreeing with the other owners about advertising, decor, tenants, etc. You may find yourself in a business environment that is not the best for your business.

Setting Up Your Office

The psychological reasons are fundamental to establishing any successful business environment. Just as significant is the efficiency of that environment.

This hinges on *design*, which is based on space, size, and cost, your personal needs and preferences, and the necessary ease of operation (as well as the ease of relocation to another environment later).

Crucial components of design are the equipment and furnishings you will buy. Not only should you "shop smart," getting the best buy for the money and establishing a suitable "look," but you should design the area, so that it functions well for your needs. While that may sound simplistic, there are items that function well because they are built well, and items that function well because you use them well and wisely.

The following pages contain information on the purchases most often needed to establish a business: computers, telephones, postage machines, typewriters, word processors, copiers, carpets, chairs, lights, and conference room setups. In addition, there are a number of tips on how to maximize your dollars in the use of this equipment. Every dollar counts, and there are some simple office economics that can make those dollars go farther for you.

The Work Pod

Between 13 and 14 million Americans now work at home, full time. Of those, some three or four million are estimated to use the computer as a part of their work or as an adjunct to their business.

While these numbers do not include all the one-person businesses in America, they give some indication of the growing magnitude of people who have opted to change their life-styles or work in a singular environment.

Whether or not your work requires a computer, it is likely that you will buy one in the next two to five years, simply to help you run whatever your business is. The PC is predicted to become as important to business as the clock and the telephone; and, with the prices continuing to diminish and the software and capabilities increasing, it is likely that all of us one-person businesses will own one before 1990. As author Paul Edwards (*Working From Home. Everything you Need to Know About Living and Working Under the Same Roof*) says, "With the personal computer, you can have the equivalent of a multiperson office. With the right software, the machine can serve as secretary, bookkeeper, file clerk, and researcher."

With that future in mind, a number of designers have concerned themselves with the "work pod." (I hate the sound of it, simply because it reminds me of so many bad B movies of the fifties.) They have come up with a design of work space different from that described in Chapter 7. It still serves many of the same functions and is offered as one of the many alternatives for organizing your business and your business routines. Here is a consolidation of some of the suggestions, which would fit in a space as small as 11 by 11 feet.

There is one other tip for work spaces that I will pass along. Ernest Hemingway used it and I have found it useful too. Have *two* desks; one that you sit at normally and one that you *stand* at (such as an architect's drafting table). Alternate between them and discover how it alleviates boredom, weariness, *fat*. When we work alone, we tend to do a lot of it *sitting* down. The standing desk is one way to fight the problems this may cause.

Determining Incoming Phone Lines

Your phone lines are adequate if no more than 2 percent of your callers get busy signals on their first try. The phone company will do a "busy" or "blocked line" study for you, free of charge.

Buying Telephones

Check your phone rates for the past three years to see how much the rate has increased (nationally, the increase is about 6 percent a year). Then you can evaluate the cost of owning your own phones as compared to renting them; when will you break even? Be sure the phones that you purchase have a Federal Communications Commission registration number stamped on the housing; this indicates that they have been certified.

Alternatives to WATS Lines

There are other companies that offer alternatives to AT&T's WATS (Wide Area Telecommunications Service) lines. They are Southern Pacific Communications (SPC), Microwave Communications (MCI), and ITT-Corporate Communication Services (ITT-CA).

They offer several advantages: simultaneous conversations, lower costs, itemized billing, off-peak rates, and quantity discounts. They also have limitations: limited geographic coverage and lack of dialing ease (sometimes you have to dial too many numbers).

Consider the WATS line if you use six to eight thousand minutes of long distance conversation a month. Don't consider it if your current long distance calls are no more than 125 to 150 percent of the cost of a monthly WATS line. Typically, some WATS calls overflow to toll call circuits and there is a tendency for the cost to average out.

When Not to Use the Phone

The average phone message is seven minutes long, and that can add up when you are talking long distance. If the message can wait until an hour, or the next day, there are cheaper ways to send a brief message: Under $1.00: Telex or TWX. Under $2.00: Mailgram, dispatched by Telex or TWX teleprinter. Under $4.00: Mailgram, telephoned to Western Union's 800 number. Under $7.00: Telegram dispatched by Telex or TWX teleprinter, or Night Letter, dispatched the same way. Under $10: Telegram or Night Letter, telephoned to Western Union's 800 number. Under $12: Express Mail.

Cellular Phones

You have been told of all the advantages of cellular phones, including the models that don't have to be held, those that can be circuited through switchboards, those with a lock that allows you to stop calls, and those with the ability to talk over a broad territory.

There are some disadvantages. First, they are not cheap ($3,000 to 4,000), and you are billed for phone calls going out *and* in. Your car insurance goes up to cover theft, and the coverage is not available in many areas. Some of the companies may not be around too long. Furthermore, your calls can be monitored, since they go through radio frequencies.

Cut Your Mailing Costs

Here are some tips:

- Check mailing scales; 9 pennies should weigh exactly one ounce.
- Use microfiche or microfilm for bulky catalogs or weighty instructions; it is less to mail and several will save the initial costs.
- Print reports and bulletins on both sides of paper to save postage (weight).
- Certified mail is one-third the cost of registered mail. Don't register unless the item must be insured.
- If you mail over two hundred items, use third class mail.
- Evaluate the cost of parcel insurance, if you are mailing many of the same thing. It may be cheaper to drop the insurance and pay for any lost items.
- If you need five thousand or fewer envelopes, buy them pre-stamped from the Post Office. They are a bargain.
- Fold all correspondence for number 10 (regular) envelopes instead of 9- by 12-inch. It costs less to mail and is delivered faster.
- Pay 22¢ for the first ounce of first class but only 17¢ for each additional ounce. Do not overpay.
- Spoiled postage imprints, stamps, or cards are redeemable within one year at 90 percent of the original cost.
- Do not use special delivery to large metropolitan areas, to large companies that pick up their mail, or to Post Office Box numbers. It is a useless expense.

Best Buys in Electronic Typewriters

According to *The Office Products Analyst* in New York, the best buys under $1,000 are now: Brother EM-85, Canon 350, Olympia Startype, Panasonic KX-E601/603, and Silver-Reed EX300. Best values in the $1,000 to $1,500 range: Adler 1020, Brother EM-200, Hermes 40, Olympia Supertype, Panasonic KX-E708, Royal 5020, and Silver-Reed EX66.

Before Buying a Word Processor

If you reproduce the same text many times (a mass mailing, for instance) you may be better off printing the material and addressing it individually. The real value of a word processor is when there is a great deal of material that is redrafted and re-edited many times. Writers, editors, lawyers, accountants, researchers, analysts all have a need for a word processor. Be sure to evaluate your real needs.

Choosing an Office Carpet

This is a major investment, if you have to furnish it yourself. You want a good buy, so pick the one best suited to heaviest use if you are going to carpet the whole place in one fabric. Nylon and acrylic are the most durable; wool is the most attractive. Low, dense, level loops wear best. Selection of fiber and color should be based on ability to hide soilage. Have the carpet treated with a soil repellent that is strong enough to stand up to heavy-duty cleaning agents. Be sure a static control system is built into the yarn; spray-ons are not very effective. Treat the fiber for flame resistance.

Selecting the Best Copier

According to *The Office Products Analyst* of New York, these are the most highly rated copiers, based on reliability: Panasonic 1300 and 1310R, 10; Canon PC-20, 9.5; Canon PC-25; and Toshiba BD-7812, 9.3. The lowest ratings were: Royal 130, 6; Royal 145, 6.6.

Chairs for the Desk Bound

A chair is as personal a purchase as shoes, and yet, many of us quickly buy one based on color, or line, or the salesperson's pitch. Here are some guidelines for the one-person owner who spends a lot of time sitting:

- The *backs* should be straight at the shoulder level to prevent neck strain, and slightly convex where they touch the spine.

- The small of your back should fit snugly into the chair back.
- Opt for a hard seat, slightly contoured to the buttocks; soft cushions roll up around and put pressure on joints.
- Arm supports should be firm, softly padded, and at least 2 inches wide.
- The height should be adjustable; get the height that is right for you.
- Look for adjustable chairs that let you move forward, tilt backward, sit upright for posture changes that allow you to rest and relax if you are sitting for hours at a time.

Planning a Conference Room

If your business requires a conference room, keep it versatile. Meetings of fifteen to twenty-five people require a room about 45 by 50 feet. The best shape for the meeting tables is a "U," made up preferably of several tables, so that they can be taken away when the room needs to be set up in "theater style" for more people. People should sit on the outer rim of the "U"; easels and podiums, screens and displays can be set up in the open end of the "U" for good visibility. The inner section of the "U" can be used for additional seating, when the principal speaker is situated at the bottom curve of the "U." Your aim is to design for both flexibility and comfort.

The Best Office Light

The best light is natural light from a window. The worst light is flat flourescent light. The best combination for keeping productivity high and boredom and eyestrain low, is to have window light (with shades and drapes to vary the intensity), wall or ceiling lights in accented areas, and lamps for special focus, with incandescent bulbs, not flourescent!

Simple Office Economics

Here are some tips:

- You can wire up to $300 anywhere in the country using a VISA or Master Charge card and the Western Union toll-free number (1-800-325-6000). The money can be picked up within two hours. This can be an effective way of controlling your cash flow until the last minute, and, in effect, delaying the use of your own money. The charge will not appear until your next charge card statement.

- Log your long-distance phone calls. Rarely are long distance telephone bills absolutely accurate. When a call is not properly identified, the phone company puts it on somebody's bill in the hope that it will be paid. Don't let the "sucker" be you!
- Keep track of and list the office supplies you use in a year. Get bids on the total amounts. You will save a bundle. (See the Appendix for suggestions.)

All of us have printing costs; some of us more than others. If you are into volume printing to sell your product or service, you know that paper costs can bury you. Here are some tips from the Center for Direct Marketing in Westport, CT.

- Buy paper from paper wholesalers and jobbers, and let them deliver it to the printer. (Average savings: 10 percent.) Buy only 3 percent extra, if using sheets; 6 percent extra, if rolls.
- Use higher-grade, lighter weight paper instead of lower-grade, heavier-weight paper.
- Prepare work to be printed using red acetate (called "rubylith") to show exactly where photos and drawings should be placed. Use overlays to show second and third printing colors. Taking these steps reduces chances of error in the printing shop and means that the printer has to do less work.
- A written agreement or contract with the printer should include separate prices for plates, makereadies, press time, wash-ups, author's alterations, overruns, additional ink charges, delivery, and, if needed, bindery and proofs.
- If one printer is to be used for a series of jobs, have him draw up a table of standard charges, so that the cost of any future work can be easily projected.
- You can get effect of two-color printing on a small catalog at a lower cost by mixing one-color and two-color pages. For an eight-page catalog, use two-color on the front and back covers and on pages four and five. Use one-color on pages two, three, six, and seven.
- Four-color printing can be imitated by printing in magenta (reddish blue) plus cyan (bluish green) on yellow pages.

Summary

Things to consider in choosing a place to work:

The Location:

- Is it right for you?

The Financial:

- What capital is required?
- What operating expenses are required?
- What are the tax advantages of the various choices?

The Design:

- Is the style suitable for you and customers?
- What is the cost?
- What is the ease of operation/relocation?

The Psychological:

- What are your personal needs?
- What are your family's needs?
- What are your customers' expectations?

The Function:

- Can it be run by one person—you?
- Can you "shop smart" for equipment and transfer it elsewhere?
- Have you absorbed the techniques of managing your expenses in a one-person environment?

Chapter 6

Tips on Marketing

Remember what we said in Chapter 1 on Planning: *marketing is the process of selling;* it is the aggregate of activities that you utilize to move a product or service from the producer to the consumer.

It is easy to fall into the trap of believing that only big businesses require an organized marketing plan with the necessary allocations of time and resources to drum up business. While I know several one-person businesses that operate very busily on word-of-mouth referrals, it is generally the exception, not the rule. Because your time and resources are more valuable than those of any company that has several or many employees, your careful consideration of *who* you want to attract, *when* you want them as clients/customers, and *how much* time and money you can spend to get them is a crucial part of your business planning.

You are interested in shortcuts and high value for your dollar, but you are not interested in a "cheap" look or an amateur impression. For example, it is very important that you spend money on good-looking stationery and business cards that are professionally designed and printed, and it is just as important that you have good telephone manners and a good telephone service—either a good answering machine and beeper system or a good answering service. You are the only person with whom your clients will come in contact; and many times their only contact with you will be a letter, a phone call, or a chance meeting at a convention where you exchange business cards. That "first impression" must be professional and attractive, or it could be your last chance to cultivate their business.

This seems like a simplistic recommendation, but so many one-person businesses ruin their opportunity for growth with cheap stationery, bad typing, unanswered phone calls, names and phone numbers scribbled on scraps of paper. The first marketing money you should spend is on your "first impression" material: stationery, business cards, telephone service, a good typewriter (or typing service). You are marketing yourself, and your manner, appearance, and attention to detail is fundamental to launching yourself properly.

Research

Whether you are starting your business, expanding or reducing your business, changing your product or service or assuring its ongoing healthy life, you will need to engage in research on a regular and constant basis.

Research is the gathering and analysis of information that is of value to your business. There are many good books written on the subject and a few are recommended in the Bibliography.

Formal and Informal Research

Research is both formal and informal. Every time you go to a luncheon or a seminar, read a book or magazine, interview prospective clients, participate in round-tables or presentations, you are engaging in research. You are informally gathering information that can be useful to you.

Keep track of it. Exchange business cards. When a card is given to you, write on the back when and where you received it and what you talked about. File it in your card box in one of several ways: by the company name (on the assumption that you would remember the company name in the future faster than you would remember the person's name); by calendar year and month (if your mind works in a chronological memory mode); by topic (consultant, supplier, industry/client, possible subcontractor); by city or area (if your business requires regional contacts); or by the person's name.

Save the seminar programs with your comments and contacts written on them, and establish a filing system to locate them (perhaps with categories similar to the above).

Clip newspaper and magazine articles, filing them by topic, area of interest, regional need, or whatever is suitable to your needs. (I always have a number of books and magazine articles "in the works," so I clip material and file it by subject and/or title.)

Formal research should be conducted with the help of a professional. While all of us think we know our business and are certain that we know the kinds of questions we must ask, a professional researcher can help us hone in on precisely what it is we are trying to discover and develop the specific method of discovering it. Suppose you are trying to match a product or service to a customer or client. The shortest distance between those two points is, more often than not, good research. Be prepared to pay for it. A few thousand dollars spent before you launch a new business can be worth many thousands of dollars to you as you proceed.

Research is generally categorized as either inside/out or outside/in. Inside/out research gathers and analyzes information that focuses on the skills and capabilities you have in your business; the outside/in approach concentrates on customers/clients—their wants, needs, and demands. Obviously, both sets of information are necessary for you to make a decision that can lead to success.

Secondary Data

Secondary data is information you can gather yourself from other sources; it is data that is already assembled and analyzed, which you can then turn to your specific uses. Some examples might be: number of college students in your city and the particulars of age, sex, income, etc.; new housing starts in your community; number and description of shoppers at a particular shopping mall, etc. Everyone needs statistical data in running their businesses from time to time, and usually you can find it without having to pay to have it gathered by a research firm.

There are many sources, such as the Chamber of Commerce (national and local); local newspaper advertising departments; the Department of Labor monthly statistics; the Department of Commerce monthly and biannual statistics on specific industries, industry publications, and banks. You can find these reports at libraries, City Hall, the Chamber of Commerce, newspaper offices, and banks.

Primary Data

Primary data is information that you have gathered and analyzed specifically for your own use. It is recommended that you use a professional researcher to help or to do it all for you. Following are the methods the researcher has at his or her disposal:

1. *Interviews.* With a few specific questions that allow for open-ended answers, a great deal of information can be discovered. (This differs from a survey because the answers *are* open-ended.) Good discovery interviews can be conducted with clients, suppliers, sales people involved with your product or service, people in advertising, and bankers.

2. *Surveys.* Specific questions with carefully defined answer parameters ("yes/no," "a gread deal/somewhat/not at all"), when properly analyzed, can reveal trends, likes and dislikes, needs, and a whole assortment of information valuable to an aggressive business person. Surveys can be conducted in a number of ways:

   - *On-site:* The questioner stands in the shopping mall and asks a random sampling of people to answer a few questions. The questioner keeps a tally sheet for later analysis.
   - *Telephone:* We are all familiar with the evening phone call during which two or three questions are asked.
   - *Warranties:* A product has a warranty card to be returned, and on it are also certain market research questions. The card is returned and the answers are analyzed to discover who the customer is. (It is called a "customer profile.")
   - *Mail:* With the purchase of a mailing list, a survey to be mailed back is conducted. The number of returns on this is typically very low.
   - *Sample offer:* An ad offers a sample of something, if the reader will write in. The reader does, the sample is sent, and a mailing list is compiled for telephone or mail surveys or for sending catalogs and brochures.

3. *Focus Groups.* Devised, conducted, transcribed, and analyzed by a professional, this is one of the most expensive forms of marketing research. It is excellent for testing ad art and copy; perception of companies, products or services; an image problem or a consumer need. A group of representative consumers is assembled in a room and led by a professional through at least one hour of questions and interchange, while also being transcribed and observed from another room. Body language as well as comments are noted.

It is unlikely that a one-person business would require many or all of the above services. However, any business requires some research and analysis throughout its life, and, although you may be your own best researcher, remember that an objective approach, another point of view, can only help to make you smarter. Besides, unless your business is marketing research, you want to spend your time running your business. Engage someone else to do the research for you.

(**Helpful hint:** Marketing research students at colleges and universities can do an excellent job in gathering, compiling, and helping to analyze secondary data for you, and the cost can be substantially lower than if a research firm did the work.)

Follow-Up as Research

Part of my business is to give seminars and lectures for groups and companies. *Immediately* after I always write a thank you note to the person in charge. It is the courteous thing to do, and it inevitably elicits a response, generally a favorable one, which can be used later in the solicitation of other business. If the sponsor also conducted a survey at the end of the session asking the participants to critique the presenter, I ask for the results of that survey in my letter. While they oftentimes provide "quotable quotes" for future business, they also help me to know what I did right and what I did wrong. It is instant research feedback and it costs me the price of a postage stamp.

Advertising

Advertising is paid news. You announce news of your product or service and pay to have it appear when, where, and how you wish.

While we will discuss the other components of your marketing plan (publicity, public relations, and merchandising), as covered in the Marketing Plan portion of Chapter 1, it is important to emphasize in the one-person business that advertising may be the most important part of that plan (after word-of-mouth and referrals). The reason is simple, but might escape notice. *You* are your business.

Your knowledge and skills are your most important assets to your clients. However, your time is your most important asset. Publicity, public relations, and merchandising take time. That does not mean that you should not use them in your overall marketing strategy, but advertising puts other resources to work for you, helping your customers and clients find you. Frankly, it gives you more time to do your business rather than to promote your business.

We all know that the challenge, the frustration, the financial difficulty of running these very special businesses is the conflict between *doing* our business and *selling* our business. Good advertising, well thought out and carefully bought, can do some of that selling for you.

Here are a few guidelines:

1. *Decide what it is you have to sell*. That is harder than you think. It goes back to the inside/outside, outside/inside research that you have done to determine your particular product or service and the target markets that can most likely use it. If you have not yet reached the comfortable level of word-of-mouth and referrals to keep you busy, then you must define specifically what you have to offer and to whom you wish to offer it.

2. *Determine the media that reach the largest customer potential you have identified as using or needing your product or service*. Your research data have helped you define your potential customers. Now you must find a "match" in particular media. (If you have created a new dance shoe, for example, you would not really want to advertise in *Sports Illustrated*. However, if you have developed a new program or seminar suitable for small businesses, you might wish to advertise in Chamber of Commerce publications or the regional Small Business Administration journals.) *Standard Rate and Data* is a publication that you should be able to find in most library reference sections. It is in three volumes; one for the print media and one each for radio and television. It contains information on most outlets, including circulation, rates, coverage, and much more. If you are not working with an advertising agency (and consider it, including bartering your product or service for their help), this publication will help you make some decisions.

3. *Use the rifle-shot approach, not the shotgun*. Don't try to cover the broadest possible market, at least not early on. Target spe-

cific groups and/or individuals whom you wish to serve and search out the specialty publications, the specific trade or interest groups, the small local publication or broadcast outlet that can reach your target. On the other hand, if you have invented a special product or implement that has broad appeal, cable television systems with an 800-number call-in have been very effective; expensive, yes, but the return for a broad market is effective, because 40 percent of the country has cable now. If you offer a service, and it is of a special nature, target those specific interest groups. Also consider classified ads in publications, rather than display ads and run the ads more than once. Classifieds are less expensive than display ads and can often serve to describe your business in more detail.

There are certain words and phrases that "send a warning" to the consumer. If the consumer sees "one owner" in an automobile ad, he is interested, but wonders why the one owner is selling the car. If he sees "doll house" or "handyman special" in a house sale, he knows the house is small or in need of a lot of repair. If he sees "exciting office" in a job ad, he is wary of the conditions or salary.

Beware of using "warning" words in your ad for your product or service. Use honest and positive words to make your pitch. The best course is to tell the truth about what you are selling; describe what it is or is expected to do or accomplish and give the particulars of its cost and source. Don't oversell and don't obfuscate (try to confuse, trick, or lead astray). While these may sound like obvious rules, the tendency or advice to oversell a product or service is rampant today. Don't be dishonest; don't oversell. If you are candid, chatty, specific, direct, you are more likely to appeal to your target.

4. *Get the most for your money*. Repeat your ads. Buy "blocks" or "flights" of ads in publications or radio and get the discounts offered for such purchases. Make it stand out. If it is a display ad in a publication, be sure the copy and art work stand out. (One writer recommends that you paste your ad in the publication and let several friends thumb through the magazine or newspaper to test whether or not it stands out.) The size determines the "stacking" and in a newspaper smaller ads are usually stacked above the fold, which is the most advantageous place.

Also, the smaller ad is cheaper. Rather than buy a full-page ad, buy one column less than full page; it is just as effective, it is cheaper, and people may stop to read the editorial material in the column, inadvertently reading your ad. In radio buy ten-second spots, adjacent to the station identification (on the hour and half-hour), and buy them consistently. Bunch the ads in calendar periods (holidays or other important periods) for effective "frequency." Put a phone number and/or address in every ad.

5. *Give something free.* Give a sample, a premium, a trial subscription, advice, an analysis, an excerpt, something. It helps you build a mailing/contact list for future sales. Depending on your business, offer participation to those who help you sell.

6. *Always request discounts from the media.* Whether seasonal, for quantity purchase, for time of day, always ask for a discount. Never accept the first "rate card" offer you receive. (Classifieds offer discounts for repeat buying as a standard procedure; all media do it; ask for it.)

7. *If you work through an advertising agency to buy display advertising, you pay later.* They do the work, place the ad, and bill you when it runs. Be sure you know who your account executive is before you commit to the agency, and ask to see other work that he has done. Check with his or her clients to see if they are satisfied with the work. Remember that ads exist to sell a product or service—not the ad. Wonderful, creative ads that are fun, exciting, and memorable often win awards, but they do not necessarily increase sales. Don't be beguiled by the creativity; check the results.

8. *The Yellow Pages.* When in doubt, do it. Telephone directory advertising still generates substantial new business, particularly if your interest is regional. Yellow pages are proliferating now that deregulation of Ma Bell is complete. It is not a question of, if, but which? Call your telephone directory representatives. Let them make you a sales pitch and make them provide you with circulation and sales figures; they will. You may want to advertise in more than one region and that's fine too, as long as you can justify the expenditure with research that shows your target market coincides with the subscribers in question. Be consistent with your ad and place yourself in the proper category (maybe more than one). Remember to monitor results and,

if you run an ad for a year with no response, consider getting out of that particular region or category.

Direct Mail Marketing

Direct mail marketing should never be used as a substitute for other advertising and promotion; it should be used concurrently. One supports the other.

It is easier to set guidelines for direct mail when you offer a product than when you offer a service. The results are more easily measurable.

1. Measure your cost per paid *order* to evaluate the true cost, not the cost per thousand of doing the mailing.
2. Measure the effectiveness by *conversion* (getting a second order from a customer).
3. Avoid direct marketing when an item is inexpensive or heavy. Shipping costs dissuade buyers.
4. Direct mail is most effective when the purchase is fun and enjoyable. Your advertising should emphasize the rewards of the purchase.
5. If you rent a mailing list, be aware that there are two kinds: compiled lists, which are lists of names developed from published sources, such as directories, membership lists, and professional associations, and response lists, which are lists of individuals or companies which have bought a product or service similar to yours. The disadvantage to the compiled list is that there is no evidence that the persons listed have ever bought a product or service similar to yours. With the response list, you may not be able to develop a qualified list for your own product or service. However, overall, the best advice is to stick to lists of people who have already bought by mail.
6. The best months for direct mail advertising are January and August, except for the week before Labor Day.

The selling of *services* by direct mail is a somewhat trickier subject. It relates to the service you offer. If you are offering a cleaning service, a landscaping service, a word processing/secretarial service, a hauling service, or the like, and focused on a particular neighborhood or area, it is worth considering a mailing at bulk postal rates to that specific neighborhood or area. You can obtain such lists,

115

which define apartment houses versus single-family houses, or by defined zip codes.

If you are a consultant (business, beauty, special industry, educational), offer special legal services, specialize in speech or vocal training, or the other myriad of one-person businesses that deal with areas of expertise rather than areas of a neighborhood or region, then you will need special mailing lists of those potential customers/clients. You can get them from the library, which carries lists of organizations and professions, from your Chamber of Commerce, from contacts with the local banks, who will consider you as a resource for clients who need help, or from other cultivated sources. Your rate of return from letters and follow-up phone calls will be low, and slow, and it will not be your only method of advertising; but you should consider special mailings to your target markets just to get your letter or brochure into the hands of the people who may, some day, need you.

Good Copy for Sales Letters or Brochures

Ed McLean of Yonkers, New York, publishes the *Direct Marketing Copy* newsletter and has offered some tips for writing stronger copy for sales letters and brochures.

A cover letter should:

- Seize the reader's attention quickly.
- Establish a bond of friendly mutual self-interest.
- Tell positively and without apology how the product or service can help the reader.
- Refer to an enclosed brochure or reply form that describes the offer in more detail.
- Push for immediate action in an order or sales inquiry.

The brochure accompanying the letter should include:

- A thorough description of the product or service, how it works, what it provides.
- A list of ways the product or service can benefit the reader.
- A comparison of the product/service with competitors, with charts, tables, illustrations.
- Technical specifications, if relevant.
- Testimonials from satisfied customers/clients.

- Commonly asked questions about the product/service, with clear, factual answers.
- The guarantee (if any) and a clear order/request form with an easy-to-find address and phone number.

An easy test of the copy: substitute the name of your competitor(s) for your own. If the copy still stands up, rewrite the whole thing. You have not made your offering unique.

Posters, Billboards, and Outdoor Advertising

In many regions of the country one-person businesses often run outdoor advertising. In my hometown, the chiropractor has had a billboard at the outskirts of town for many years. It must get business, because he keeps it there. On the other side of town, the insurance agent for a national carrier has run a billboard—with his picture—for many years. Again, I have to believe that there are some results or he would not continue the expense.

There are small, portable, electrified billboards that have become fashionable on state highways in recent years (averaging as much as $250 per month), which have great appeal to one-person businesses. I don't know if I live in a part of the country where humor is paramount or not, but I have enjoyed some of the slogans on these very personal billboards. (Their value is that the message can be changed quickly and by the owner.) An automobile service stop recently advertised before winter: "Plan ahead. It wasn't raining when Noah built the ark"; a hairdresser on the road announced: "Let me get into your hair"; a small antique shop proclaimed: "Customer wanted; no experience necessary"; and a small gift shop stated: "My mom told me to get more customers in here. Help!"

While I don't advocate this as the quintessential form of marketing, it is obviously memorable, or I wouldn't remember it. It aims to attract the attention of the passerby to shops and services that depend on walk-in or drive-in traffic. Variations on the theme are worth considering, and, while humor may not appeal to you, it does have the advantage of standing out in the neon-saturated world we live in.

Most of the signs are white with black letters. The good ones are either black with yellow letters or yellow with black letters—the absolute, market-tested best way to be seen in a traffic situation. They are, of course, illuminated.

Store/Office Signage

If your business is conducted in a store or office where signage is possible or desirable, there are certain simple rules: (1) have it painted by a professional (2) have it duplicate (if possible) your stationery and your business card design; (3) have it visible for the walking or driving traffic (on a perpendicular to the building, if possible); and (4) use colors that are appropriate for the neighborhood, but that catch the eye; such as black and yellow, gray and maroon, green and gold, gray and black, maroon and white, dark blue and gold, or red and white.

Trade Shows

With over nine-thousand trade shows held in the United States in 1985, it is important for a small business to consider participating in one or more of them. However, don't even think about going into a trade show unless you intend to use it to sell (sign up buyers, sign up prospects, sign up distributors). If it can fulfill some of your sales goals and be cost-effective, then you should analyze it as a part of your marketing plan. However, here are some questions you need to answer before you make the commitment.

1. *Which show should you be in?* You have regional and national options. Which offers the best sales prospects for your product or service? Write to the sponsors of shows that are possibilities and ask for an audit of the previous show: companies that appeared, names of visitors (if available), attendance and attendance flow—anything they can provide. If one or two still look promising, attend them and make your own audit. Interview exhibitors and attendees (informally, of course), observe the ambience and organization, survey the flow and competition.
2. *Will your product/service be well presented by the people you hire?* As a one-person business, you cannot do it all by yourself. You will have to hire people to "man" the booth for two or three days. You have to hire them in advance and train them to repre-

sent you. (You certainly are not going to let them "wing" it or leave their presentations to chance.) If the expenditure of that time and money seems likely to produce sales prospects, then you can analyze the cost-per-contact.

3. *Will your customers/clients know you are going to be there?* If you decide to participate, send a mailing at least two months before the event. One company announces its participation on the envelopes of every piece of mail it sends out for a month before the show.

4. *What are your specific and achievable goals for the show?* Write them down, work out the strategies, and train your helpers accordingly. What can you afford to give away? What do you plan to have as "take-aways" by the people who come? How do you plan to get people to sign up while they are with you.?

5. *Can you afford to make the booth attractive and professional?* If you cannot afford a professional look, don't go; you will do more harm than good. However, if you plan to be in more than one show, there are portable display walls and racks that can be carried and shipped in very manageable cases, the cost of which can be amortized over several appearances.

6. *Are you prepared to follow up?* If you don't have the time and resources to follow up on every contact immediately after the show, perhaps you should reconsider. Nothing is staler than last night's beer and last week's show. One exhibitor comes to a show with the follow-up material already packaged. As soon as the names are obtained, he addresses the package and mails it off, so it is waiting at the attendee's desk within two or three days. That's follow-up!

Organization Programs

If you are an active member of your community or want to be, you will be asked to buy ads in printed programs for special events. While it is unlikely that these ads are going to deliver much business to you, it is often important for your business image and visibility to be associated with these special events.

You cannot buy an ad in all of these programs, and the size of the ad you might be able to buy is probably too small to make an impact. You might discuss it with the person who is selling the ads and ask him or her to set aside several pages for business cards. These are ads obviously smaller than the usual full page, half page, or quarter page; they are the size of business cards and have a special rate. It saves you the cost of a mechanical and allows you to group yourself with other persons or one-person businesses who wish to support a community effort, while participating at a greatly reduced rate. Most advertising directors of such programs will welcome the suggestion because it allows them to "find" other advertisers/subscribers.

Public Relations

Remember, we said in Chapter 1 that public relations is a means of inducing your various publics to have an understanding of and goodwill toward you. Public relations is about *image*—the perception that other people have of you and your business. It is hard to measure, but there are things you can do to earn the respect you desire in your community and among the clients/customers you wish to serve.

1. *Teaching*. More often than not, the easiest way for a one-person business owner to build a reputation and following is if he or she teaches a course at the local college or university. If you choose to do this, obviously, it should be in your area of expertise. It will be particularly helpful if it is in the "continuing education" programs, where adults (usually professionals) come to enhance their skills in a particular area of information. You not only have the pleasure of working with adults who are interested in your realm of business, but you also have the opportunity to cultivate potential clients/customers for your business.

2. *Lectures*. From such teaching and from your association with various organizations will come the opportunity to lecture to various groups. While your teaching will provide an income, albeit modest, your lectures, at first, may be gratis. As your reputation grows, you will ask for an honorarium for your lecture appearances, no matter how modest, to put yourself in the professional category and to place a value on your time and knowledge.

Be prepared. Write your material in advance; read it, time it, be familiar with it. Type it double- or triple-spaced in capital letters, so it will be easy to read. Use 5- × 7-inch cards to keep from rattling papers at the lectern. If you are good at ad libbing, then adapt the material to an outline form, and prepare it on five by seven cards. You might put important phrases, quotes, or figures on the backs of selected cards, so you won't forget or misquote.

If you require audio-visual equipment, chalk board, flip chart, stand for displaying cards, etc., check it out with your sponsors well in advance, so that they can have the necessary equipment or materials ready. Be a good stage manager; check the room, the equipment, the seating, the hand-outs at least thirty minutes before you are to "do your thing." If something is missing, you are the one who suffers, not the sponsor. If you use slides, filmstrips, film, exhibit cards, or any other kind of visual or audio material, have it professionally done. What they see and what you give them can mark you as an amateur or a professional, no matter how brilliant your lecture or how well-spoken it may be. Don't skimp on this item. Ideally, you will be able to use your presentation materials at an assortment of places and presentations, thereby amortizing the cost.

3. *Column/comment placement.* As a teacher and speaker/lecturer, you will gain confidence in yourself, but also, you will gain status and recognition as an "expert" in your field. Become familiar with all the newspapers, magazines, trade journals, local "shoppers," business publications, etc. in your region or community. Buy them, read them, become familiar with their content, styles, and the names of their editors and writers. If it is feasible to meet some of these people in an informal setting (lunches, meetings, cocktail parties), do so. Introduce yourself; compliment them on recent writings; discuss a topic of recent interest; give them your business card. Try to direct the conversation in such a way that the door is open and there is a logical "hook" or opening for you to follow up with a letter, an article, a phone call in the future. Your objective is to get an interview about yourself and/or your company or to offer to supply an article or a series of articles in your area of expertise. Many local papers and journals cannot pay their writers and welcome columns

written by interested readers. Your "pay" will be the appearance of your name and your company's name (with luck, on a regular basis) to a public you might not otherwise reach.

4. *Interviews*. The obvious spin-off from the above is that you will become better known as an "expert" to be called upon by writers in the area who are looking for "in depth" information, "comments," "background material," and other information that they may need for something they are writing. How do they know you are available? Every time you have an article written, announce a lecture, or have an interview, send copies to the major writers in town with your business card clipped to it and "FYI" written on it. They may toss them away, but pretty soon your name will become familiar to them. You should also include on this mailing list the names of interviewers at the radio, television, and cable stations in the area. Keep this special PR mailing list up-to-date and use it regularly to let the media in the area know who you are and what you do.

5. *Special events*. Every community in this country has numerous special events during the year that businesses participate in, from the United Way, to marathons for hospitals, to banquets for arts organizations. How can you compete against the big companies in the area for visibility without their financial and human resources? By *volunteering* to serve in a committee chair capacity, where you and your company can gain recognition. Having said that, let me pass along a few lessons learned the hard way. If you cannot afford to give the *time*, don't do it. Time is all you have to sell. Realize that this will take away earning power, so it is a substantial contribution; be sure you are also going to get substantial recognition. Don't volunteer for something that will require lots of phone calls, office help, mailing costs, or office supplies; you don't have any to give away. Don't volunteer for something you are not really interested in. With time slipping away, it had better be something you *care* about. Be selective; don't volunteer for everything that comes along; choose one or two things a year that really matter. Be professional; don't volunteer just to get your name on a roster. Really work and really do a good job. Remember, you are seeking visibility, and you want to be visible as a professional.

6. *Joint Ventures*. Be alert to opportunities to promote your busi-

ness in cooperation with someone else or others. This can take a variety of forms: cosponsoring a seminar or conference, if you are a consultant/lecturer; printing the season tickets for the high school football season (with your company name on the back of the tickets), if you are in the advertising, design, printing, or newsletter business; running a joint sale of your product or service with some other that is compatible; bartering your services for logo credit for the local hospital, Kiwanis, or MADD chapter. You get the idea. Keep in mind that the objective is to keep real cash costs low, visibility high, and personal time and expertise as the commodity you contribute.

7. *Contributions.* The 1986 Tax Reform Act eliminates the deduction of contributions for individuals who do not itemize their personal tax returns. Further, the deductions for charitable contributions on company income taxes must now pass much more stringent tests. For instance, a charitable contribution deduction for travel expenses is allowed only where no significant element of personal pleasure, recreation, or vacation is involved. What does this mean to the one-person business? First, you review your previous deductions to see if they conform to the new law. If some of them do not, you must reappraise them to see if they still have worth to you, both as a community participation project and as a tax value. Please remember, however, that the United States has the most extensive charitable contribution record of any nation in the world. We are a nation of people who give and care. It is unlikely that you will make your decisions solely on the basis of tax advantage. You are interested in your *image* as well as what makes you *feel good.* Good citizens in this country are those who do good works. You wish to be known as a good citizen. Your best decision is to be selective and to target your modest resources to those issues and organizations that matter most to you.

Publicity

Publicity has been called "having a good flak beat the drum to tell your story to people who might not otherwise hear it." It requires good reading and good writing. You must read and listen and watch the many news and information outlets in your community or marketplace to determine what sort of audience each of *them* has. Then you can determine which outlet is right for the audience you wish to reach and concentrate on them. That is the good reading part.

The good writing part is a bit more technical and detailed. Once you decide which outlet is right for your product or service, you must write for their audiences, and write well and interestingly and grammatically correct (and must we add, typed professionally?) to get them to consider including your story in their time and space.

Publicity, you see, is free. They print or tell your story. However, the trade-off is that your story must be interesting to their readers, viewers, listeners.

It is an art, and a craft, and a good publicity person is worth whatever you have to pay. (Fortunately, the work can be measured: by the inch of newspaper or magazine space or by the coverage by radio and television.) If you are good at the craft yourself, fine; you can devise the publicity campaign, write it, and hire part-time help to get it out to the contacts you designate. However, we are back to a discussion of the good use of your time. Do you want to be running your company and doing what your company does, or do you want to be doing publicity? I urge you to *hire* it done.

1. *Be alert to publicity campaigns in your community or market.* Who does it best? If it is done by a large company, undoubtedly they have an in-house staff. If it is done by a small company, call the president and congratulate him or her for a campaign that is particularly well done. First of all, they will be flattered, particularly if they designed it themselves. In the course of the conversation, you may discover which outside firm did it, if such is the case.

2. *Call the two or three persons of firms whose names you have obtained.* Tell them that you are considering hiring out some PR work. They will take you to lunch; they will make presentations to you. Review their campaigns. Ask them which ones failed. Get names of clients and call for references and satisfaction. Pay particular attention to clients who have similar products or services to yours. Call those clients and ask if the campaigns helped *sales*. Maybe they will tell you and maybe they won't, but you won't know unless you ask.

3. *Ask the PR firms to make a presentation to you of the kind of campaign they would suggest.* Evaluate it on the basis of how it would increase your market reach, extend your customer potential, result in sales. Ask them to help you in that evaluation. Please be aware that some firms/persons will be reluctant to give you a campaign presentation. All they have to sell is their creativity and contacts. Obviously, they will be wary that you will take their ideas and use them yourself, or that you will give them to someone else (cheaper) to do for you. Their doubt is understandable, because it happens all the time. That does not make it right; in fact, it is disgusting. You don't want to behave that way. You want to conduct all your business dealings in an ethical way. In addition to being the right thing to do, it is the smart thing to do. Crooks and cheats get found out; that is not the reputation you want. Assure them in writing, if necessary, that their ideas will be held in confidence. You may also want their assurance that the information you give them about your company will be held in confidence and never used against you in another campaign.

4. *Be honest about the money you have to spend.* A good PR person will devise a campaign to get the "best bang for the buck" if you level with him or her. They will focus on those areas of a campaign that can maximize your exposure for the amount of dollars you have allotted.

5. *Remember one thing: there are no guarantees in PR.* The best person with a terrific campaign, impeccable contacts and diligent follow-up may not be able to place your story in the media of your choice—or anywhere. Sometimes your story is of no interest to the media outlets at the time you send it out or that you need it. Be prepared for that. Don't put all your marketing budget into a PR campaign. Remember, it is one element of an all-inclusive campaign to sell your product or service. This is usually the hardest part of marketing for a new company or a small business person to understand. Every dollar is so important that we expect results when we hire experts to work for us. Remember, your press agent does not control the radio community calendar, the television station production schedule, or the assignment desk editor at the paper. They can only entice, cajole, and try to persuade. When they succeed, it is terrific.

When they fail, you know that you also have your advertising budget operating for you, as well as your promotion activities, and, possibly, merchandising.

One other word of caution: When dealing with the press, print, or broadcast media *be prepared.* Don't expect them to know your business. Be prepared to tell them about it, succinctly and clearly; and have "hand-outs" for them in case they need additional reference. In some cases, it is not a bad idea to prepare a list of questions too! They look better, and so do you.

Reporting and interviewing is a hard business; they have to be "instant experts" in many fields. Anything you can do to make their jobs easier, and make them look better is usually greatly appreciated. (One caveat: don't let them think you are "leading" them. That is an insult. News should be unbiased, and they strive very hard to attain that.)

Press Releases

The key to good PR usually rests on a properly written press release. The Sperry and Hutchinson Company (330 Madison Ave., New York, NY 10017) publishes a splendid handbook on publicity (geared to nonprofit organizations) that is invaluable for the neophyte. Although you are a for-profit company, you might wish to order one.

There are certain "guidelines" that all of us can use to make our announcements attractive to the outlets we seek.

1. Use a letterhead that has the proper company name, address, and phone number. If you are using a PR firm, they will use their own letterhead.
2. Be sure it is typed accurately, spelled and punctuated properly, and that it is double or triple spaced.
3. Put the words "PRESS RELEASE" at the top-center of the page under the letterhead. On the top-left corner type "CONTACT:-----" and put the name and phone number of the person who can give additional information. On the top-right of the page type "FOR IMMEDIATE RELEASE." If the timing is important, you should type, "FOR RELEASE AFTER ---------."
4. Unless it is a particular complicated story, try to hold the release to one and one-half or two pages of copy, stapled together. The first (and possibly second) paragraph of the release should supply

the who, what, where, when, and why of the release. Although your main objective is to be creative and to catch the attention of the reader, this is the most important part of the press release. Hundreds of such press releases are received each day; these first two paragraphs encourage further reading. The succeeding paragraphs will supply important details, additional names, supporting data—the things that make your press release worthy of being considered "news." Put the most important elements first and continue your paragraphs in descending order of importance (to you). Editors crop copy from the bottom up. If the writer puts your story into the system, it will be cut to fit time or space. Put the most important first, the least important last.

5. Target your reader. Don't just send it to the newspaper or the radio station. Get a name or get a title to send it to. You want the person who can do something about it to read it. If it floats around the shop for a few days, it will get lost anyway.

6. Good material for press releases includes new products, achievements, prizes, promotions or additions to your client roster, findings from research, speeches, participation in community activities.

7. Stick to the facts. Do not editorialize. Opinions have no place in a news story. Be careful about using adjectives. There *are* ways to inject an opinion into a story, however. Use direct quotations for example. Quotations are also a good way to get a mention of your company in the story, as well as a way to draw conclusions from the facts you have reported in the story.

8. There are certain styles of writing for the news media. Ask your local paper for a style book. They will probably give you one, and you will be able to write your press releases in an accepted style, making them more likely to be accepted.

9. For the print media, photographs are truly worth a thousand words. Editors will often run a photograph to brighten a page, even when it has less than spectacular newsworthiness. The most effective way is to encourage the publication to come and photograph the event. If a person (you) is important, the publication will generally invite you to the publication studio for a "head shot." Be sure to take along a prop or an award to liven up the photo. More often than not, you will have to take care of the photography yourself. Hire a good photographer who knows to get a sharp picture, the composition uncluttered, and the focus of attention in the center of the photo. Also hire one who is fast. If you have an event on Friday afternoon, it will probably not see the morning paper. It *may* get in the afternoon paper, if the 8

by 10-inch black and white glossies (with captions, which we will discuss) arrive at the paper before 7 or 8 o'clock in the evening. If timing is not important—two or three days later is okay—then the photos have to be interesting. They take on a different significance, because they are no longer "news" and have become "features."

10. Captions are crucial and should be prepared in a very specific way. All photos must have captions in order to be considered. Every person must be identified (from left to right, with properly spelled names and appropriate titles) and the event the photo captures must be described succinctly! Type the caption on a piece of paper as wide as the photograph. Leave about 2 inches of space at the top of the paper. Spread some rubber cement in this space and affix it to the back of the photograph with the caption showing below. Then fold the caption up over the face of the photograph. If you are sending more than one copy of the picture, be sure every photograph has a caption attached. (Don't use carbon paper; it smudges.) Never use paper clips or staples on a photograph and never write on the back. These practices render the print unsuitable for reproduction. When mailing, protect the photo by putting it between two pieces of stiff cardboard cut to size.

The Broadcast Media

Many times public affairs departments and community calendars will announce events in the community, if the events are of broad interest, such as seminars and conferences, special parties to which the public is invited, etc. If your product or service falls within a station's guidelines for such announcements, a typed announcement, written along the lines of a press release and sent to the appropriate person at the station, can get you, at the very least, an announcement on the air.

A news conference is a dramatic way to announce an important story. However, it should be reserved for those special occasions when the topic is too complex or too important to be covered in a news release. Obviously, a press conference includes both print and broadcast media, but your desire is to have broadcast coverage as soon as possible (that night on the early news, or live, if a radio station is interested). It takes careful planning, in terms of meeting space, preparation of the announcement, and the way you will answer the questions. Let the media know at least two weeks in advance through a written "notice of press conference" that gives all the particulars, and follow up with phone calls to see who is coming. Be sure you know who will attend and that they know what the event is about. Have press kits available with plenty of information, and be sure that "exclusive interviews" can be handled before or after the event. Keep it to thirty minutes and *know what you are talking about.* Prepare possible questions and know what your responses will be. Try to second-guess the questions so you will be prepared for surprises. Use news conferences very sparingly. The media picks and chooses the time it spends; don't waste it. They will not come back if you try to fool them.

Interviews on the broadcast media (in their "Public Service" local interview programs) are a lot easier to arrange and can have significant PR impact for you. Know who the interviewers are and keep track of their programming. Watch as often as possible to see what kind of people they have on the shows and how they conduct their interviews. We have already decided that you are going to keep them on your "FYI" mailing list, building up their awareness of what you do, who you are, and the special things with which you are involved. When you have a special need to increase your visibility, develop a "hook" and call the station. Ask for the producer of the particular show. (We are talking about local programming, not network.) Introduce yourself, ask if he or she has seen your previous material, tell them how much you like the show (particularly a recent interview you have seen), and ask if you can send some information that might be of interest to them. Although you may get turned down or be treated like the village dolt, it is unlikely. Even if you are, be polite and send the information anyway. If the reception has been pleasant, send the material to the show producer and follow it up with a phone call in an effort to arrange an interview on-air. If the reception has been unpleasant, send the information to the on-air personality with a copy of your letter to the station manager. It is likely that the personality will not see it, but the manager will, and the producer who opens and reads the mail will have to give it some consideration. Tread lightly with this; but there are so many broadcast interview programs in the average city, that your reception will undoubtedly be good somewhere. They *need* program material; and they need people with an interesting story to tell, an interesting personality, a new idea, a new service. This is a particularly good outlet for you, if you have volunteered to chair some charitable committee and you go to talk about that. In the course of the conversation, you *must* describe who you are and what you do for a living. It is a "tie-in," and it is important to you because it is free.

Wire Services

Chances are you have a wire service bureau (or two or three) in your hometown. (A list of wire services is in the Appendix.) Know whether or not you do, what the service is, where it is, and the name of the bureau chief. If you don't have a bureau, you may have a "stringer" in your town. (A stringer is a person who does stories on a part-time basis for one or more of the wire services.) Ask your local newspaper editor if such is the case. If possible, get to know the bureau chief or stringer, perhaps socially, or go to the office and ask for ten minutes to introduce yourself.

If you feel you have a special story to tell, something unique, funny, interesting, different, that has an impact outside the confines of your own community, that bureau chief may receive it with interest, rewrite it, and "send it out on the wire." That does not mean it will get printed, but it could be picked up by newspapers, TV, and radio stations all over the country. Friends of mine started a magazine devoted to inspirational and informational material for women who had experienced breast cancer. Their budget was modest and their marketing was slow and tedious. However, the AP (Associated Press) Bureau chief in their hometown liked what they were doing and thought it was a special human interest story; he "sent the story out on the wire." It was picked up by a score of papers all over the country and their subscriptions made a quantum leap. They focused their advertising in those areas of the country where the stories had run and began a second dramatic phase of building their magazine. Wire services can make a real difference in outreach, if national coverage is of interest to you. *Know* that bureau chief.

Merchandising

Merchandising is a sales promotion activity, usually oriented more toward advertising than toward sales. The purpose of merchandising is to induce your customer/client to make multiple purchases, usually in different products or services.

The most typical kind of merchandising is in couponing for free samples or discounts, sales discounts on products or services, or "two-fers" (two for the price of one). If these activities are suitable for your business, you need little advice about how to proceed. There are myriads of examples around you.

I offer one reminder: when you discount or offer samples, two-fers, or other forms of cost reduction, you *decrease your income*. There are different ways of planning and accounting for this discount or loss: as a discount item on your gross revenues (when you prepare your monthly income statement) or as an advertising cost (as an additional expense on the P&L). However you plan to account for it in your financial records, you must never lose sight of the fact that it costs you something.

Your appearance at meetings, conventions, and exhibitions can be considered a form of merchandising, and we have discussed that earlier. Besides paying for an exhibit booth, there are other ways of merchandising yourself, your product, or service at conventions and conferences. They are:

1. *Prizes and gifts*. All conventions look for small gifts for the "goodie" bags given at registration or for door prizes to be awarded in drawings. These can range from pens or pencils with your company name imprinted, to copies of your newsletters, to a free consultation at your financial planning office, to a free lawn mowing, to a free admission to your next seminar. The opportunities are limited only by your imagination and the willingness of the sponsor to include you in their convention.

2. *Entertainment*. At monthly meetings, conferences, or conventions of particular target market groups, you have the opportunity to attend, mingle, leave your card. That is a typical "networking" expenditure of time and money. Another wrinkle on this has been used successfully by several small businesses: they take one or two college students to such a luncheon or dinner meeting, paying the tab, of course and introducing the students as their guests and career interns. It helps, of course, if the students are interning with the company, working part time, or have some connection. It allows you to be helpful while getting help, and to introduce yourself and your company as a caring organization.

3. *Hospitality Suites.* At the right kind of convention, one in which you feel you can cultivate active sales leads, you can consider the expense of sponsoring a hospitality suite at the meeting hotel. They don't work unless you preannounce them (write every member a month before and invite them to your suite), register everyone who comes into the suite, give them a little gift when they appear (one company took Polaroid pictures in a fun setting for years), and follow up with material and phone calls promptly afterward. In addition to the cost of the hotel suite, the refreshments, and the letters and follow-up material, you should also budget helpers for the occasion. You cannot do it alone, and you will want to spend some time and money training the help before the event. Remember: the goal of such expenditure is active sales leads.

4. *Special store displays.* In every community almost every merchant (particularly privately owned stores, rather than chains) will allow special store displays under certain circumstances. If you sell a product that they carry, they, of course, may be receptive to an attractive display that does not take up a lot of room. If you offer a product or service that is not sold at their store, but that has a tie-in (it is up to *you* to "sell" them on the tie-in!), they are oftentimes receptive. For example, the photocopy shop that I use regularly has a prominent, but tasteful, area in which they display announcements of word processing experts. Friends of mine make a magnificent furniture polish in their garage, which they sell by mail. Many antique shops around the country display their tasteful announcement, because the stuff works so well on antiques, and because antique dealers do not usually sell furniture polish. (Of course, they receive a "sample" each Christmas from my friends!) Most major supermarkets have a "Community Bulletin Board" on which are displayed small announcements of goods and services; so do laundromats and car washes. It may not sound sophisticated, but it can reach thousands of people in your community each day. If you have a publication, product, or service that would not seem too out of place, doctors, optometrists, dentists will sometimes allow a discreet, tasteful card or coupon box in their waiting rooms. Think about it; and don't be shy; ask!

5. *Novelties.* An acquaintance of mine imports and customizes nov-

elties (pens, pencils, playing cards, tie tacks, cuff links, etc.) for clients. He belongs to or attends every civic and organizational meeting in town, or so it seems! He is personable and outgoing. He circulates and "works" the room and leaves his card, which is a fun, playing card, with his name and company on the back, or hands out pens with his name and company on it. Everyone knows what he is doing, but everyone takes the pen or "collects" the cards, and he has a great portion of the novelty business in town. He advertises in the business journal in town, and he is also in the Yellow Pages, but his personal efforts supply the real "pay-off."

You can use novelties (note pads seem to be in vogue right now) to leave at conventions, luncheons, every call you make— to remind your potential clients who you are, where you are, and what you do.

One of my books is on business planning, and I give seminars around the country on "how to write a business plan." When we have finished a long day or weekend on the tedium (and excitement) of writing a business plan, I give the group "one more exercise." After the groans have subsided, the laughter starts; the exercise is a cryptogram puzzle of all we have worked through. I call it "The Planning Puzzle" (copyrighted), and it is a "take-away"—something for them to do on the train or plane as a reminder of the principles we discussed. Is it a novelty? Yes. Do they do the puzzle? Many do, because I hear from them. Does it serve a purpose? I think it serves two: it reinforces what they have worked on, and they have my name, company name, and address on the puzzle. If they use it back at work, it reinforces their memory of me, and that is what novelties are for. It is also what public relations is all about.

Product Exposure on TV and in Movies

Products appear in movies and TV shows, and they did not get there accidentally. Someone (the creator or distributor) worked to get them there. It costs time and money, but the exposure can be widespread beyond your wildest dreams. (Clark Kent ate Cheerios in *Superman* and millions of people saw it.)

How does that relate to a one-person business? If you own or have created a particular product that could benefit from national and international exposure, it is worth trying. You will have to work through a broker. Here are some names:

For movies: Associated Film Promotions, 10100 Santa Monica Blvd., Los Angeles, CA 90067; Donald Degnan Company, 400 Madison Avenue, New York, NY 10017.

For TV: Donald Degnan Company (see above); Larry Dorn & Associates, 5550 Wilshire Blvd., Los Angeles, CA 90036; Game Show Placements Limited, 901 N. Seward St., Hollywood, CA 90038; Edward E. Finch & Company, 880 Third Ave., New York, NY 10022.

Summary

Marketing is a two-edged sword for the one-person business. It is the "fun" part of your activity (second, of course, to the doing of the business itself, which you enjoy or you wouldn't be doing it), because it allows you to "sell" yourself and your business to an ever-widening public. It also takes time from the business, however, and poses the ultimate question: Do you want to *do* what you do or *sell* what you do?

We all know that we cannot do it without selling it, so it comes down to choices. That is where your marketing plan can make a difference. Review Chapter 1 and coordinate it with these tips. Decide on those elements that *you* can do best and those that will best sell your business to your target market. Then you can concentrate on those activities that will take the least of your time, the minimum of your dollars for the most reach into the marketplace you have researched and targeted.

Frankly, there is no business without marketing it. Selectivity is your major challenge, but in researching and discovering what you have to sell to your select public(s), you rediscover yourself. Perhaps that is the greatest satisfaction in your marketing effort.

You redefine and reaffirm yourself, and why you got into this singular activity in the first place. Everyone is unique and your marketing efforts should be spent in reaffirming that.

Chapter 7

The Most Valuable Asset—Time

As in all businesses, your major concerns must be the allocation of time, resources, and what you *like* to do. In the case of the one-person business, these concerns are of particular importance because you are all you have. Spreading yourself too thin, running out of time, getting hung up on tasks you hate, instead of doing what you like (and that, presumably, is the business itself) can be devastating to your growth, your reputation, and your profitability.

There are hundreds of books on library shelves and scores of seminars that purport to tell you how to use your time more effectively and channel your resources, both personal and financial, into profitable activities. I suggest you read them, attend some seminars, and choose those that are most appropriate for your personality and your business.

However, if you don't have time for that (doesn't that sound familiar?), the following chapter is a distillation of a lot of reading, a number of seminars, many interviews with one-person business owners, and a few years of experience.

John Donne gave the best advice when he wrote, "Know then, thyself." Gather ideas and information from wherever you choose; then put them through your personal analysis machine and make your own choices. Each person has his or her own life-style and individual goals and needs. Your work habits and personal skills will ultimately dictate how you run your business. At best, the following ideas will be grist for your creative mill and will allow you to devise those tricks and mechanisms that will best serve you.

"Time spent on what you love is not wasted time." I don't know if I read that or made it up, but it is true. Don't ever forget Chapter

2 and why you got into this in the first place. You *want* to be a one-person business, because it satisfies particular needs that you have. It allows you to work the way you want to work in a business you control and you enjoy. It allows you to allocate your time to the things that matter to you. It allows you time to love and to create and to "smell the flowers." It allows you to be your own boss and set your own priorities. Look carefully, however; all those words are "active verbs." They imply that you are in control. The danger is that the *business*—or the details of business—take control, and you are no longer in charge of your time.

Inevitably, you find yourself relying on other people to do some of the tasks of running your business. That takes money, and, although you know that you have allocated those funds in your budget, you want to be sure you don't overspend, just because you are losing control.

You want to be efficient. Economy of scale is what the one-person business is all about. You may *like* or be good at a task that could be done more efficiently or economically by someone else. You also could do some things very badly and be better off paying to have it done.

Let's talk about problems and solutions.

What Wastes Your Time?

Reading the Mail

It arrives six days a week, and, whether your business is mail order or not, the mail is one of your most important outlets to the world. It can get piled up, lost, become overwhelming, unless you set up certain techniques and procedures to control it, rather than the other way around. Sorting, trading, separating the letters from the bills and solicitations, answering the letters that need answering, paying the bills, dumping or analyzing solicitations—all the myriad of things connected with the mail can take an enormous amount of time, and depending upon the *kind* of business you run, can make a difference (service or product, local or national, immediate or long term).

As a one-person business, it is unlikely that you will allow this important activity to be done by another person. You have to organize yourself, your office, and your time to deal with the situation.

1. *Organize Yourself.* When is the mail delivered? If possible, be there at your office at the appropriate time. (I know! That is not always possible.) If it is a morning delivery and you can (generally) keep your mornings free, you can do an initial sort.

- *Set up a sorting table.* It can be a simple table with a chair and lamp for easy work, but it has a significant purpose. Along the back is a series of file boxes in which you will do a preliminary "sort" of the paper you generate and the paper that arrives in the mail. Depending on your business, it will vary from "payables" to "billables" to "correspondence" to "other." This is the way you sort your paper work so that you can manage the filing in the absence of someone to help.

  The following is a variation on the sorting table that may be useful to you.

  At the back of the table you may wish to set up five holding bins on a filing wall:

- *Personal.* You put everything in it that is personal—letters, or solicitations, invitations, etc.—and you take it home with you for reading at a later time.

- *Checks.* These can be ascertained by looking at the return address. Put them in a second bin, open them promptly, and arrange to deposit them *that* day.

- *Letters.* Put them in the appropriate bin, open them promptly, and mark them (in pencil) for specific action. After you have finished opening all the mail, put the letters in the appropriate dated bin on the wall for the day you plan to follow up. Perhaps it will be by telephone, but, if you plan to answer letter with letter, you will want to set aside dictating time or typing time. *Schedule* it by putting the material in your daily "tick" bin.

- *Business solicitations.* Put them in a bin marked for the purpose. If you file them back to front, you can pull out a timely batch for reading while traveling, waiting for appointments, or taking a coffee break. I keep a soft zipper pouch for such use; I stuff a few in and have them handy to take with me.

2. *Organize Your Office.* After you have organized your office with these holding bins, you will want to organize the rest of the space in a more efficient way. We are talking about space design, so bear with me. No matter what your business is, the de-

sign of your personal work space is crucial to utilizing your time (and, therefore, your productivity) efficiently.

- *Preserve one wall for schedules and mail.* Place the mail bins previously discussed in a handy position. You will work these bins every day.
- *Place a calendar board on the wall; it should have the fifty-two weeks of the current year.* The best one I have seen is about 5 feet long and 4 feet wide, and is divided by week. It allows you to write in the days, dates, commitments in felt pen on a white plastic surface. Set up a code of colors: red for travel, black for appointments, green for sales presentations, whatever is right for your business. Log in your schedule as you set it, so that you can see your year at a glance (and adjust your schedule to your written business plan discussed in Chapter 1).
- *Put thirty-one numbered bins along the wall.* This is your "tick file." As you read your mail and your bills, solicit business, get calls or sales, commit to travel, receive invitations, etc., drop them into the appropriate bin. If you drop a bill into the bin marked "9", you will pull it out on the ninth day of the month and pay the bill (or answer the letter, make the plane reservation, or make the follow-up phone call). These bins become your daily agendas for each day of the month. Obviously, as you work your way through them, the "9" you complete becomes the ninth day of the following month. (Don't be put off by the tedium of these suggestions. They work, simply because they take the place of a full-time secretary.)
- *Put twelve bins along the wall under the thirty-one.* These have the months written on them, and these are the bins that you use for letters, notes, memoranda, bills, etc. for action in a future month. On the second day of each month, you will go into the bin of the next month and pull out those items that are relevant for the *current* month. They will be put into the daily files numbered 1 through 31.

If all of this sounds tedious, remember that the initial investment in the calendar and bins to organize your activities takes the place of a full-time assistant, or the scattered notes and reminders that you will find yourself accumulating as a one-person business. Of course, they will not work unless you use them.

- *Organize a second wall for sorting and filing.* This is the wall along which you put your filing cabinets. The files should be alphabetical, but to your own specific needs. I use "current," "regional," and other specific designations for each drawer, but I also tape a 3 by 5-

inch card on each drawer that summarizes the particular files within it.

• *Filing.* There are two schools of thought on filing: (1) do it *now;* (2) do it all at one scheduled time. I prefer the latter, as it allows you to keep control of your time—the object of the exercise. I use the bins that stack—they help do preliminary organizing, they take up less space, and they fill up fast enough to force me to cope at least once a week. (I find Saturday afternoon during the opera broadcast a good time.) One is marked "Accounts," all paid bills, and receipts go in there. One is marked "Correspondence"; staple all related copies together! One is marked "Projects."

You will work out your own best divisions. The hard fact is that most of us do our own filing. It is how we keep track of things. If someone else does it, you should write the name of the file in pencil in the upper right corner, so you will know where it lands and can get it quickly later.

At this point, you have organized yourself and your office in order to take care of the mail. Let's continue our discussion of the kinds of things that waste your time and that you must control in order to be productive.

The office tools you have installed can help facilitate mail sorting and filing. How you *use* them and disciplines you use are even more important in saving your most valuable asset—time.

Answering the Mail

The mark of a true professional is a prompt response. Don't let clients and creditors chase you. Don't let requests and invitations pile up. Set aside time each day to pull the letters from the daily tick bin and get to it.

If you can respond by telephone in a productive way, do it. In the long run it is cheaper, more personal, and apt to clear up a lot of questions that could take days or weeks by letter. Use a good long-distance service to cut down on your long-distance expense; and, if the material requires something in writing, then confirm later.

Make the call with your appointment book and the initial correspondence in front of you. Don't scribble on note paper; it can get lost. I write on the back of the initial correspondence, putting down the date and time of the call, with whom I talked, and what was said. Write as you talk. Put the notes in the appropriate project file for further follow-up.

If you must send letters, use a "correspondence" file. I keep a manilla folder on the left side of my typewriter. When I finish the letter, I staple it to the original material and put it in the correspondence or project file bin for later filing. I am a night person, so I do a lot of my letters after 11 P.M. at night. A friend of mine is a day person and types her letters in the 5 A.M. quiet with her first cup of coffee. We share one trait: we do it when we are not likely to be interrupted by phone calls or business appointments.

Every town and city has splendid secretarial services. If you have neither the time nor the skill to do your own typing, you can get a lot of mileage out of a dictating machine. Pick a good time to dictate your correspondence on tape and let a service do it for you. There are services in my city that will do the job for $3.50 a letter, with copy and envelope. If you are doing a "mass" mailing, anything from ten to one thousand letters of the same text to different people, the price can drop to a few cents a letter, because the services do the work on a word processor. It is a much more attractive alternative than photocopying a letter and adding the address yourself. Remember, you are buying your time, and it is a very valuable commodity. If you dictate well, you can save hours and hours, and thus, lots of dollars. Caveat: shop around and find a service that will work on a personal basis with you. They will take better care of you, do it properly and promptly, and will also probably give you a good "rate," if you use them consistently.

Answering and Screening Calls

This is another time waster. You will likely answer your own phone, but you may want to screen them with an answering machine. (Record a friendly message! "Hello, this is XYZ Services. Don't hang up. Your call is very important to us. After the tone, give your name and number and we'll be right with you. Here's the tone.") You can pick up immediately after you hear their names and continue the conversation; or you can call back *promptly*. Please understand that the answering machine is the bane of all communication and *no one* likes it. If you use one, keep this in mind:

- Check in with your machine at least every hour, unless you are traveling, in which case, record a new message.
- Pick up immediately, if you have screened the call and know that it is an important client or contact.
- Make sure your "message" is right for you and your business. Change it regularly so people can find you when you are in another location.
- Don't pay too much for one. You can get an excellent machine for about $100 at discount outlets.
- Don't depend on it entirely. Use other means to stay in touch with the world.

Put the *call-forwarding* feature on your business telephone. However, remember that it has some definite advantages and disadvantages. The advantage is that you can be reached when you have gone to another location. However, that location may not be a good place for you to take business (or personal) calls, so it is not the ultimate answer. The point is that you should *buy* the service. It is another alternative that allows you to keep your business running while you run your business. Just remember that it is not the ultimate panacea and use it with discretion.

You should also consider an *answering service*. Having said that, there are some definite things to consider.

The advantage to the service is that you have a live human being talk with your callers and relay messages and information in an efficient and "human" way. This will work, obviously, if you keep your service informed of your whereabouts and relay messages through them to the proper person. We can all remember the Broadway musical, *Bells are Ringing*, and the romantic associations of an answering service. You want a service, not a buddy. The secret is to find a really efficient service. Sadly, that is not as easy as it should be. Check the services that doctors use and then call the doctor and find out if he or she is satisfied! Service just ain't what it used to be! Get a good one or they can do more harm than good.

The advantage of leaving specific messages with a service for specific people can be outweighed by the cost. You can have a service from 9 to 5 Monday through Friday; or twenty four hours a day, seven days a week; or variations in between. Before you buy, analyze your real needs and buy the coverage that is best for you. (I have a friend who teaches two days a week. She uses a service for those two days because she wants to "stay in touch," as well as leave specific messages for people. It's worth it to her. You must decide what is right for you.)

Later in this chapter, we will discuss the options of an office service location and an "incubator." These are two alternatives to answering letters, answering telephones, and a variety of your needs.

Sorting and Paying Bills

This takes time. If you do it all, it can take a lot of time away from your business. Let's break it down into segments and see if we can find the elements that are time wasters and time savers.

1. *Opening and sorting.* I suggest that you keep this part of the exercise under your control. Your cash flow is crucial to your success and the timing of your bill paying is the key. When you have sorted your mail as we have discussed, put the bills in the proper daily "tick" bin. The payment date is determined by several things: do you get a discount for paying early? Would you rather spread out the payments, such as insurance, and pay the slight interest charge in order to keep your cash? Do you want to pay precisely on the due date in order to keep the cash in your account as long as possible? These are questions you should have answered early on, so that you know how to pace your payments.

The following procedures will help keep track of your accounts as well as save you time and money:

- Put the pay date on the bill.
- Mark the amount to be paid on the bill.
- Keep the envelope and bill together. Use the vendor's envelope; put your return address on with a rubber stamp.
- Put the bill in the proper daily bin for payment. I use a manilla envelope for bills, so they will stand out from the rest of the material in the file. You may have bills in the first day, the tenth day, and the thirtieth day or others that are important for your cash flow control.

2. *Bill paying.* Be sure you pay and *mail* on the day you planned to. The postmark may be important. Some more tips:

- *If you pay the bills yourself, schedule a time to do it.* I find early in the morning a good idea. It gets the stack out for the postman in a timely manner, and I can go on about my business. Put the check number and date on the bill before you put it in the file box for later filing. I work with both my checkbook and ledger in front of me. I write in the bill ID number on the check stub, as well as an explanation of the payment. I also make the entry in the ledger immediately, under the proper category (insurance, contract worker, telephone, entertainment, etc.). This saves time later when I am posting cash items (postage, supplies, etc.) in my ledger.

• *If your accountant pays the bills, follow some of the same procedures.* Mark the bills "OK" to pay, put down the date to pay, and the amount on the bill. Be sure that the bills get to the accountant on time and be sure to review your cancelled checks to ensure that they were paid on the dates you specified. The monthly report you receive from your accountant should identify each transaction sufficiently. It should have at least the check number, the vendor, the amount, the bill ID number, a word or two of explanation ("utility charges," "auto insurance," etc.), and the date it was paid.

Whether you or someone else pays the bills, there are some tips to remember in managing your money:

• *Plan the date the bill is to be paid.* Don't get a penalty for late payment. Neither should you pay in advance and let another company have your money. If you can get a discount for early payment, do so; take the discount right off the check and indicate it on the check with the identifying bill ID number.

• Keep the bulk of your monthly cash in an interest-earning account. A friend of mine runs a small newsletter business. She puts all the receipts in the bank money market fund, where they earn a good interest. Only three checks a month are allowed on that account. She writes one large check at the first of the month for the checking account. From that she pays the bills coming in for the prior month. Late in the month, she draws another large check from the money market account into the checking account for incidental petty cash expenses that have been incurred during the month. In this way she maximizes the number of days her money earns interest, and she incurs no penalties for writing more checks than are allowed.

• *Keep your accounts current.* It is the only way you will be in charge of your business and your cash. Don't be sloppy; don't get in arrears. If you don't manage your money, it will manage you. It also establishes your credit and credibility in the business world. Your creditors become your references when you go for a loan, try to lease office space, etc.

- *Use charge cards for certain expenses, but use them carefully.* Pay them every month and do not incur interest. It is no longer deductible on your income tax, and, at over 18 percent annually, it is ridiculously expensive. Charge your automobile costs, entertainment costs, plane tickets, gifts, office supplies, telephone (if, for instance, you use MCI or American Expressphone) on your credit cards. Pay the full amount promptly (by the due date indicated) when you receive the bill. You have operated on their money for a month and you have avoided interest payments. Your money has stayed in the bank for thirty more days earning interest.

Keeping Accounts

This is a boring and time-consuming job for most of us. Even the best accountants admit that their own records take a back seat to their clients'. However, as this is the life blood of maintaining your business, you should adopt a few rules to make it as efficient and painless as possible.

- *Post your check payments in your ledger at the same time as you write the checks* (as we have discussed). It saves time, it keeps you current, and it assures you that you are in charge of the situation.
- *Schedule one time every month to post the cash outlays from the "receipts" file, which you keep on your sorting desk.* (Every time you pay a parking fee, buy postage, get photocopying done, buy supplies, etc. you get a receipt, don't you? Put those receipts in the "accounts" box on your sorting table and post them in your ledger at least once a month. (Once a week is better, but you know that.)
- *Bill your clients promptly.* Send them one copy, put one copy in the project/client file, and put one copy in the accounts receivable file. When the check arrives, you will deposit it promptly and staple the deposit slip to the accounts receivable copy of the bill. This can then go into an "income" file for your quarterly tax reconciliation. The day you receive that check you will also post the date, amount, and billing number in your ledger.

Doing Errands

If you have ever worked in a company/corporate environment with the attendant support staff, then starting your own one-person business can be one of the major culture shocks of your life. Have you noticed?

The key, of course, is organization, and we arrive at that realization the hard way. I remember a college friend who wrote to her parents "I ran out of money before I ran out of week!" In our peculiar kind of business, we often run out of week, before we run out of work. In our business, time truly is money, so we cannot let ourselves run out of time.

There are some specific errands that seem innocuous at a glance, but that can eat up our assets: photocopying, going to the post office, purchasing office supplies, fulfilling client requests, traveling (local and long distance), filling in for contract workers who do not show up, and delivering "stuff" to clients when the immediate, personal touch is important.

There are some time-savers (and ulcer preventers) available, if we think and plan ahead.

1. *Try never to do one errand for one thing.* Plan your day. The use of a day planner or similar business calendar is crucial for the one-person business. Each appointment and notation becomes the raw material from which to set your *daily agenda*. Every call, every letter, every contact may result in an entry into that daily calendar. The best ones (kept on your desk and kept up to date at all times) allow you to enter your appointments, your calls to be made, and the calls you receive, and, of course, you review tomorrow's schedule the day before.

   I also keep a tablet on my desk, next to the calendar, with a list of things to buy. Materials and supplies are noted before they are needed and I try to keep them in categories (stamps separated from office supplies separated from presentation materials separated from equipment repairs, for instance). I ran out of typewriter ribbons one Saturday night at 10:30; the article was due to be mailed on Monday morning. I have never made that mistake again!

   Each afternoon I review tomorrow's agenda. If there are errands to be run—if I need to do photocopying, if I need to deliver material, if I need to go to the post office—I put it on tomorrow's schedule. I plan enough time to do several things at once. This sounds very simplistic, but organizing what you need to do and where you need to do it saves your most valuable commodity—time.

   I keep two boxes at my office door: one for outgoing mail and one for material either to be copied or to be taken elsewhere. When I leave for an errand I take it all. Sometimes I use a brief-case with compartments. One friend of mine uses a camera bag; another uses a duffle bag. (In this age of Reeboks with mink coats, the overexposed "power image" of the Gucci briefcase has become a little fuzzy.) The point is to organize as you plan and produce. Then continue that organization in your departure on your rounds. Put the shopping list in one compartment and make it a part of planning your activities.

2. *Don't waste your time doing things others can do for you.* Analyze what your time is worth to you and don't waste it doing menial tasks that can be purchased for less than your own time is worth.

Keep an accurate weight machine and a postage meter in your office and handle your mailings yourself, particularly if you have a cooperative postman who will pick up the material at your office. Sometimes larger packages must be taken to a postal drop, and the planning of such a trip must be made with the same care as above.

Analyze the price of photocopying. If the price of leasing equipment (or amortizing the purchase), plus convenience, paper, maintenance agreement, and electricity come to less than 3¢ per copy (that is what I pay at my twenty-four-hour-a-day service), then you should have your own copying machine in your own office. If the cost is more than your local service, then you must weigh the advantages of saving time against saving money.

If the personal delivery of material is important to your business image, then you must plan that delivery on your daily agenda. If you don't need to be there personally, however, investigate your local delivery services. Get to know the owner and build a relationship. Although you may not match the volume of their larger clients, they will care for your needs if you use them consistently, and they help you save time for the productive needs of your business.

3. *Build a list of helpers; don't depend on one or two people.* A friend of mine runs a research survey company. Her greatest need is for dependable people to conduct telephone surveys at all hours of the day or night. She keeps a roster of housewives,

who can work in the daytime; students, who can work at night and weekends; and retired persons, who have very flexible hours. She contracts with these part-time workers when the jobs come in, but, inevitably, one or two of them are not available when the work begins. She always has at least one standby under contract for each job, not at full fee, but at a standby fee. It costs a little money, but, if she needs the person to fill in for someone who does not show up, it is worth it. If she does not need the person, she pays them the small standby fee for being available and they go on about their business. (She builds the cost into her fee and never misses a survey. Further, she does not have to jump in and make phone calls herself.) There is nothing unusual about it; the theater has paid standbys for years to be available at "half hour" in case the star cannot go on. Don't fall into the trap of doing the work yourself when contract workers fail to show up. Have a dependable list of standbys available, pay them, and build it into the fees you charge. Your clients are buying your talents and organizational skill, not your manual labor.

4. *Don't waste travel time.* This is probably an unnecessary piece of advice to a person as motivated as the one-person business owner. We have already talked about using travel time on planes, trains, and buses for reading the tons of material that flood your office. However, there are some tricks to getting work done on public transportation, and I will pass them along.

Sit on the aisle seat of a plane and the window seat (two-seater, if possible) on a train. Sit in the smoking section if you can stand it to avoid as many families with children as possible. Try to preserve the seat next to you, if possible, to avoid conversation and to have a place to put your material. Take a Walkman or similar tape player and some soothing music (Mozart is particularly good) in order to dissuade people from talking with you. Don't drink liquor, or, at least, hold it to a minimum. The more alert you are, the more you get done. While dictating in a tape machine is virtually hopeless on a plane, it can work very well on a train or bus. Take only the material you know you can work on; it only frustrates you to take more than is possible in the chaos of the current travel environment. Put all necessary instructions on the written or taped material and send it express mail to your stenographic service immediately, so that your work will continue in your absence. Hotels will help you with this service. Check with the office services in your city. Many of them can receive and duplicate material by telephone and modem, even if you do not have the capability in your own office. Use their services, in conjunction with a bank or hotel in your destination city. The promptness will oftentimes more than outweigh the costs.

Planning and Marketing

These are the most important things you can do, and, as must be evident from Chapters 1 and 6, they should occupy a great deal of your time. Further, they are both ongoing activities and should be done on a regular basis. If you have written your plan (including your marketing plan), which we discussed at length in Chapter 1, there should be an obvious review time, at least on a monthly basis, of the financial status, the marketing results, the changing internal and external environments, image and quality of your product or service, and the personal satisfaction you are enjoying from your work.

In a company or corporate environment, these reviews are scheduled as a part of the working month. In the one-person business, there is a tendency to avoid them on a regular basis because they "take too much time" and we "know what's going on." *Wrong!*

You can be blind-sided by surprises this way, without the security of a large corporate capitalization or staff to cope with the unexpected. Your regular review of your progress, therefore, is more important than in a group environment. How do you make yourself "look at the numbers"? Planning and scheduling is, of course, the answer.

Some time around the fifteenth of the month is probably the best time to do this. The bills have been paid, the bank statements are back, the contracts for that month are already signed, and you are plotting the next month's activities.

How do you force yourself to review your progress? It is so easy to slough it off because you have no one to talk to.

One way is to make appointments. Set aside time in advance, at mid-month, to talk with your accountant, your advertising/PR/marketing representative and your financial advisor or lawyer to review your activities. Since you may have to pay them for their time, it will force you to review it yourself and prepare to discuss what has been going on. The important thing is the discussion. It is an exchange of information, based on preplanning and a summary of what has happened. Therefore, it requires analysis and preparation and a comparison of results to the goals that were originally set. It may take a day out of your life, but it is worth it to the success of your business.

There *are* certain businesses that can be reviewed quarterly, rather than monthly, but you should consider this carefully. In Chapter 9 you will see suggestions of how to best utilize the advice of professionals. The point to be made in this chapter is that the time must be scheduled in an orderly and regular way in order to stay in control of your business plan. Chapter 9 will offer some suggestions as to how to do that economically.

Lunches, Dinners, Entertainment, and Meetings

These can take a lot of your time, but are very important to you, as you *are* your company. Your public image, your community and business contacts, your reputation rests on the exposure you have in social environments. In Hollywood phraseology, you can "do lunch," "work out," and "buy drinks" six or seven hours a day, not to mention the "power breakfasts" that are now the rage. There are no easy solutions to the demands on your time for social interchange, but a few suggestions may help in the crucial element of scheduling. (Remember: we are talking about time, your most valuable commodity).

For one thing, select the clubs most valuable to you. These fall into two categories: social and professional.

Your professional clubs will undoubtedly schedule meetings once a month, either at breakfast, lunch, or early cocktails/supper. This advance scheduling will permit you to write in the meetings monthly (and sometimes for the full year) on your schedule calendar thereby allowing you to preplan these meetings in conjunction with your other business appointments. In all candor, you will not go to all the meetings. When your mail arrives and you are screening it, you will choose those meetings with speakers/programs that interest you personally or that you think will deliver the kind of audience with whom you wish to mingle and make contacts.

I find that, if it is a breakfast meeting, I am better off getting back to the office to handle mail, calls, and other business work. If it is a luncheon meeting, I utilize my time better by scheduling other meetings in the afternoon, while checking in to the office regularly. If it is a cocktail/dinner meeting, I prefer working in the office till the last minute, which allows me to maximize my time. You will find your own best routine, but the secret is to not let the social event take you away from your work base for more than a couple of hours.

Your social clubs (exercise clubs, luncheon, country clubs, etc.) should be for your purposes and should not place demands on you. This does not mean, of course, that you don't serve on committees and boards; that is how you increase your exposure and outreach. Be selective. Use these clubs as an adjunct to your office. They become your executive dining room; the "perks" you can offer clients; your "home away from home" when you travel to other cities (if they have reciprocal arrangements with other clubs). If done with care and finesse, under the new tax laws, this also offers a good way to keep accurate records of business expenses.

Socializing and entertaining can present a fine line of decision-making for the one-person business owner. The temptation is to be everywhere, and, perhaps in the first year of your business, that is what you should do. However, as a part of your business plan, you will evaluate the benefits of those activities and define the pay-out. How much is it worth to your business? Your image? Your contacts? Your place in the community? Some of that is tangible; some intangible. It must be evaluated, because it all takes time (and money). Be as tough on that evaluation as you would on the productivity of an ad in a publication, and schedule your participation accordingly.

Time to Analyze Your Time

While a good deal of what we have just covered may sound like a lot of tedious detail, it is necessary to analyze the first element of your capability of managing the one-person business: the expenditure of time.

We have explored eight broad categories that can either be wasteful or beneficial, depending on how you analyze, organize, and utilize them. You could, undoubtedly, add more elements to the list and I invite you to do so. Each one-person business is unique and requires specific details and substance to make it function properly. However, I hope the foregoing has sparked your enthusiasm for identifying those details that can waste your time.

As we discussed early in this chapter, there are some things that you like to do but should not do, things that you do well, but that should be done by others, and things that you have to do and no one else can do them. Following is a simple checklist that will summarize those details with your real feelings about each. Fill it out honestly, and you will have a better idea of where you must spend time and where you must spend money.

Checklist

Things to be Done	Like	Don't Like	Good at it	Not Too Terrific
The Mail				
The Telephone				
Paying Bills				
Keeping Accounts				
Filing				

Checklist

Things to be Done	Like	Don't Like	Good at it	Not Too Terrific
Errands				
Stocking/Supplies/ Shipping				
Correspondence/ Communications				
Planning				
Marketing/Sales				
Entertainment				
Interviewing Helpers				

Managing Your Resources

As the foregoing exercise made clear, there are some things that you cannot do and also run your business efficiently and productively.

There are some things that you must pay for. How you pay for them and how much you pay for them can make a difference in your profitability.

Unless one of the following businesses is your own business, it is likely that you will pay for all or nearly all of the following services. It is best to identify them up front, so that you can develop alternate means of paying for them or utilizing them to their fullest.

Persons and services you pay for:

- Lawyer
- Accountant
- Broker
- Insurance agent
- Typing/clerical/copying
- Messenger/delivery
- Answering service/paging/car telephone
- Construction/renovation/decorating
- Contract help
- Supplies/materials
- Automobile (leasing/buying)

One of the ways of paying for these services is to pay full price, when billed, no questions asked. Of course, you are not going to do that. While none of the following suggestions will be new to you, perhaps one or two will spark a little creativity and encourage you to rethink some of your business expenses. Remember, you are striving to get the best value for the dollar and the best value for your time. The following suggestions have nothing to do with "cheap;" they are suggestions for value.

Barter and Exchange Goods and Services

There are a number of barter and exchange clubs and organizations throughout the country. You can usually find them in the local classifieds and sometimes in display ads in the Sunday paper. You can also barter or exchange services or products with other services that supply to you; it has been going on for millennia. (We assume it was the first form of commerce.) The IRS looks at it very carefully, and, before you engage in it, you should know that. The Service would like you to place a dollar value on the goods or services that you exchange, and each party is expected to declare that value as a part of income. Further, the IRS is trying to obtain the membership lists of barter and exchange associations so that they can audit the exchange as it relates to income. Be alert. Friends helping friends must do so with discretion and honesty.

Use Family and Friends

Your family and friends are your most important support system when you run a one-person business, if only because you can feel so alone otherwise. You must be very careful not to abuse that dependency in your desire to run your company efficiently. Having said that, also remember that it is just good business to do business with people you know and trust when you are out in the river of competition all alone. If members of your family or your friends have businesses that can supply goods or services you need, it is sensible to use them; you know the quality beforehand and it is likely that you will get a "price break" from them, at least in the early stages. There is one caveat: don't expect to go "on the cuff" with people you love and care for. If anything, be more assiduous in your promptness. That way, the support system will never fail.

Paying by the Job

Paying by the job, instead of by the hour or by "cost, plus," is a better way of controlling your expected expenditures, provided that you know the requirements thoroughly, get a number of competing bids upfront, and put the arrangements into a letter agreement or contract. The advantages are that you know the total cost before you begin, and any overages, accidents, redos are paid by the contractor, if the arrangements are put into the contract before work begins. The disadvantages are that you may forget something in the contract, you may pay a bit more if you have a really efficient contractor, or, you may end up with an unhappy contractor should something occur that is in a "gray" area and you hold him or her responsible. The technique is definitely worth considering, however, if the job is complex and likely to run a long time. Candidly, independent contractors tend to work more efficiently if paid by the job, simply because they are in control and are apt to perform quickly in order to move on to another job. Just know the requirements, so that short cuts will not be taken.

Paying on Discounts

We have briefly discussed paying on discounts, but it is worth repeating. Some companies allow substantial discounts if payment is received within ten days. While it has become more and more fashionable to delay payments as much as ninety days in larger companies, it is worth it to the small business owner to review the advantages of discounting, simply because it cuts your real costs. Also, other small businesses, such as office-supply houses and wholesalers, will usually discount to "preferred" customers (those customers who always buy those goods and services from them). If you don't ask, you won't get. Build a track record and a personal relationship and you will surely be granted a discount. Further, you will be billed at the end of each month, so that you have the best of both worlds: postponement of payment till after delivery and discounting for prompt payment.

Take Advantage of Discounts

Discounting has become a way of life in American retailing, from electronic equipment, to automobiles, to clothing, to office supplies. In the Appendix are some interesting mail order sources, and the major chains, such as K-Mart, Wal-Mart, Caldors, and even Sears, are well known. Every city has one or more "discount warehouses," to which membership is available, the prices are a few dollars over wholesale. If you are a company, you can buy a membership, usually for $25, and buy at remarkable prices. If you are to resell the material, you don't even pay sales tax. Check your friends, the yellow pages, the local ads, and the Appendix for purchases substantially reduced in price.

Use Interns

Most high schools and colleges have an off-campus work program to help their students make the transition from academia to the real commercial world. The "vocational" students in high school are generally available after school hours during the week and on Saturdays. You are expected to pay them the minimum wage and you will find them to be enthusiastic and willing workers. Remember, you will have to train them and supervise them, but then, that is what managers do anyway. It is even more interesting to work with college interns. Many times they come to you *free*. They are on scholarship or intern programs, training for a particular career. They are dedicated and intelligent and devoted to the work, because their grades and scholarships sometimes depend on their performances. Don't hesitate to approach the colleges and universities in your area to inquire as to their availability. Many schools have "interim" terms (the month of January), during which you can get a student for thirty-two hours a week for four weeks, to dedicate him or herself to a particular project or activity. Don't ignore this free (or inexpensive) possibility.

Investigate Full-Service Office Complexes

Like a lot of things, full-service office complexes began in California in the 1970s and have spread all over the country. To the best of my knowledge, they began with lawyers, but they now encompass every kind of business and are particularly suited for the one-person business. You will find them in classified ads, display ads, the Yellow Pages, and through word of mouth. Shop around. Many of them are run by real estate people and offer little more than an office (which you will have to furnish either by renting or buying furniture), copying service, and telephone-answering service. However, many of these complexes opening up around the country are becoming more sophisticated; they offer typing service, as well as other amenities, such as travel arrangements, stenographic service, parking, conference rooms, bookkeeping, and others you may require. The "basic" office service complex might be right for you, because you have other suppliers to take care of your many needs, but there is a good reason to explore the more "full-service" complexes. You build a relationship with the staff and they, in effect, become your staff. You are not obliged to hire, interview, manage, direct, fire; but you can take advantage of a well-trained and well-managed staff as if it were your own. This is a major phenomenon that has developed in this latter quarter of the century that allows the one-person business to flourish. In effect, you can have all the amenities of a full office complex with a support staff at your beck and call, but you are still a one-person business, buying services, not people. It gives you credibility, professionalism, and full service without demanding that you take a lot of people on your payroll. I invite you to investigate the possibilities.

Use Incubators

A number of state governments and universities have combined to create "incubators" for new businesses. These are jointly funded complexes that provide office space and a number of services to the new business for a modest cost. The "catch" is the kind of business you are starting or running. As the funds come, partially, from state treasuries, the type of business nurtured in these environments is, more often than not, calculated to grow into a larger employer or to bring more money into the state. While the one-person business may not fit the bill in terms of plans for employee growth, it is possible that you could appeal in terms of monies brought into the state. For instance, import-export, commodity trading, a patent, or franchise development might qualify. Explore the possibilities through your state's Department of Industry or Commerce or Business Development, your city's Chamber of Commerce Small Business Development Consortium, or your local university's Business Administration Department or Small Business Development Department. Don't assume that you don't fit. The criteria vary from state to state and from administration to administration. Personal contact and exploration may open up the avenues for you to work in a professional and sophisticated environment at a greatly reduced cost.

Have Accessible Lines of Credit

Some of us were reared in the days when owing money was considered shameful. Those days are gone. We now live in a generation in which we must owe money or we have no credit; and credit is the name of the game. We must have access to additional funds, promptly, when we need them, in order to keep our business thriving.

There are several ways to build credit ratings and to develop lines of credit. Under the Tax Act of 1986, our homes are our most important assets. If the residence is paid for or if it has a mortgage on it, investigate its market value and take advantage of the sales pitches being made by your local commercial banks. Many of them will

157

waive the survey and closing costs on a new loan on your house, if you will do business with them. It is worth looking into. The costs can be in the $1,000 range, and, if they will waive them to get your business, let them. Remember, you are not looking for a loan, you are looking for a line of credit. Under the new law, your home is not only an appreciating investment, but an asset upon which you may borrow in the future at an interest rate to be set now. Take advantage of the competition that is going on among commercial banks and apply for that line of credit. You may never use it, but it is nice to know it will be there.

Bankers are also impressed with written business plans and contracts for future work. If you have both, take it to your friendly neighborhood banker and see what kind of line of credit will be extended. Several of my clients have been pleasantly surprised at their reception. Their written plans coupled with their written contracts for future work have made them very welcomed at local banks.

Investment real estate, bought with the object of improvement, offers another means of securing lines of credit. Bankers understand the potential of such property and are often willing to extend lines of credit to develop it.

Remember to pay your bills promptly. Your creditors automatically become your credit references when you are looking for loans. Your track record of payment becomes your security in the eyes of loan officers.

Buy your insurance on a yearly loan and build your credit rating with prompt monthly payments at the bank that loaned you the money. They will invite you to borrow more money from them.

All of this is not a suggestion that you go into debt, overextend yourself, or borrow more money than you can pay back. It is an encouragement to build your credit rating in an orderly way, so that you can extend your business and take advantage of opportunities when they arise.

Use Credit Cards Judiciously

Credit cards can be a disaster or a boon to your business, depending on how you use them. The interest rates of 18 percent or more are ridiculous, so they are not the way to run your business over the long haul. As we have said earlier in this chapter, they are the way to keep your cash for one month, keep accurate records of your purchases, build a track record of prompt payment, but *not* to buy over an extended period of time. Use them every month; pay them at the first of the month; avoid the excessive interest rates; and take advantage of the delay in spending cash during the month. The most fearful debt in America today, other than the National Debt of two trillion dollars, is the individual credit card debt. We are a nation that spends more than it can possibly earn, because we are sent "free" credit cards. They are not free! Don't let your business boat founder on the shoals of that disaster. Use them, don't abuse them; and take advantage of the free month's cash flow they offer you. Pay them off each month—you will make money on your money, while using *their* money.

Take Advantage of Free Offers

There are free offers everywhere you turn. Most of them arrive by mail. Most of them are worthless. However, there are some free offers that may be useful to you and that you should consider. Many of the business magazines offer free books as a "come on" to their subscriptions—planning guides, tax tips, investment tips. Many of the business magazines also have free offers in the classifieds. Suppliers offer free trial offers. Manufacturers offer free secondary merchandise with the purchase of a major item. Is anything free? Rarely, because we tend not to pay attention to deadlines or to the details of the offer. There are usually trial periods, cancellation dates, return deadlines. We are busy and don't notice. Either we "blow it" and don't take advantage of the deadlines, or we are leary of the whole thing and don't send off for the offer at all. Neither action is a good idea. Some "freebies" are useful and should not be dismissed out of hand. If there is a tax-planning book that is free with a trial subscription of a magazine, then give it a try, if you are interested in tax planning. Look over the magazine and, if you don't like it, cancel it before the "trial" subscription becomes a permanent subscription. The issue is not whether there is anything free in this world, but whether or not you can control your time and attention sufficiently to take advantage of it. If you can't put the deadline into your "tick" bin and decide whether you want the whole offer, then don't get involved in the exercise. If you are organized enough to make evaluations, then take advantage of the many free products and services that are available to you. Don't forget the Chamber of

159

Commerce in your city, as well as the colleges, universities, and professional organizations. They offer many free services and publications that can be invaluable to a business—particularly a one-person business. Read the papers, the flyers, the brochures and take advantage of the products and services available to you.

Leasing and Leasing-to-Buy

Leasing and leasing-to-buy is a handy way to preserve your capital resources while running your business. You can lease almost anything these days: office furniture, office equipment, shop equipment, cars, trucks, heavy equipment, party furniture, plants, decor, and accessories; you name it, you can lease it.

It is not a bad idea. While your business is permanent, your location may not be. Oftentimes you can create a better image with rented items than you could with long-term capital purchases: the monthly payments are better for your finances than an initial capital outlay.

There are some guidelines. How long do you plan to stay in your current environment? Will your equipment/furnishings/car fit your needs in six months, one year, two years? Even under the new tax laws, a five-year amortization of costs is probably necessary. Will you change before that? Will you want to buy up? Cut back? These are questions that should be answered in your business plan.

The most expedient plan is simply to rent what you need when you need it. In addition, you may want to develop a lease-to-buy contract, which is somewhat more restrictive, but still not as demanding as buying everything you need and paying for it as a capital outlay.

If your business is new, these questions are very important. You want to preserve your capital for your business, not for things. Your surroundings/image will evolve with the life of your business. Leasing or leasing-to-buy is one of the major capital preservation tricks for the one-person business.

Specific Tips on Necessary Expenditures

There are people and services for which you will have to pay, no matter how cleverly you bargain or barter. However, you do not have to *overpay*. Following are some tips for getting the most for your money.

Paying Professionals

There are three schools of thought regarding the payment of professional fees to lawyers, accountants, consultants, financial advisors, etc.: The choices are to pay by the hour, pay by the job, or pay on a monthly retainer basis. Your professional may have a set way of billing and the decision may not be yours to make. A law firm or accounting firm, for example, will charge you on an hourly-use basis for one member of their staff; a consultant might want to charge you by the job. While there are no hard rules, your bargaining position should always be from your point of view. Shop around to find the person who is sympathetic to your needs and wants to build a relationship with you! If you need an accountant on an ongoing and regular basis, then a monthly retainer may be best for you; if you need a lawyer only occasionally, then a fee-per-performance basis is probably best. Don't be afraid to ask for client references before you hire somebody, and call the references to see if they are satisfied and for how long they have worked with the person. Don't be intimidated.

Managing and Investing Money

Managing and investing your money is as important as earning it. I come from the do-it-yourself school (with lots of reading and consultation and attention to my personal goals). That is why I use a discount broker for most of my trading; I do maintain a full-service brokerage for special trades, and, more importantly, to receive all the latest analyses and recommendations. It helps me compare trends with my other reading. If your bank has a competitively priced brokerage service, it is usually a good idea to use it; this helps build a more well-rounded relationship.

Buying Insurance

Buy your insurance from a full-service agent (insurance is covered in Chapters 3 and 9). Don't buy from agents who sell only one or two companies; they have no incentive to get you the best price. Remember, buy insurance for insurance. With the exception of a few current annuity offerings, it is rarely good as a part of your financial planning.

Keeping Typing/Clerical Costs Down

Unless you keep typing/clerical help on a regular part-time basis and pay them by the hour (we discuss these "employees" in Chapter 8), it is best to shop around for the best "job" price. There are a lot of other one-person businesses out there that handle typing, word processing, graphics displays, messenger service, answering service, paging, etc. who will give you a good "per job" price if you shop around. Find someone dependable, build a relationship, use them regularly, and you will get a price break. Don't hop around once you find a good one; and remember, if your work can be done during off-hours, during the slow or "down" times of their regular business, you will get an even better price. They are interested in constant cash flow too.

Keeping Travel Costs Down

Travel costs, particularly plane fares, are highly unpredictable in this era of deregulation. Your first necessity is a good working relationship with a full-service travel agency that can "shop" for the best prices for you on a computer. Obviously, the farther in advance you order your ticket (these days), the better price break you get. There are other ways to help save travel money. Belong to as many Frequent Flyer programs as you can and always take advantage of them. They are so competitive now that the mileage points build up quickly, particularly if you also use them in the member hotels and with the member car rental companies. Many of the airlines now have travel clubs that offer discounting in hotels, restaurants, and car rentals. It is probably a good idea to belong to the one with the fullest airline service in your hometown; you will be using it more often. Belong to AAA (American Automobile Association) for auto travel protection, but also because it usually offers other travel discounts or price breaks. If you or anyone in your family is fifty or older, join AARP (American Association of Retired Persons). They have excellent discounts on travel, as well as drug purchases and insurance. There are software packages that work on PCs and help you access the airline schedules and rates. Unless you travel all the time, it is probably too expensive to purchase (although it presents an interesting opportunity for a travel consulting business in itself!) The secret to cutting travel costs is to plan ahead. You are going to pay full rates if you wait until the last minute.

Shop around for a travel agent who will handle all your travel needs, by getting the best prices available. They need the business and you need the time.

Auto Leasing

Auto leasing is done by the car rental companies as well as by most local car dealerships. The secret is to shop around. Remember, the lowest price is not the only criterion for your selection; you also want service and dependability. Ask for the names of people who are leasing and call a few of them to check it out. If the dealer will not give you the names of any customers, maybe you had better go to another dealer. You are looking for other satisfied customers.

When you lease, the depreciation of the car over the lease period is calculated and payments are made on the depreciation amount only. Then, at the end of the lease, you have the option to buy the car for the remaining value or trade it in. For example: if you bought a $10,000 car, you might expect to pay $300 per month over 60 months. To lease that same car, if the resale value after five years was set at $4,000, you might pay only $250 a month, eventually paying for only the $6,000 depreciation, or, as car dealers say, "that part of the car that you use." The leaser then has first option to buy the car for the remaining $4,000, or turn it back in and lease a new car. You can put the $50 a month that you have saved into savings and accumulate that $4,000 when the lease ends. If you lease another car, you are $4,000 ahead. For the one-person business, there is little capital tied up in a down payment and all the lease payments can be deducted as business expenses. You must use the vehicle at least 50 percent of the time for business in order to count the expense, and most leases require that you do not exceed a certain mileage. Under the new tax law, sales tax and interest expense on buying a car are no longer deductible, so the advantages of leasing far outweigh buying a car.

Saving on Telephone Calls

Under equal access, phone users designate a primary toll company. The selected carrier handles almost all interstate calls, as well as some within states, that are dialed in the usual manner—1 + area code + phone number. Let's say you have picked MCI as your primary company, but want to place a collect call. However, AT&T, the only carrier to employ operators, is the only one capable of offering operator-assisted services. AT&T's carrier code is 10288, so, to place such a call, dial 10288 + 0 + area code + phone number. Codes for other major toll firms are: MCI, 10222; All-net, 10444; US Sprint, 10777; ITT, 10488; and Western Union, 10220.

Remember that too much use of other access codes will reduce your discount rate with your designated toll company. A summary of code-dialing rules can be found in the "Long Distance Comparison Chart," published by the Telecommunications Research and Action Center in Washington, D.C. Its number is (202) 462-2520.

Bringing the Computer Into Your Work Environment

Many of the activities we have discussed, those that you do or those you must hire other people to do, can more quickly and accurately be done on a computer.

There are a number of PCs on the market and scores of software packages that are indispensible to the one-person business. Much of the software is particularly helpful for the accounting tedium that afflicts all business.

Before you buy a PC, I suggest that you *rent* one and try it out. While many products are advertised as "user friendly," not everyone is comfortable with a computer or a keyboard. Renting will allow you to try out several models of hardware and to experiment with a variety of software. It may seem an expensive way to "audition" a product, but it is less expensive than buying something that the sales clerk loves, but that may not be right, either for your business or for your temperament. You will undoubtedly be able to "borrow" some software from friends or shop owners to try it out. It is almost as easy today to copy software as it is to copy audiotapes.

I have been able to try out a variety of software copied for me by friends (including Lotus, Wordstar, and others) to test my needs and capabilities.

Analyze your specific needs. Do you require a good word processing system so that you can do letters, manuscripts, presentations? Do you need graphic capability so that you can do designs, layouts, presentations? Do you need a spread sheet for the weekly, monthly, quarterly, annual activity of your business? Do you want to be able to "post" all your transactions as you receive payment, pay your bills, contract help? Do you want to be able to interface with your bank, so that you can do your banking transactions directly to the bank or broker or agent? Do you want to be able to list your product or service on the national and international "bulletin boards" that are interconnected by modems and telephone hookups throughout the world? These and many other questions will determine whether you computerize your business activities. I encourage you to consider the possibilities.

The final question or, maybe the first question, you should ask is, am I comfortable doing business this way? Try it. You may like it, but don't get hung up on it. I wrote four books on an old IBM Executive typewriter instead of a word processor, because I was working under deadlines and knew that my concentration had to be focused on the *books* and not on learning a new creative environment. In the peace of no deadlines, I will be able to transfer my bookkeeping, my billing, and check paying, my creative juices, to something that will ultimately make my work place more efficient and less cluttered. Timing, as they say, is everything. Computers are becoming so inexpensive that they can also become "impulse buying items." What is right for someone else may not be right for you. Rent and audition. Never lose sight of your principal interest . . . you . . . and your continuing productivity.

Let's assume that you are comfortable in the computer environment. The personal computers have become so sophisticated that it is unlikely a one-person business would need anything larger.

Your first consideration must be the IBM PC family of computers; not because they are necessarily better for you or cheaper or have the most innovation (in fact, they were late arriving in the field). You will consider it because it is IBM; they are the largest computer manufacturer in the world (with some 80 percent of the market), and they have the most extensive distribution and service system in the industry.

Please note: I said you would *consider* IBM, for the above reason and because more software is designed for IBM or is "IBM compatible." Under their new marketing policies, they now allow their PCs to be sold in large computer stores along with other manufacturers. That gives you the advantage for a change.

There are several steps you should follow in picking a computer:

1. *Write down all the things you would like the computer to handle for you—word processing, spread sheets, graphics, games, billing, accounting, mailing list maintenance . . . the works.* Why do you want one? Do you want access to the national "bulletin boards"? Do you want to be able to transmit information by telephone lines? Etc.

2. *Try to talk with several people who do what you* do. See what they have. Ask them questions about use, complexity, downtime, service, flexibility, satisfaction. See if you can visit, observe, and maybe sit down at their computer.

3. *Watch the papers for sales.* August and January seem to be good times. Go to the big stores that carry several brands. Talk with the clerks and have them show you some activity on several kinds. Keep your list in hand of what you want it to do.

4. *Read Consumer Reports.* They are available in most libraries and, since 1985, they have done extensive testing and analysis of computers, modems, monitors, etc. You can compare their evaluations with your needs.

5. *Lease a computer and peripherals for a certain period of time— a year at most; six months if you can.* There is nothing like a "test drive" to see if you really like it. You may have trouble leasing for such a short time; most companies want to put you on a lease-to-buy contract. You might be able to make a deal by assuring them that you plan to lease (to buy) a computer; you just want to decide which one by trying it for a while with the option to switch to another, within the lease contract, should it prove unsatisfactory. It is a hard sell, but you can probably do it.

Buying the computer is only the start of your purchase. There is the monitor (color or mono) for viewing your work, the printer (dot matrix, letter quality, laser), hand or self-feeder (silent or noisy), the modem (for connecting to the world, through telephone), hard disk drives (as opposed to "floppy disks), diskettes, connecting cables, files, a "mouse" (on some systems) to trace your work, and more. You can spend between $1,000 and $15,000 to set yourself up, so analyzing your real desires and needs is crucial to getting what you need now, while also having the capacity to grow, when you need it. Don't overbuy, if possible, but buy a system that allows expansion when needed.

There are brand names and model types to investigate:

- IBM Personal Computer, PC; IBM Personal Computer XT; IBM Personal Computer XT, 20MB Hard Drive System.
- Compaq Portable 286, Model 2; Deskpro 286 Model 20; Portable II, Model 4; Deskpro 386.
- Epson Equity I; Equity II.
- NEC Advanced Personal Computer IV.
- Apple IIc, Apple IIe, Macintosh 512K.
- ATT personal computers.
- Tandy computers/Radio Shack. 1000 EX, 1 disk, 256K, IBM compatible; 1000 SX, 2 disks, 384K, IBM compatible; 3000 HL, 1 disk, 512K, IBM compatible; 3000 HD, floppy or hard disk 8 MG, IBM compatible.
- Atari 520ST (for smaller capability and much lower price).

The new phenomenon called "desk top printing" has occurred because of the development of the Apple LaserWriter printer and a variety of software (including The PageMaker at about $495.) Hooked to a Macintosh computer, these printers are allowing the creation of newspapers, books, presentations, all sorts of written material to be produced—with graphics and layout—as camera-ready for cheaper printing, or even printing out of the LaserWriter itself. At $6,000, the price seems high, but it depends on your business and how much you spend on graphics, layout, art work, mechanicals, and printing. It is also safe to assume that the price will go down, the quality will improve even more, and other competitors will follow suit. Meantime, Apple has provided another breakthrough in the world of computer communication.

Summary

This is a long and sometimes tedious chapter about the ways you can maximize the use of your time and your resources so that you can spend most of your efforts on what you *like* most—your business. Review this chapter often, and review your own activities in light of these suggestions. It is a safe bet that every time you read it, you will find a new idea to save time or money, and, more importantly, these ideas are intended to spark your imagination in that direction. Sharing ideas is usually a luxury in a one-person business. This chapter is intended as a sharing forum, to spark other ideas—and better ideas.

Chapter 8

Hiring Employees, If You Must

The object of being a one-person business is to *be* a one-person business. As the PR consultant said in Chapter 2, "For now, I prefer to manage my work, not workers."

We all know that there are occasions, however, when we need additional help. We have explored in detail the buying of services, not people, in Chapter 7, but even with the careful cultivation of the many suppliers that are available, sometimes you find yourself needing a specific person, either over an extended period of time or for very regular periods of time.

This chapter will deal with some of the techniques and rules that apply when you become an employer, either of contract workers, flextime/temporary/part-time employees, or full-time employees.

Writing Job Descriptions

Before you even think about hiring an employee, you should write a job description. It should be done with care and detail, because it is the means by which you will recruit the person best suited for your special business, and because it provides you with written, accurate, and continuous details by which to judge that employee's performance objectively.

There are a number of ways to write a job description and I will provide you with several suggestions.

Defining Jobs by Task

Using a large sheet of paper, make a matrix similar to the one below and list all the tasks that you need to have performed. Don't just list

169

the largest or the most obvious; list the detailed and the trivial, if you expect it to be done by someone.

Inside the Company Daily	Weekly	Monthly	Quarterly
Outside the Company			

After you have completed that exercise (and it can take quite a while—maybe a couple of days—to identify every task), then take the list you have assembled and put it on another piece of paper divided by category or "task family," such as the following:

Clerical Manual Supervisory Travel Technical Sales Creative (etc.)

These lists will provide you a wealth of information about the job: (1) whether it is full time or part time; (2) whether it can be done by one person or more than one person; (3) whether or not it divides itself up more easily as a series of projects thereby telling you that you need an independent contractor, as opposed to an employee.

Defining Jobs by Components

Larry G. McDougle, who writes for *Supervisory Management*, (135 West 50th St., New York City, 10020) suggests listing the following factors:

- Position, title, and classification (See FLSA guidelines later).
- Description of proposed duties and responsibilities. (These might include activities organized according to frequency.)
- List of the skills and special knowledge necessary for the job.

- Outline of working conditions, especially any that are out of the ordinary.
- Description of the type of supervision that the position requires and who will give it. Also, to what extent there is supervision of others.
- Qualifications: Education and work experience required.
- Full or part time; permanent or temporary.
- Salary scale. (Make it competitive to your area.) Allowances and benefits.
- Nature of contact with other groups, such as the general public, other firms, government officials.
- Type of personal judgment, initiative, resourcefulness required.

EMPLOYEE STATUS DEFINITIONS (Based on Fair Labor Standards Act (FLSA) definitions, which are revised periodically by the Federal Government.

Exempt (from overtime)/Salaried:
Executive:

- *Primary duty:* The management of the enterprise in which he or she is employed, or of a customarily recognized department or subdivision thereof.
- *Supervision:* Regularly directs the work of two or more employees.
- *Authority:* Can hire or fire other employees, or whose suggestions and recommendations as to the hiring or firing and as to the advancement and promotion or any other change of status of other employees will be given particular weight.
- *Discretion:* Customarily and regularly exercises discretionary powers.
- *Salary:* $225 or more per week, inclusive of board, lodging, other allowances, and facilities.

Administrative:

- *Primary duty:* The performance of office or nonmanual field work directly related to management policies or general operations of his or her employer.
- *Other duties:* Regularly and directly assists an employer, or an employee employed in a bona fide executive or administrative capacity (e.g., employment as an administrative assistant), or who performs under only general supervision work along specialized or technical lines requiring special training, experience, or knowledge.
- *Discretion:* Customarily and regularly exercises discretion and independent judgment.

- *Salary:* $225 or more a week, inclusive of board, lodging, other allowances, and facilities.

Professionals:

- *Primary duty:* Performs work requiring knowledge of an advanced type in a field of science or learning customarily acquired by a prolonged course of specialized intellectual instruction and study, as distinguished from a general academic education and from an apprenticeship, and from training in the performance of routine, mental, manual, or physical processes, or a person whose work is original and creative in character in a recognized field of artistic endeavor, and the result of which depends primarily on the invention, imagination, or talent of the employee.
- *Other duties:* Performs work predominantly intellectual and varied (not routine).
- *Discretion:* Consistently exercises discretion and judgment.
- *Salary:* $250 or more per week, inclusive of board, lodging, or other facilities.

Sales reps:

- The employee must customarily and regularly work away from the employer's place of business in making sales or obtaining orders or contracts for services or for the use of facilities for which the client or customer will pay.
- Work other than making outside sales or obtaining orders or contracts for services or facilities must not exceed 20 per cent of the hours worked in the work week.

Nonexempt/hourly:

- These employees do not fall under the "nonexempt" rules listed above and must be paid overtime for hours worked over the maximum (generally conceded to be forty hours per week).

Recruiting

How do you find the person you want? While it is easy to say that there "are a lot of people looking for work out there," they are not necessarily the person(s) you need in your very special business.

1. *Associations.* It is likely that the person(s) you will need fall into the "professional" category (definitions above). Your most efficient, inexpensive, and rapid source of such a professional is a trade or industry association. Check your telephone book, your

Chamber of Commerce, and the library of your local newspaper to get the names and addresses of associations related to the position for which you are recruiting, such as public relations, accounting, photographers, and researchers. Most of them have newsletters and are happy to list your job, (usually, for free).

2. *Academia*. For almost any kind of position, the Placement Office of the local colleges, universities, trade schools, and academies are happy to take your job specifications and refer interviewees to you. Because of the growing enrollment in night classes and continuing education programs, the pool of talent is enormous, with a great range of age and experience.

3. *Word of mouth*. You are out in the marketplace all the time, selling your business. If you are in the market for a certain kind of employee, tell the people you meet. You can screen their referrals on the phone and, if they sound like likely candidates, you can forward them a job description and ask for a resume and letter of application. After you have looked at that, you can decide whether or not to spend time with them.

4. *Advertising*. The secret to a good classified ad is where you place it and what it says. Use trade publications for special skills; use the Sunday classifieds for more general requirements. Put it in the right location ("handyman" is pretty useless if you are looking for someone to help you in your landscape business). Talk to the people at the classified department. I have always found them to be cooperative, informed, helpful, and very skilled at making your ad sound like the person you really want. Be specific about hours and pay; you will get more applications than you could ever want, so try to screen out some of them with the specifics in the ad.

5. *Agencies*. As a last resort, use an agency. In my experience they have generally not been too helpful with clerical and nonskilled jobs. They can be helpful if you are looking for specific professional and technical skills and want someone to help you screen out the unqualified.

Interviewing

You have narrowed down the applications, phone calls, and resumes to an interesting few and you are ready to begin the interviewing process. Where should you meet?

Your office, unless there is some overriding reason not to. (Perhaps you have a herd of envelope stuffers at work this week and there is no room, or you are in the process of expanding or changing offices and don't want to present the wrong impression.) All things considered, your office is the best place for the interview.

Sometimes you want to meet someone at lunch, dinner, cocktails to get to know them on a more informal level. This may work when you are hiring a financial officer or a PR director for your company, but I would not recommend it if you are searching for a secretary. It could be misconstrued; the person might not drink; the person might feel awkward socializing with someone who is a potential boss. Save the social interviews for the executives you wish to hire, and only then, when you have narrowed the list down to a precious few.

Private clubs have meeting rooms and parlors that can be used for interviewing, particularly if you are out of town. As a last resort, get a small meeting room at a hotel or use the living room of your suite. Don't ever invite anyone to a hotel bedroom to be interviewed! In addition to the danger of the invitation being misconstrued, it is simply gauche. Rent a suite or a meeting room.

Now that you are ready to start interviewing for employees, what should you ask the interviewees to bring? What kind of records should you keep?

It is assumed that you already have received and reviewed the candidate's letter of application and resume. When you call them to set the appointment, you might ask them to bring in any samples of their work when they come, if relevant, and you could send them a copy of the job description so that they will have a focus on the topic of the interview. Some people like to "spring" the job description on a candidate at the first or second interview. In your position, I think it saves time and builds a groundwork for good conversation if you send a copy.

You should keep an employment interview log (including race, sex, and your actions) to keep track of the candidates and your impressions, as well as to keep records for any legal question that might arise. You should use an "interview report" to make notes during the interview and to attach to the candidate's resume when the interview is over, or write your impression on the back of the resume.

The Thirteen Best Questions to Ask a Job Applicant

(From *Business Confidential,* published by Boardroom Reports, Inc., 1985; see Appendix.)

1. "What did you do at your last job?" "What were your responsibilities?"
2. "What aspects of your last job did you like best?" People are usually prepared to discuss their accomplishments, not their attitudes.
3. "What aspects did you like least?" If these coincide with new job requirements, you immediately know enough to reject the candidate.
4. "Why did you leave your last job?" Watch out for excuses, in which the applicant blames other people or circumstances for his/her own failures.
5. "If you could have made one suggestion to management, what would it have been?" An answer of "I don't know" certainly indicates lack of initiative, probably lack of motivation, and not a very good attitude toward work.
6. "What have you done that you are proud of?" No proud accomplishments signals excessive modesty or limited abilities and attitude.
7. "Describe the best boss you ever had." If the shoe fits, great.
8. "Describe the worst boss you ever had."
9. "Would you tell me about the ups and downs of your health in recent years?" Ask, "How's your health?" and they will always say, "Fine."
10. "What do you consider your greatest strength?" If the answer is "good with people," and it is not a people job, you have to explore further.
11. "What kinds of things bother you the most?" Again, compare with job realities. If it is a mismatch, better to find out now.
12. "What else should I know about your qualifications. About you? Is there anything else you want to tell me about yourself?"
13. "What else would you like to know about this job?"

Interview Questions That Produce Revealing Replies*

Questions for job applicants that reveal characteristics they may not be aware they are disclosing:

*From: Interview with Robert Half, Robert Half International, Inc., 522 Fifth Ave., New York City 10017.

1. "Why are you giving up your job?" Beware of candidates who bad-mouth their current employer.
2. "What did you like about your last job?" A superficial answer here may indicate inability to get beyond the basics of the job.
3. "What improvements would you have made in your last job?" This is a good barometer of a candidate's creativity and sensitivity.
4. "What was your most interesting job or project?" The reasons are more important than the answer. They indicate, for example, whether the candidate likes challenges.
5. "Describe the best person who worked for or with you." Difficulty with this may show a lack of understanding people.
6. "In what way would you like our company to help you if you join us?" Be wary of those who ask for a lot of help or suggest that they do not need any.
7. "Describe emergencies in the past for which you had to reschedule your time." This is the question to ask instead of, "Are you willing to work extra hours if necessary?"

Questions You Cannot Ask

In order to avoid the accusation of discrimination, there are some questions you must not ask and some statements you must not make in an interview.

1. "How old are you?"
2. "I am looking for (or, I prefer) a young person for this job."
3. "Are you married?"
4. "Do you believe in God?" "Do you go to church?"
5. "Do you have any children?"
6. "Do you plan to have children?"
7. "What are the ages of your children?"
8. "We don't hire women to work at night."
9. "You are pregnant, so we cannot hire you."
10. "Where did you learn English?"
11. "Who will take care of your children while you are at work?"
12. "What does your husband do for a living?"
13. "Have you ever been arrested?" (You can, however, ask if the person has been convicted of a felony, if you have reason to suspect it.)
14. "Do you have any credit cards? Charge accounts?"
15. "What religious holidays do you observe?"
16. "Where did you live before this address?"

17. Do *not* tell jokes during an interview, especially racial, ethnic, or sex jokes. They can be construed as discriminatory, particularly if the candidate is not hired.
18. "Your husband is tied down on his job here, isn't he?"

Reference Checks*

Fear of lawsuits now makes former employers extremely wary of saying anything critical of ex-employees. As a result, reference checks reveal little more than where the applicant was employed, for how long, and the job title.

It is, therefore, better to arrange a face-to-face meeting with references, if possible. The facial expressions and tone of voice can give important clues. Plus, as rapport builds, answers become more truthful.

Phony references can easily be arranged. One common ploy: A believable story is told about how the previous boss is always traveling, but the applicant suggests phoning him away from the office and gives a number. The result is a glowing recommendation from an impersonator. Rule to follow: The reference must be called at the office of the company.

One fail-safe measure is to verify educational credentials, professional memberships, and honors. Someone who lies in these areas is probably not telling the truth about more important matters. It takes time and often must be done in writing on a firm's letterhead.

Avoid vague questions that can be met with equally vague answers. For example: "What kind of guy was Ed?" Instead, ask for concrete instances of what Ed did. For a marketing director applicant, ask: "What was Ed's contribution to any new products put out during his tenure?"

Listen carefully to the former supervisor's tone of voice over the phone. Hesitations or false heartiness may be warning signs, but do not jump to this conclusion. Many managers are unused to giving recommendations and they respond awkwardly.

Do not settle for a reference from the personnel department. It knows almost nothing about the applicant's day-to-day performance.

*From: Robert Half, Robert Half, International, Inc., New York City and Harry Davoid, H.D. Associates, Washington, D.C.

Double-check an overly negative response to a reference call: the person may personally dislike the applicant.

Four questions that may bring an informative response:

1. "Why did the employee leave the job?"
2. "Would you rehire?" (A pause before "yes" says more than words, usually.)
3. "How would you rate the candidate in comparison with other candidates as to (whatever quality is important to you?)"
4. When an answer sounds deliberately ambiguous: "Why did you say that?"

Following are two samples of reference sheets to use when you are checking out a potential employee. While it is assumed that you will get very few or very incomplete answers to these questions, you can at least ask them. Be polite and cordial; be brisk so that you don't waste someone's time. Thank them for whatever help they are able to give you.

Following are two forms which offer suggested questions to ask when you do a reference check on a potential employee. You may wish to consolidate their contents with some of the questions indicated earlier and come up with a set of questions which is most right for your company and your particular employment needs. The idea of using a blank form during the telephone conversation is a good one, to help you in remembering all the questions you wish to ask, and to help you keep all the answers on one piece of paper.

Verification of Previous Employment

Name of candidate _____ Date _____

Name of Employer _____ Phone _____

Person called _____ Title _____

Relation to candidate _____

Was candidate employed by company? From _____ To _____

Regular in attendance? _____ Punctual _____

Nature of work _____

Performance in position _____

Initiative _____ Follow through _____

Learning ability _____ Work habits _____

Communication skills (oral) _____ (written) _____

Compatibility with superiors _____

Compatibility with co-workers _____

Reason for leaving _____

Disclosed earnings _____ Is this correct? _____

Chances for re-employment _____ Reasons _____

Employee assets _____

_____

Evaluation of reference: Reception to call:

Factual, objective _____ Receptive _____

Vague _____ Indifferent _____

Insufficient knowledge _____ Uncooperative _____

Willing to give information _____

Prejudiced against candidate _____

Telephone Reference Check

Applicant _____ Date _____

Company _____ Tel. No. _____

Person Contacted _____ Title _____

The applicant states he/she worked for your Company from _____

to _____ as _____.

Is this correct? YES ( ) NO ( )

If not correct, what were the dates? from _____ to _____

Have former employer evaluate the applicant on the following items:

Suited for job by training/experiences _____

Attendance/Punctuality _____ Efficient work habits _____

Ability to get along with others on the job _____

She/he said she/he left because _____

If not correct, why did she/he leave? _____

_____

Any problems outside the office that interfered with her/his

work? _____

_____

Would you re-employ her/him? _____

Special Working Arrangements

Independent Contractors

Employers can realize important savings by using independent contractors rather than employees for the right kind of jobs. An independent contractor may save you 15% or more over a full-time employee. You pay no Social Security, unemployment insurance, medical insurance, vacations, other fringe benefits, or workmen's compensation.

But be very careful. IRS considers the use of independent contractors to be a tax loophole and it may claim that they are really employees. In that case, the employer could be liable for withholding taxes that have never been withheld, and for other payroll taxes, interest and penalties.

The crucial test is control. If the employer closely supervises what the worker does and how and when he/she does it, then this can be construed as an employee. But if the person is free to control the work schedule and methods and is paid for the result, rather than on an hourly, daily, or weekly basis, then the independent contractor label is probably safe.

Other factors supporting independent contractor status:

- The worker provides the tools, equipment, and motor vehicles.
- The worker acquired skills on his own, not through training provided by the company.
- Work is done off the company's premises.
- Worker selects, hires, and pays the assistants.

Examples of independent contractors:

- Carpenters, plumbers, or electricians who supply their own tools, are paid for completed jobs, and are not closely supervised while doing the work.
- Salespeople who represent two or more manufacturers or companies and are paid on commission only.
- Truck or taxi drivers who buy their own gas and take a percentage of the revenues collected.
- Freelance magazine writers, commercial artists, draftsmen, designers, and the like.

Note: In borderline cases, it might be wise to ask the IRS for a ruling.

Guaranteed trouble: An employee already on the payroll is shifted to independent contractor status without any real change in work schedules or pay arrangements.

For a one-person business, the independent contractor is the preferred means of hiring the kind of staff support you need without getting involved with payrolls, taxes, insurance and all the rest. Following are some suggested letter agreements that are suitable for you to use (with modifications to fit your own business) either as the employer or the Contractor.

ACKNOWLEDGEMENT OF INDEPENDENT CONTRACTOR

The undersigned acknowledges that it has been retained by
_____ , (Company) for purposes of:
(Describe)

In consideration of the foregoing, the Company agrees to pay the undersigned payment as follows: (Describe amount and method of payment)

It is further acknowledged that:
1. The undersigned shall be deemed an Independent Contractor and is not an employee, partner, agent or engaged in a joint venture with the Company.
2. Consistent with the foregoing, the Company shall not deduct withholding taxes, FICA or any other taxes required to be deducted by an employer as I acknowledge my responsibility to pay same as an independent contractor.
3. I further acknowledge that I shall not be entitled to any fringe benefits, pension, retirement, profit sharing or any other benefits accruing to employees.
4. As an Independent Contractor I shall maintain the following insurance in amounts not less than those specified below.
(a) Workmen's Compensation and Employers' Liability in accordance with applicable law.
(b) Comprehensive General Liability. (Optional) Bodily injury liability in amount of $_____ for injuries sustained by one or more persons in any one accident. Property damage liability in the amount of $_____ for each accident and $_____ aggregate for each year of the policy period.
(c) Comprehensive Automobile liability. (Optional) Bodily injury liability coverage of $_____ for each person in any one accident and $_____ for injuries sustained by two or more persons in any one accident. Property damage liability of $_____ for each accident.

Signed under seal this _____ day of _____ , 19 ___ .

_____

Letter from Employer to Independent Contractor (Who Formerly was Employee)

SAMPLE

Date _____

Dear _____:

As previously discussed, this is to advise you that your position as "salesman" with our firm is being discontinued. However, rather than lose your services completely, we would like to develop a "working arrangement."

We will pay you a commission of 10% on all sales generated by YOU on behalf of the Company in the state of Pennsylvania. You will pay all your own expenses and will not be reimbursed by us.

We understand you will represent other manufacturers and will in no case represent yourself as an agent or employee of this Company but instead hold yourself out to the General Public as an Independent Contractor.

Term of this agreement is one year and may be terminated by either party through a written 60 day notice. Unless this agreement is terminated, it will continue for successive one year intervals.

In the event of a dispute about this agreement, both parties will abide by the Rules of the American Arbitration Association and waive their rights pending a decision by an Arbitrator appointed under its Rules.

Please sign a copy of this agreement and return it to us.

I look forward to a long term, mutually profitable relationship.

Sincerely,

_____

_____

If you pay *one* Independent Contractor more than $600 in one calendar year, you must file a 1099 form with the IRS to that effect, notifying them and the Contractor of the amount paid. It's still a lot less time and paper work and money than if the person were an employee.

Flextime and the Four-Day Week

Before plunging into the uncharted waters of alternate work schedules for your employees, be aware of some of the pros and cons.

183

The basic appeal to employees is that it gives them more control over their lives. From the employer's point of view, it offers the potential of reducing absenteeism, tardiness, and turnover, as well as improving morale and productivity.

Most common schedule rearrangements:

Flextime allows employees to choose hours (within limits) they will work. Usually scheduled around a core of common work time (9:00–3:00, 9:00-12:00, 1:00–3:00) when other workers are available. To fill out the eight hours, employees can come in early or stay late.

Lunch breaks can either be fixed or converted into flexible hours. Flextime programs put great emphasis on the role of the supervisor, who must see that previous production standards are met and that there is no falloff in productivity. When all goes well, flextime can result in more productivity, according to American Management Association surveys.

In terms of employer benefits this eliminates the need for short-term absences and tardiness. The facility is staffed over a greater period of time without increases in over-time pay. It sometimes makes it easier to recruit good, high-quality workers.

The four-day, forty-hour week is popular with unions, since it is seen as a means to creating more jobs. It is also popular with many employees, who vastly favor a three-day weekend (Friday is the preferred day off). Still, the four-day week is definitely not for everyone. Mothers don't like longer days, even if they are fewer in number. The four-day week is also not successful where work is too physically exhausting to permit ten-hour days. The four-day week is most successful in firms with high start-up and shut-down costs. It may gain momentum as more companies adopt it. A major objection of employees is that their schedule is different from the rest of the world's.

Permanent, Part-Time Employee

A permanent part-time employee is one who works in one job, generally five days per week, but no more than twenty hours per week. This employee is not entitled to company benefits, paid vacations, paid holidays, sick leave, or personal days (unless special concessions are made by the employer). In no case may a permanent part-time employee work more than 1000 hours in any calendar year. (After that point, they are considered full-time employees and are entitled to all company benefits available to other employees.)

Temporary Employee

A temporary employee is one who works for a specified period (with a beginning and ending date) to perform a particular function or project. The temporary employee is not entitled to company benefits, paid vacations, paid holidays, sick leave, or personal days (unless special concessions are made by the employer). In no case may a temporary employee work more than 1000 hours in any calendar year. (After that point they are considered permanent employees and are entitled to all company benefits available to other employees.)

Employee Relations

Employee relations is more than recruiting, hiring and firing. It also includes the contractual agreement, employee benefits and performance evaluations, at the very least. The following tips may help you develop the best procedures for your business.

Contracts

Employment contracts are usually good for the employees, but not always for the company. That is because they are very difficult to enforce (according to James Freund, Skadden, Arps, Slate, Meagher and Flom, New York City). For example, suppose an employee leaves after two years of a five-year contract. The court will not order the employee to work. The company has a theoretical claim for loss of services, but it would have to prove it could not replace him for the same money. Since damages are hard to prove, employers rarely sue.

Still, most employees honor the contract as a moral obligation, and the noncompete agreement puts some teeth in it for the company.

Situations in which employees have enough clout to get contracts:

• In mergers, top officers of the acquired company ask for contracts.

The acquiring company is usually glad to give them, because it wants experienced management to stay.

- An experienced or mature executive going to a new company that has come courting. If the executive is over age fifty, the executive really requires one.
- Chief executives who do a good job are sometimes rewarded with employment contracts by a happy board.

When negotiating an employment contract, remember:

- The agreement not to compete if and when the employee leaves the company should be sharply limited in time and geographical area. If it is not, it may not be enforceable.
- Try to get the noncompete agreement to end if the executive is let go at the end of the contract.
- The company will want the right to fire an executive "for cause." One useful provision: If there is a dispute on what constitutes "cause" for dismissal, it goes to arbitration and the executive collects salary until it is settled.

A wide variety of employee forms and employment contracts are available through Enterprise Publishing of Wilmington, Delaware.

Benefits

As a one-person business owner, you may or may not have developed a long "menu" of benefits for yourself. You are certain to have secured for yourself medical and dental insurance, long-term disability, accident and life insurance, liability, and some form of pension or annuity planning (see Chapters 3 and 11 for some concrete suggestions), but you may not have formalized in any way the number of holidays you take, whether or not you get a "paid" vacation (Chapter 10 explores *how* you can take a vacation!), how many paid "sick days" you are allowed (most one-person business owners are notoriously healthy), and whether or not you give yourself a bonus at the end of the year.

All of this probably seems like unnecessary twaddle to people like us who are busy running our businesses and trying to be smart enough to protect our current and future security with a few insurance policies. However, once you have decided to hire a full-time employee, all of these questions become important. While it would take too much space to enumerate all the nuances of the new tax act with regard to the proportion of benefits for each employee, suffice it to say that if *you* have some protections and extras that can be construed as benefits, then your employee is entitled to the same things. (Talk with your tax advisor to get the specifics.)

What does that mean? It means that the insurance you carry on yourself will now be carried on someone else also. It means that you may go into the office to work on the Fourth of July, but your employee is entitled to that legal holiday off (unless, perhaps, you agree to pay overtime). It means that you may work when you have the flu, but your employee may expect to be out for real illnesses and, furthermore, will expect to be paid for a reasonable number of days off. If you carry a pension or profit-sharing plan on yourself, you must also make plans to include that employee (with certain percentages off and certain provisos; talk to your tax accountant.)

If you must hire a full-time employee, give that person a "company policy" memo or booklet at times of employment, listing the benefits, the expected work schedule, the amount of paid vacation and paid days off (holidays, sick days). By putting it in writing, you avoid misunderstandings later.

Hiring a full-time employee can be an expensive item. Benefits (which also include FICA, unemployment taxes, worker's compensation taxes, as well as your own company benefits) were once calculated at 15 percent of the base salary of a worker. Those days are long gone. The cost of benefits now ranges from 29.2 percent of salary in the textile industry to 44.5 percent of salary in the petroleum industry, with other industries falling somewhere in between. If you plan to hire someone to help you at $30,000 per year, you can expect that person to cost between $38,000 and $42,000 a year, and they certainly will not be working every day.

Is there a way to maximize your dollars? Here are a few suggestions:

- Analyze your condition carefully to be sure you need someone to help you. Then be sure that you need a full-time employee, rather than an independent contractor.
- Define the job description carefully so that you will recruit, interview, and hire the person who is best suited for the tasks you have available.
- Keep the employee informed and a part of the planning and implementation process. Motivate and challenge him or her to be a part

187

of the company's growth. Treat the person fairly, evaluate the work regularly and reward him or her for extra effort.

If your business is to grow and prosper, it will undoubtedly require additional people to help you. You must be aware, however, that taking on an employee or employees changes the nature of your business operation completely. That does not mean that the change is *bad*, but the complexity and expense of creating payrolls should not be ignored.

There are a number of books listed in the Bibliography that can aid you in managing your personnel more efficiently.

Evaluations

One of the most efficient ways of managing your personnel well is to give them periodic and fair performance evaluations based on the job description, which should be updated every couple of years. Following are samples of evaluations for nonexempt (hourly wages) and exempt (salaried) personnel.

Performance Evaluation Nonexempt Employees (Nonsupervisory)

Name of Employee: _____ Date _____

Rate the employee in each category by a (√) mark opposite one (1) of the five descriptions listed for each rating category. *Keep in mind routine demands of job and employee's typical present performance.*

I. *Job Knowledge:* (Consider knowledge of work gained through experience, general education, specialized training, special sources of information.)

_____ 4. Knows essentials and details thoroughly enough to perform without assistance.

_____ 3. Knows job well enough to perform with a small amount of assistance.

_____ 2. Adequate grasp of essentials; requires some assistance daily.

_____ 1. Limited understanding of job; requires considerable assistance.

_____ 0. Inadequate understanding of job; requires constant assistance.

II. *Quality of Work:* (Consider accuracy, neatness, thoroughness and dependability of results regardless of volume.)

———— 4. Practically always good enough to use as a "model"; exceptionally neat and accurate.

———— 3. Occasionally good enough to use as a "model."

———— 2. Usually acceptable; usually neat; occasional errors or rejections.

———— 1. Often unacceptable; frequent errors or rejections and/or untidiness.

———— 0. Practically worthless; usually untidy and/or full of errors or rejections.

III. *Quantity of Work:* (Consider volume of work produced under routine, day-to day conditions. Disregard errors. Check whatever production records are available.)

———— 4. Unusually productive; turns out much more than accepted standard.

———— 3. Output usually somewhat above demands of job.

———— 2. Satisfactory for demands of job.

———— 1. Output somewhat below requirements of job.

———— 0. Production far below that which job requires; barely satisfactory.

IV. *Working Characteristic When Under Pressure:* (Consider ability to turn out satisfactory work under difficult conditions.)

———— 4. Practically always speeds up and works under pressure.

———— 3. Occasionally does better work under pressure.

———— 2. Usually keeps calm; turns out satisfactory work.

———— 1. Tends to become rattled; as a result, speed and accuracy often not up to usual level.

———— 0. Breaks down under pressure; unable to perform satisfactorily.

V. *Adaptability:* (Consider quickness to learn new duties and to adjust to new situations encountered on the job.)

_____ 4. Exceptionally fast to learn new duties and adjust to changed conditions.

_____ 3. Rather quick to absorb new material and adjust to change.

_____ 2. "Catches on" and adjusts to changes fast enough to perform work satisfactorily.

_____ 1. Rather slow to absorb new material and adjust to changes.

_____ 0. Extremely slow to adjust to changes or to learn new duties; becomes confused.

VI. *Industry:* (Consider the degree of effort which employee applies to the job.)

_____ 4. Always busy; whenever regular work caught up finds a job to do.

_____ 3. Usually busy; occasionally finds extra work for self.

_____ 2. Keeps pace with regular flow of work.

_____ 1. Requires occasional prodding to keep up with regular duties.

_____ 0. Shirks work; puts it off; must be continuously prodded.

VII. *Adjustment to Fellow Worker:* (Consider all working relationships.)

_____ 4. Tends to act as and be accepted as a leader in constructive achievement of department's work.

_____ 3. Works well with others in the group; voluntarily helps others.

_____ 2. Maintains satisfactory relationships; willing to help others when asked.

_____ 1. Has difficulty working with others.

_____ 0. Won't or can't work with others; antagonistic.

VIII. *Attendance/Punctuality:*

_____ 4. Totally dependable and never watches the clock.

_____ 3. Rarely watches the clock; concentration on work to be done.

_____ 2. Keeps regular hours; covers absences.

_____ 1. Occasionally late, does not always inform before absence.

_____ 0. Rarely arrives on time; does not keep proper hours.

_____ *Total of Points Checked:* $\div 32 = $ _____%

Course of Action:

_____ Merit Increase

_____ Promotion ......

_____ Training ....

_____ Separation .....

This Progress has been Discussed with the Employee on (Date) _____

Employee's Signature: _____

Annual Performance Appraisal Exempt Employees

Date: _____

Name: _____ Position: _____

Present Salary _____

Rating Code:

4—Superior—on par with the very best
3—Above average—occasionally something to be desired, but no problem
2—Average—satisfactory
1—Below average—needs improvement
0—Low—not suitable to job

I. *Job Knowledge:*

_____ A. Understands job requirements, responsibilities and degree of authority

_____ B. Applies basic skills to full use of ability

_____ C. Possesses necessary experience to perform work duties

II *Administrative Abilities:*

_____ A. Ability to plan, organize, control flow of work

_____ B. Promptness in completing assignments; follows-up on problems promptly

_____ C. Willingness to accept responsibility

_____ D. Capacity to delegate authority with responsibility

_____ E. Motivates subordinates to maximum effort

_____ F. Promotes harmonious working relationships

_____ G. Extent individual's methods achieve results

III. *Judgement:*

_____ A. Exhibits good judgement in arriving at conclusions

_____ B. Discriminates in doing important tasks first

_____ C. Can make objective and unbiased criticism of others

_____ D. Makes independent decisions when precedent or direction not available

IV. *Cost Control:*

_____ A. Degree of awareness of importance of cost factors

_____ B. Guards against unwarranted increases in expense

_____ C. Reduces expenses when and wherever possible

V. *Dependability/Professionalism:*

_____ A. Conscientious in the absence of supervision

_____ B. Extent instructions are followed when important to do so

_____ C. Intellectual honesty when reporting results of work

_____ D. Respect for confidential data

_____ E. Prompt/on time

VI. *Adaptability:*

_____ A. Willingness to accept constructive criticism and suggestions

_____ B. Flexibility—performs various tasks simultaneously within scope of job

————————— C. Ability to understand and make use of new changes in method of work content

————————— D. Seeks/Accepts direction

VII. *Relations with Others:*

————————— A. Extent of tact and diplomacy when dealing with associates and customers

————————— B. Ability to express oneself well in conversation

————————— C. Degree of respect received from associates

————————— D. Cooperative with other people

VIII. *Professional Development (Where applicable):*

————————— A. Attends and participates in meetings of Technical or Professional Societies

————————— B. Keeps well informed on current trends in field of endeavor

————————— C. Extent formal education is being continued

————————— D. Contributes to professional conferences/seminars

————————— Total Points Given: $\div 32 =$ —————%

Appraisal Discussed with Employee: ————————— Date: ———

Employee's Signature ——————————————————————

As is probably obvious from the foregoing, being committed to the freedom and uniqueness of running a one-person business, I have a bias against hiring permanent employees. That does not mean that I don't require help in my business on occasion, and that you won't require help. It is what kind of help you require that becomes the crucial question, not only in the matter of expenses, but in the matter of supervisory time, emotional commitment to another person, and concerns about constancy of performance.

That is why I feel this new age of service businesses offers such great opportunities for those who want to run businesses alone; they are ready-made to take care of your needs!

Failing that, we always have the opportunity to hire independent contractors, temporaries, part-time or flextime workers. In my view, your decision of last resort should be the hiring of a full-time permanent employee. A friend of mine said it well when she took on her employee, "Now I have to work twice as hard, because now there are two of us to feed!"

However, if you *do* decide to take that step for the betterment of your business, then I hope this chapter has offered some tips and shortcuts in making the experience an efficient, economical, and enjoyable one.

Chapter 9

How to Use Your Accountant, Banker, Broker, Consultant, Insurance Agent, Lawyer

Throughout this book we have talked about the interrelationships you will have with a variety of people, particularly the six mentioned in this heading. It is difficult, if not impossible, for a one-person business to operate without the assistance of these people (as well as a number of others, including Financial Planners, whom we have discussed in other chapters).

This is not a chapter about how to get them "for free." There is an old saying that "you get what you pay for," and if you don't pay a professional, either in money or reciprocal kindness, it is unlikely you will get a thorough and dedicated job. You would do best to treat them as you wish to be treated—as a professional, remunerated properly for your expertise.

However, there is the issue of what you get for your money. Few professionals are mind readers, and, although the good ones will strive to do what is best for you, they will not be truly effective without your help. All good professional relationships are joint efforts. You have to know what you want in order to get the best advice from your professional advisors. They will ask you a lot of questions in order to lead the discussions to the best possible solution. However, you have to ask a lot of questions, too. In fact, that is what this chapter is about . . . questions.

Twenty Questions for Your Accountant

1. "Can I keep books in my business in the cash method as well as the accrual method?"
2. "Which method would be best for me to help me maximize my profits?"
3. "What percentage of last year's taxes must I pay quarterly this year, since last year's taxes were low?"
4. "Does my company's tax year have to be the same as the calendar year?"
5. "Can I set up a reserve account for anticipated bad debts?"
6. "Can I set up my installment-payment income to be accounted for as I receive it?"
7. "I've heard of the LIFO (last in, first out) method of reporting inventory. Is this of any value to me?"
8. "I'm involved in science (or engineering). Do I qualify for the 'research and development credit' while I'm working on a project? What do I count in it?"
9. "What would you suggest I keep in my reserves (retained earnings)? What are the advantages and risks?"
10. "What options do I have in depreciating office/shop improvements? Equipment and vehicles? Furniture?"
11. "Do you see any problem in my budget? What other company(s) could you give as examples?"
12. "Will I always deal with you or will I be switched around from person to person?"
13. "How often will I talk with a principal of the firm?"
14. "How many companies like mine do you handle? May I call several of them for a reference?"
15. "What is your firm's position on a tax audit? Will you accompany me? What do you charge?"
16. "Are there advantages to late-filing extensions? Or do we not wish to call attention to the return?"
17. "Should we investigate charitable remainder trusts on my house or some stocks?"
18. "What is your method of charging companies my size? By the hour, by the job, by the year? Could we discuss the advantages and disadvantages of each?"
19. "If I had things in my business that are no longer valuable—tools,

machinery, vehicles, inventory, supplies, certain intangibles—what is the best way of handling that? Abandonment with write-off? Flea market sale? What?"

20. "How much of my equipment purchase should I write off in the first year, now that the new tax law is more liberal? Will it help my tax position?"

Twenty Questions for Your Banker

1. "How many 'activity charges' will I have on my account each month?"
2. "How do you charge for those items? May I have a list?"
3. "How do you calculate my basic balance each month? May I see the formula?"
4. "Will you send me a breakdown of the 'profit' each month on my account?"
5. "If you multiply the account's average monthly balance by a monthly interest rate, what bank reserve requirement do you reduce from the interest earned? What do *I* net?"
6. "How do you calculate average balances? By average collected balance or by average current balance?"
7. "How long do you take to clear checks from other banks? In town? In state? Out of state? What cities clear overnight? How many days do you hold the float from small banks or small cities?"
8. "What balance must I maintain to collect your maximum interest?"
9. "What are your monthly charges in case I don't wish to maintain that balance?"
10. "What days and hours are you open? Do you have a credit card teller machine for business accounts? If so, where are the machines?"
11. "What is your 'actual' money market rate yield?"
12. "If I keep with you substantial balances, far in excess of your requirement, what extra advantages will this yield me?"
13. "If I buy CDs through you, what loan advantages does that give me? One percent over the yield of the CD? One-half percent?"
14. "What is your formula for company borrowing?" Typically, it must not exceed the sum of 10 percent of the net working capital, plus 5 percent of cash and receivables, plus 10 percent of one year's net income; less 3 percent of the long-term debt. See how your bank stacks up.
15. "Do you work with the Small Business Administration?" If they

197

do, up to 90 percent of their loans to small businesses are guaranteed. So be persistent and shop around.

16. "I'd like to negotiate my loan as a package. Let's start with the loan rate, and then 'plug in' the repayment schedule, collateral, compensating balances, fees for services, etc. OK?" The idea is to trade off higher balances and other items for a lower rate. Get the banker to give the rate first.

17. "How much do you charge for bounced checks? What is your rejection time?" You don't care about the cost of bounced checks; you don't plan to bounce any. *You* need to know that, if someone bounces a check on you and your bank doesn't notify you within thirty-six hours, they have to pay for it. That is the Uniform Commercial Code. Watch for it.

18. "Do you have a bank lock box?" This way your customers can send checks to the bank's postbox and you are credited the day the bank receives the check. It speeds up your use of your money.

19. "Can I borrow the money to buy your money market certificates?" You can still make money if you put up some of your money and some of theirs, if they charge no more than 1 percent above the certificate yield on their money.

20. "What is your policy on borrowing from an IRA carried with you? What is your interest rate?" You can borrow on your own IRA for under sixty days without a withdrawal penalty. The exact amount must be replaced. Since it is your money, you should get a good rate.

Twenty Questions for Your Broker

1. "What is your scale of rates for buy and sell orders? May I have a copy?" Check your bills against the list when you trade!

2. "That's an interesting investment offer. Is your firm underwriting it? How long have you had it? When does it close? Are any other firms underwriting it?"

3. "Will you put me on your newsletter list?"

4. "Will you put me on your special offering list? What is the minimum investment to be on that list?"

5. "Will you put me on your municipal bond offering list?"

6. "What is your borrowing policy?" Remember, you should be able to borrow up to 50 percent of the value of your stocks and up to 70 percent of the value of your bonds. Find out the interest rate. It should be less than any local bank's.

7. "Will you hold the security or deliver it to me at no charge?"

8. "Do you carry SIPC insurance* and what is your insurance coverage per client?" $500,000 per client is the industry maximum.

9. "If I have a cash balance on my sales or trades, what is your policy? Do you refund it to me and, if so, how quickly? Do you have a money market fund, and what is its current interest rate?"

10. "What is your margin trading interest rate?" It can range from 1/2 to 2 percent over prime, so shop around if you plan to do margin trading.

11. "Do you have Keogh and/or IRA plans? What is your interest and dividend performance over the past five years? What are your charges?" Some charge $25 to set up and $25 annually to maintain, or even a percentage. Usually, you can do better at banks or with mutual funds than with that sort of charge.

12. "You say this is a 'special' today. Could you please send over a research report and I'll get back to you?" Beware of "specials." The firm is usually unloading something they are unhappy with, and the brokers will be paid extra commission for moving it fast.

13. "I'm a relatively small investor with you. When your company recommends a 'hold' on a stock, would you call me? I will probably want to make my decision to sell then."

14. "Do you follow the OTC (over-the-counter stocks) and issue any recommendations on them? Can I obtain 10K's (financial reports furnished by a company to the investment community) or reports through you?"

15. "What are your hours of telephone operation? How early can I call you to place an order? How late in the day?"

16. "Do you have an 800 telephone number that I can use in other cities? What are your other office numbers and do you have a 'relationship' with other firms in other cities?"

17. "Do you conduct special investment program seminars for your clients? How do I get on your announcement list?"

18. "Do you have other investment programs? Tax shelters? Public utilities?"

19. "How many days from a buy or sell transaction do I have before you must receive payment? If the payment arrives late, what happens? How do you treat a check? Is there a delay in crediting or processing? What kinds of checks are acceptable or unacceptable?"

20. "How soon after my buy or sell order can I expect written confirmation?"

*Securities Investors Protection Corporation, the stock brokers' equivalent of the Federal Deposit Insurance Corporation at banks.

Twenty Questions for Your Consultant

1. "Have you done this kind of consulting before? Could I have some references?"
2. "Have you worked as an adjunct with another consultant/one-person business before? Could I have references?"
3. "Do you wish to bill our potential client yourself or will you bill me?" You would rather make the deal with the client yourself and have the adjunct consultant bill you.
4. "Do you prefer to contract for the full job? If so, what kind of payment schedule do you usually prefer? Weekly? Monthly? When certain points of the job completion are reached?"
5. "How do you bill for your expenses? What is included? Excluded?"
6. "Do you prefer to contract for individual pieces of the job? If so, how would you structure the delivery and payment schedules?"
7. "Do you carry life insurance, liability insurance, employee FICA coverage? Will you verify?"
8. "Are you willing to sign an Independent Contractor agreement? Will you sign the one I draft?"
9. "Are you able to 'put up the money' for initial research, development, preliminary studies? Will you need an advance? How much? In what increments?"
10. "Can you clear the time on your calendar that we will need to do this project? What other projects will you be doing at the same time?"
11. "Who will you be using to help you? Can I see their credentials?"
12. "Have you worked for this client before?"
13. "Have you worked for this client's competitors? Is there a possible conflict of interest?"
14. "Will you supply the necessary materials, transportation, clerical assistance? Is it built into your expense projections, or will you bill the direct costs?"
15. "Do you have the necessary business licenses to do this work?"
16. "If you have to travel, will you bill on actual expenses previously agreed to, or will you accept a per diem? If so, what is your per diem?" The average consulting per diems range from $100 to $150 per day. Obviously, the city in which the work is done is important, as well as where the consultant is required to stay. Some hotels cost $150 a day and this does not count meals and transportation. Per diems are preferable, simply because they eliminate collecting receipts and arguing over details. The best bet is to find out the current federal per diem for government employees and mark it up 10 to 15 percent.

17. "Do you charge for travel time, or simply the time spent with the client?" Generally, clients don't like to pay for travel time, since they are paying travel expenses. The best arrangement is to be sure that the fee or hourly charge for time spent with the client covers the travel time. With a consultant, time is money. If the usual daily rate is $500 and it takes half a day to get there and half a day to return, then the charge should be somewhere between $750 and $1,000 to cover the consultant's time.
18. "May I see a sample of your billing sheet?"
19. "May I see a sample of your presentation to a client similar to this one?" Be careful! They may think you are trying to "lift" their ideas. This is when your integrity is absolutely essential.
20. "Do you think we'll get along well together?" (If it is your client, you want to be in charge of the relationship and have the assisting contractor defer to you.)

Twenty Questions for Your Insurance Agent

1. "Do you represent a particular carrier or carriers?" The idea is to buy insurance from an agent/broker who deals with every carrier. You want them to shop around for you.
2. "Why should I drop my old policy? It serves my current needs very well." Like stock brokers, insurance agents sometimes "churn" accounts because they are usually paid at the front end of a sale. Your old policy does not help them any.
3. "I presume that my old policy will not be cancelled until I have received and reviewed the new policy and its premiums. Could I have that in writing?" Beware. When you switch policies, you can be in for a rude surprise. The old one is cancelled and the new one has some "front-load" fees and a premium that you were unaware of—even if you have the ubiquitous "computer projection" provided now by most agents. If it happens, fire him, notify his company and the new carrier of the misrepresentation, and also demand that your old insurance be reinstated without increase. There is a "grace period" any carrier will allow when they think there has been misrepresentation. They don't need any problems with state insurance commissions.
4. "Why should I switch carriers just because you have? I have a low claims record and a low premium. What's better about this new coverage?"
5. "Why shouldn't I make a small loss claim? That's what I buy insurance for." If the agent advises against small claims, something

is wrong. Go directly to the company and cite your coverage, as well as your good claims record. Then get a new agent.

6. "I'm buying (all/most) of my insurance from you. Could you provide me with a 'certificate of insurance' until the policies arrive?" This is a form of "malpractice" insurance that all big brokers should be willing to provide in writing. Then if something occurs that was not in the original arrangement, you have recourse to that insurance.

7. "I've looked at your major medical insurance and I've looked at several HMOs (Health Maintenance Organizations). They look like a better buy for me and my family." Have the agent review the differences point by point. Then do the same with the HMOs you are investigating. If you basically work in one city, particularly if it has a good reputation with hospitals and private practitioners, it is sometimes much better to buy HMO coverage, particularly for an entire family.

8. "You've offered me fire and theft insurance on my business place. But what about improvements and betterment clauses? What about business interruption? I lease the place; what about leasehold insurance? Can you get me some bids?"

9. "On this disability policy I want to be sure that the definition of disability makes sense for me. I need one that defines disability as 'the inability to perform any of the duties required by my occupation'; not the 'inability to perform any occupation.' "

10. "Well, okay. Let's split the difference. What will it cost if the strict definition is used for six months or a year, and then the general definition takes over?"

11. "What is the length of the benefit period? Will it still pay if I'm over sixty-five?"

12. "What's the waiting period before the benefits start paying? How much lower are the premiums if I can wait ninety days instead of thirty days?"

13. "What if I get hit by a car and, after six months, can go back to work, but only part-time? Does this policy take care of that?" In such a case you would need a policy with a "residual benefit" to fill out your income needs.

14. "I need to insure for my 'net income,' not my 'gross income.' Let's figure the rates on that."

15. "Does this disability insurance have any relationship to Social Security? If I collect Social Security disability, does it reduce this payment?"

16. "I'm told that there's a formula for deciding on the amount of life insurance I need. Could you tell me what it is?" You should be

prepared with your own formula: cash needs for settling your estate; paying uninsured medical costs and funeral expenses; outstanding debts, such as the mortgage, car loans, installment loans; outstanding company debts and loans, using 6 percent inflation as a factor for the future; an income for surviving family; amount to cover buy out or liquidation of your company; education for your children, if applicable; liability if certain of your assets are destroyed; your age (in case you will be collecting Social Security or a pension soon). It is tempting to buy term insurance when you are young, because it is cheaper, but whole life may be more manageable. Review every year, and remember, the difference between buying $1 million in insurance and $5 million is very modest on a monthly basis.

17. "How much fire insurance do I need?" Insure for at least 80 percent of the replacement value, otherwise you will not be able to collect the full value of the policy in case of disaster.

18. "What outside coverage do I get on my homeowner's policy?" Most policies cover theft and certain kinds of accidents away from the home. Know the limits and opportunities.

19. "Surely we can save some money on the insurance at my place of business. I'm sure title insurance was written on it during the past five years; let's check and see if we can't get a reduction, since they don't have to do a full title search again. Also, I'd like a deduction because I have a smoke detector, a burglar alarm, we have weekend security, and I'm a nonsmoker." Ask for special rates when you are a "good risk."

20. "My major medical has a high deductible (to keep down rates). Shouldn't I have some kind of 'excess' or 'wraparound' plan to pick up that little bit of expenditure?"

Twenty Questions for Your Lawyer

1. "How big is your firm?" A firm of two lawyers may be friendly and intimate, but chances are they will be so busy making a living that your time with them will be very limited. Conversely, a firm with 150 lawyers would more than likely look upon your business as a hobby. You need to be taken seriously and you need the benefit of several attorneys with a variety of specialities. A firm with between twenty-five and one-hundred attorneys would be the place to look.

2. "Will I be dealing with a principal?" Unless you have a really big

problem or lawsuit, you may want to see a principal on rare occasions, two or three times a year. The prices are prohibitive.

3. "Will I have one person who is 'my lawyer' in the firm, even though he or she may use the expertise of other members?"

4. "Have you handled other businesses such as mine? May I call a couple of your clients?"

5. "How do you bill your clients? By the hour? By the job? On retainer?"

6. "I would like to be billed for specific services. Is that okay?" You would like to pay a different rate for a consultation in the office with a principal, some research done by a paralegal, an updating phone call between you and your contact lawyer, and the preparation of agreements, a good many of which are probably "boiler plate" that come out of the computer/word processor, courtesy of a good secretary. Each of those activities should have a different rate, if the firm is interested in a long-term relationship, and you should receive the bill at those rates.

7. "I'm 'shopping' for a firm to handle my business. Could we talk for a few minutes?" If the lawyer or firm suggests charging you for an introductory interview, you know already you have got the wrong firm.

8. "I need very little legal work, but my clients require a lot. Could we talk?" Some companies, such as real estate brokers, use lawyers all the time to "close" on sales; yet, they personally rarely need legal work. If you are a "referral agent" to a lawyer, you should expect certain courtesies in return: preparation of occasional legal documents for your company; the opportunity to use their admission to luncheon clubs or business seminars. Don't mistake this for barter or "kickbacks." It is pure professional courtesy and should be treated that way. Don't be shy about suggesting it, after you have referred a number of clients.

9. "How prompt are you in delivering the necessary paper work for my deals? Are there any problems I should know about?" It is unfortunate that some lawyers, like a lot of other professionals, blame their delays on "their secretaries," or "computer breakdown." If ever you have a piece of legal work delayed and you hear either of those excuses as a reason, quietly prod the lawyer until you get what you want, and then change lawyers. Both secretaries and computer maintenance are under control in a professionally run office. You should not have to be delayed, just because they can not control staff or have a mediocre maintenance program. Let's be honest; those excuses are just that— excuses. Paper work is usually late because the lawyer did not get

it out on time. Harry Truman had the right idea: "The buck stops here." The sign was on *his* desk!

10. "Can I expect to have you return my calls promptly? The same day? That night? I'll give you my home number." "Telephone tag" is the dreariest professional game in the world. Don't call another professional and leave your number if you cannot be reached in a reasonable amount of time. Conversely, if you leave a message for a lawyer and don't get a return call for twenty-four hours or longer, you really need another lawyer. It is a great way to find out the value placed on your account.

11. "I'm looking for a permanent advisor to my company. Here are the problems and opportunities I see. What do you think?" When choosing a lawyer, you should get at least "a second and third opinion." You will be amazed at the differing suggestions. Which one to choose? You have to do your homework, too. Make your decision based on the business plans and personal needs you have already defined. Who understands you and your business best?

12. "Does your firm represent anyone who is a competitor to me?"

13. "Can I use you for special assignments only?" You may want to retain a "big" firm for serious work and use a "family" lawyer, even in another town, for more personal work.

13. "So-and-so is my accountant. Have you ever done business with him or her?" Your advisors should be friendly, but not necessarily "pals." A little friendly disagreement between them can sometimes go a long way in working out the best "deal" for you.

14. "If you don't have the specialist I need for a particular problem, who would you call in? What are his or her credentials?"

15. "Are you on any boards of directors in this city or elsewhere?" Is there a "hidden agenda" you should know about?

16. "What other firms have you worked for? When did you come here?" This could be important some day. People keep contacts and friends wherever they go.

17. "Do you represent any work at such-and-such bank?" Your bank may be their client. You have to decide whether or not that is good or bad.

18. "Does my business interest you?" The lawyer may hate it! See if you can find out.

19. "If you were to leave here, who would inherit my account?" Touchy! If you are in a "firm," however, you need to know the junior who's coming along who can help you.

20. "May I show you some of my work? My workshop? My office? My references?" Whatever is necessary to make the point that

you are a real professional and have splendid credentials. Like bankers, lawyers (particularly those in larger firms) don't really understand one-person businesses. Is it a hobby? How serious are you? Can you really make a good living doing this? Can you really pay your bills? Are you worth wasting time on?

You should play "Twenty Questions" with every supplier, every professional who provides goods or services to you, and, of course, you can come up with a lot more questions than those included here. Perhaps these will get you started.

Is there a lesson in this chapter? Yes. A very simple one. Never accept an answer just because a professional gives it. You would not want that to happen with people who are hiring *you*. Ask questions—particularly questions that have a value to *you* in your business.

Chapter 10

How to Take a Vacation

During the time I was writing this book, I ran into a friend at a luncheon who also runs a one-person business. When I told her the topic of the book, she was delighted and said, "Why don't you tell us how in the world we can take a vacation?!"

I thought that was a splendid idea, having had the problem myself. I told my editor about it. She agreed it might be a good chapter to include in the book.

So . . . the time came to write the chapter. I dutifully went through all my references and periodicals to see what other "expert" advice was available. Nothing.

I sent my researcher to the library, confident that the problem had been addressed by time planners, writers of management procedures, time/motion experts . . . somebody. After two days, he came back quite unhappy and very chagrined. (He is a very good ferret and was afraid that he had let me down.) The fact was, he could find nothing about vacations or time off or breathing room that had any remote relationship to this particular problem. Most of the suggestions on time management had little to do with the need to "get away from it all" every now and then without seeing the business go down the tubes (or, at the very least, losing a particular plum of a job).

That is when I decided to invite some people to "tea" and have a little free wheeling discussion. All of them run one-person businesses and are very sympathetic to the problem.

A lot was said that night, and I am not sure we reached any meaningful conclusions, simply because we all run so many different kinds of businesses. If I can share with you some of the highlights of the discussion, perhaps you will glean some ideas for managing this very important aspect of your life.

First I would like to share with you some of the definitions we developed about what a vacation really is. Its root word, of course, is to "vacate," and that was the starting point of our discussion. There is a need in every business person's life to *vacate* the business premises on a more or less regular basis, if for no other reason than to come back to it with a new or renewed perspective. Things look different when you have been away for a while and have taken the opportunity to mingle with people who have other interests, other ideas, other needs. Just seeing a different place and doing a different routine, particularly if you work basically alone most of the time, is very rewarding and refreshing.

There was a good deal of talk about this. Getting away from home and into a new environment was considered very important to the concept of a "real vacation."

There was talk of needing to spend time with family, a close friend, that "special" person, because most of the time we carry our work with us, at least in our heads, twenty-four hours a day.

Then the word "recreation" came up—doing something "different" than you do all day long, all week long. Of course, this comes from the root words "to re-create," and it has a wonderful, soothing ring to it. My group took up the theme of a vacation as a time to "re-create" themselves—to come back refreshed, with new perspectives, new energy, new will and determination. To "go to the well" of our own personal beings and find those new resources that can re-energize us for the months ahead.

After we had gotten that off our chests, we had to put on our thinking caps and get serious about how this wonderful event could be accomplished.

Things got a little harder.

"How do you take a vacation?"

"I don't. I take long weekends."

"But is that enough?"

"No. But I try to take a bunch of them during the year."

"Do you take them on the long federal holiday weekends?"

"Usually. I know that most people are away and that I won't get many calls."

"But that means that you're away when everybody else is trying to get plane reservations and hotel rooms."

"You got it."

"That's the pits."

"What about taking long weekends when nobody else is traveling much?"

"That's what *I* try to do. We have a place on the lake, and, if I can leave on Thursday night, I can spend a whole day by myself and two days with the family."

"You're still fighting traffic on Sunday night."

"No. I get up at 3 A.M. and drive back on Monday morning."

"I couldn't see the steering wheel at three in the morning!"

"Well, we have to do what's right for our own metabolism. I'm best in the morning."

"Do you call in on Friday?"

"Well . . ."

"Admit it!"

"Well, yes I do. But I leave an honest message on the machine. I say that I'm out of town, but, that if it's urgent, I'll be in touch. Otherwise, I'll check in on Monday. It's worked out pretty well."

"But what about longer times? Do you have more than three days away at a time?"

"Oh, sure. In my business, everybody's "out to lunch" from Thanksgiving through New Years. I couldn't get a client to look at a job if I offered it for free. We usually plan a trip away in early December and take at least a week."

"That's when I'm the busiest."

"Why?"

"Because many of my clients find that they still have some budget left and they're frantic to spend it. Otherwise, it will be cut out the next year. I hold hands and do projects and could work seven days a week if I wanted to."

"So do I. That's the busiest time for our parties. My problem is finding enough people to help with the work. They're all in demand."

"When do you do your Christmas shopping?"

"July."

"By mail."

"Gift certificates!"

(General laughter.)

"Do you think we're stuck with always having short vacations?"

"I hope not! My kids aren't going to know me."

"Well, my work is a little different. With the seminars and consulting, I can agree to a schedule and then take time off anywhere in between that I want to."

"Is it really when you want to? Or is it just when the work is a little slack?"

"A little of both, I guess. I like to travel abroad and that takes at least a week, and preferably two. So I try to carve out chunks of time to allow that."

"But what if someone calls or writes while you're away?"

"Someone answers my mail while I'm away. And I have call-forwarding to a colleague. He has my schedule and can answer the basic questions in my absence. If they want information on the seminars, he sends it. If they want to set a tentative schedule, he makes a note and I answer as soon as I'm back."

"Do you pay him?"

"We have an arrangement. We expense whatever time he spends on my behalf and, if I get a job out of one of the contacts he talks with, he makes a small commission. The nice part is that I do the same for him when he's away."

"Does he ever try to take business away from you?"

"No. We don't do the same thing."

"That's lucky."

"I wouldn't call it lucky. We planned it that way."

"It *is* lucky. The only people I know who could handle my calls are in the same business I'm in. I'm not sure I could trust them."

"That's depressing."

"It's reality."

"Couldn't a member of your family help?"

"I like to be with my family!"

"No. I mean your mother. Or your sister."

"I never thought of that."

"Lord knows, they have your best interests at heart. And I'll bet your mother would love to have something to do."

"That's an idea. She always knows where we are, and I could brief her on the things to say and to take note of."

"Wasn't she a secretary for many years?"

"A legal secretary."

"Then she's got to be pretty good. I'll bet she could handle things very well for you."

"I'd like to get back to the idea of a colleague taking care of your business for you. In our business, we're accustomed to sharing commissions. It's no problem."

"How does it work?"

"If I've made the initial contact and the colleague does follow-up, the commission is one combination; if my colleague accepts the call to me, the commission is another. It's understood and it works very well. Several of us 'trade off' with each other, and it means I can go skiing when I want to."

"But what if your profession doesn't have that tradition?"

"Then you start one with several people you know and trust. Hey! Let's face it. All of us have the same problem. I'll bet you know people who would love to have time off, just like you would. Work out an arrangement, and it would make it simpler for everybody."

"Do any of you have employees who could handle things while you're gone?"

"I don't have employees."

"The only person I work with on a regular basis is my accountant."

"My principal helper is very good. But she has another job that takes a lot of her time."

"Could she pick up your mail and messages?"

"I've never asked. I'm one of those that never takes a vacation."

"Do you think she could?"

"I think she'd love it."

"You'd have to pay her, of course."

"I pay her a commission now, if she brings in a job. We'd just work out some kind of arrangement."

"Of course, if your business is self-running, you can leave for a while and let it run itself."

"Whose business is self-running?"

"Lord, if I thought it could run itself, I'd leave for Hawaii tomorrow!" (General laughter.)

"No. I mean that there are certain businesses that can run for a few days without constant supervision."

"Name one."

"Oh, I don't know! If you set up an ad campaign, the agency can surely follow it through without your constant supervision. I'd think an accountant could take a week or two off, unless he does weekly payrolls. I know my doctor takes time off several times a year, and he leaves the name of his associate to handle problems."

"Actually, doctors and dentists should be a lesson to us all. Although they *do* work weird hours when there's an emergency, they always take their golfing date on Wednesday and their two vacations in summer and winter. They share their fees, obviously, with the colleague who covers their office or their patients. We should be just as smart."

"Sometimes we can be. But if someone wants me to do a research project, I'm the only one who knows how much time it will take me and what the cost will be. No one else could give that information."

"But is it necessary to give it in a preliminary call?"

"You have to at least give them a 'ball park.' "

"Can you have a rate card?"

"A what?"

"Could you develop a presentation or a card or a letter that would give a range of services and prices, so that if anyone called, you could have a service or a colleague send it out?"

"Maybe. I'm a little leary of giving out prices. I'd prefer to negotiate."

"Then maybe you should have the 'all purpose letter,' thanking them for their call and setting aside a date to talk with them about serving their needs. That could be sent out by almost anybody, and with the postal service the way it is, you could be back from vacation in time to follow up with a phone call."

"That's a good idea. But I'm not too good at writing letters."

"I am. We'll trade off."

"That's the name of the game."

"I want to get back to vacations. What's wrong with taking time off in your own home, and tending the flowers and going swimming and . . ."

(General pandemonium.)

"A vacation at home is *not* a vacation!"

"I *like* my home! We have a lovely pool and I enjoy my gardening and I get a lot of rest and relaxation out of it."

"Can't we admit that different people need different things?"

"But I thought we said that a vacation was being *away* from our usual environment."

"I'm away from that environment too much. I spend ten to twelve hours a day at my office! I love the opportunity to be home with the family and the rest of the things I love."

"Wouldn't you call in to the office every day? Or have the calls forwarded?"

"Yes. I do. But I set aside one hour a day to do it. The rest of the time is my own."

"That's not a vacation to me."

"I don't know which is worse, taking a vacation at home or taking your work with you on vacation."

"Yeah. I can remember sitting on the beach trying to write a proposal in the glare of the sun, while everybody else was enjoying the water and the surf! *I* wished I was somewhere else, and so did they."

"Well, I take work with me when I go away."

"It's a drag."

"Then you aren't really getting away."

"Some vacation!"

"Wait a minute! I *like* my work. When I go away to a different environment, I seem to get inspired anew. I think of new ideas and I look forward to jotting down new proposals. And then I go sight-seeing or out to a terrific dinner or off to the track or the theater. It's a wonderful mix of experiences and, since it's so different from what I normally do, I enjoy the vacation, and I get some great new ideas in the meantime. What's wrong with that?"

"Obviously, nothing. It works for you. And that's really what we have to understand about this whole discussion. We're different from the norm or we wouldn't be running these businesses by ourselves to begin with. Surely we realize that we're different from each other, too!"

"Of course we do. And we haven't even talked about shutting down altogether."

"What do you mean?"

"I just remembered: When I was a kid, my father owned a bowling alley, which he ran by himself. On the weekends, my mother helped keep scores and sell refreshments. But when deer hunting season came in the winter, he shut it down. Why bother? And in the summer, when people went to the swimming pool, he didn't keep it open, except on the weekends; and we traveled and did a lot of things together during the week. Does that qualify as a one-person business?"

"It's close. But you bring up the major point, that some businesses can be seasonal."

"Yeah. Like resorts in the mountains in the summer."

"A beach cottage in the winter."

"Those people can take some *real* time off, if they want to."

"That's what they do. That's why they love that life. They work really hard for several months out of the year and then they can play really hard or rest really hard in the other months."

"Are you saying to close down when you're really not needed?"

"If I thought I wasn't needed, I'd shoot myself!" (Boos and hisses.)

"I don't think that's what she meant."

"No! I mean, all of us must have *some* time of the year when business is slack and, if we *really* admitted it to ourselves, we could plan our lives around it and really get away . . . away . . . and enjoy it."

"Sure. But it takes really knowing your business."

"October is a real drag time for me. School is open and all the supplies have been bought by the interns and I'm just sitting by the phone, feeling sorry for myself. If I were really smart, I'd go away and have a blast, and then come back in November and have a giant 'year-end sale' on the stuff I had left."

"Have you ever done that?"

"No. I just thought of it. I think I'm so indispensable that I never registered on the opportunity. It could probably also help me unload the surplus before the end of the year."

"If you need a good sales campaign, call me."

"If you need some good travel planning, call *me*." (More boos and hisses.)

"Have we come up with any answers?"

"I think so. It means knowing our businesses inside out, but we ought to know that anyway. And it means knowing ourselves; knowing what *really* matters to us, and how we react to different needs and stimuli."

"Oh, wow. That's what I need is some good stimuli."

"I think it's time to say good-night."

Did we learn anything in the session? Yes. We learned that, although one-person businesses have a great deal in common with each other (as I hope this book is showing), they differ greatly from each other, particularly in the use of time and the manner in which each owner/manager deals with the customer/client. We learned that some businesses are seasonal and some are not. We learned that we have very personal relationships with our clients, more often than not, and leaving them in the hands of strangers is not the best thing for our businesses.

We learned that we are different and have different ways of satisfying that desire for renewal, that need to re-create ourselves so we can jump into the fray with renewed vigor. One person's vacation may be another person's "drag." "Know thyself" becomes very important in developing schedules and attitudes toward vacations.

Did we learn any tips? I think so. There are some ways of freeing ourselves from the business without sinking the business. The secret is to find the ways that are compatible with the business and with our own personalities. Here are some:

- Take long weekends. Sometimes these will inevitably be on the long, federal holiday weekends, when everyone else is scrambling to enjoy themselves. If you can carve out your *own* long weekends, in a place that gives you a sense of renewal and that is without the maddening crowd, you can make three days seem like five or ten.
- If your work is demanding all year long, you may have to adjust to many *short* vacations (long weekends and the like) instead of some longer times away. If they are planned and scheduled, with a definite change of environment, they can be very rewarding.
- If you have the option of scheduling your work, it is much easier to carve out several one/two/three-week periods to "get away from it all." The secret is to take the scheduling of the vacation as seriously as you take the scheduling of your work appointments. Have your mail opened by a commissioned colleague or a contract helper. Bills should be paid; letters requesting information should be answered with a standard form about your business and with a promise to follow up with a phone call. Phone requests should be call-forwarded to a knowledgeable colleague who can answer questions, send your information, and keep the prospect "live" until you return. Commission-sharing or bartering services is the best way to accommodate this activity.

- A member of the family can serve in the same capacity—answering phones, taking messages, relaying messages, opening mail, sending flyers, etc.—in your absence. They have your best interests at heart and would be remunerated in a number of ways agreeable to both of you.
- A part-time assistant or service could handle the telephone and mail, if they were trained properly in what to do and what not to do.
- Establish a "rate card" for certain of your services, so that they could be sent out in your absence. You could follow up as soon as you return.
- Always let your referral service (whoever it is) know how to reach you immediately in case of an emergency with family or client. (They would have to be taught what a *real* emergency was.) Then you could be contacted and decide whether or not to follow up.
- Develop the "all purpose letter," thanking a caller for an inquiry and promising to follow-up by phone in a few days. That will give you the "breathing time" to follow up personally, after a colleague, hired help, or family has sent out the letter.
- Take time off in your own home or your own hometown. Check in to the office once a day. This is not the right solution for everyone, but for people who enjoy their home environments and would like to be there more often, it is a viable solution to the problem of "getting away from the office."
- Take work with you on a vacation. Although this is not the best idea for everyone, some people *are* renewed by new locations and new people. They get work done more quickly and more imaginatively, and they still have plenty of time (for them) to enjoy the vacation environment.
- Shut down altogether when business is slow, and let your customers know it. A big, splashy ad campaign or sale when you get back can bring them back to you, and you have probably saved a lot of "maintenance" costs in the meantime (while having a good time on a vacation).

There were no absolute answers, and we did not come up with anything that you don't already know. The gist of the evening was that we need to know our businesses, we need to know ourselves, we need to plan our vacations as hard as we plan our businesses, and we need to be as tough on ourselves about time off as we are about time on. Don't ever forget: you are the boss. It is your own fault if you are not enjoying this!

Chapter 11

What if Something Happens to You?

Sometimes we must be reminded that we are mortal. As one-person businesses, that mortality can place an unexpected burden on those we love, unless we make some plans and take certain precautions.

This is *not* a chapter about how to do estate planning. I suggest that you spend a considerable amount of time with your lawyer, your accountant, your financial planner, and your insurance broker to work out the arrangements that are best for you and your loved ones in case of your death. We have touched on a number of options in several of the chapters in this book, but *you* ultimately must make the decisions regarding the allocation of your estate, should that become necessary.

We assume you have a will (updated and reviewed at least every two years), an arrangement for the disposition of your company and its assets (buy-sell agreements, insurance for family and/or other owners), and a ready file of your business activities (at the very least, your accountant).

This is a chapter about files. This is a checklist of those things that should be available in an orderly way, for the benefit of those people who will need to make arrangements and to carry on.

Death is not a pleasant topic for discussion, but it is a necessary one. In our businesses, incapacity is also a disaster of considerable stature. How does another person "carry on" when necessary?

Well, enough of the reasons. We are all adults. Let's get on with it.

If You Are Incapacitated

The business must go on. Someone needs to know the following:

217

1. *Your principal customers/clients.* This should be complete with names, addresses, and phone numbers. It would help if their current status was noted, too. The simplest way of keeping this information is on an address card wheel (under clients/customers) and a simple file in the file cabinet with their billing or activity under their names.
2. *Your principal suppliers.* The same system can work; namely, an address card wheel and a file cabinet reference by name or company.
3. *Your contract laborers, consultants, work force.* Again, their names, etc., and some information about their expertise on an address card wheel will make it a lot easier for someone "stepping in."
4. *Your business papers and where to find them.* Someone should have a list (updated regularly) with the following information: your social security number; your employer ID number; your bank accounts, by bank, location, and account numbers; your loans, by creditor, location, contact, loan number, and phone number; your credit cards by number and expiration date; your company insurance by identifying title, policy number, policy carrier, broker name, and phone number; the location of your corporation papers/partnership papers/proprietorship papers; your company investments, by title with broker name, company, and phone number; the location of your tax reports for at least the last three years; the location of any deeds or leases held by your company; the location of any mortgages held by your company or owed by your company.
5. *Your advisors.* There should be a list of the names, addresses, and phone numbers of your lawyer, your accountant, your financial advisor/planner, your insurance agent/broker, your investment broker, your banker, and any other advisors you use.

In Case of Your Death

The list above will be crucial to anyone taking over the business in the event of your death. In addition, there are a number of other pieces of information that will be crucial to that person's ability to succeed.

1. The name(s), address(es), and phone number(s) of your executor(s).

2. The location of your tax return worksheets for the past three to five years.
3. Your insurance benefits spelled out in simple language, as they relate to the company and as they relate to your family and/or estate.
4. Your pension, profit-sharing, retirement benefits spelled out (as they relate to residual payments), as well as the location and contact(s) for such benefits.

Immediate Action

In case of your death, someone must know where to locate information (in written form and, preferably, signed and notarized) to provide guidance in a number of actions that must be taken immediately.

1. *Donor designations.* You may wish that organs be donated to the aid of others. The Uniform Anatomical Gift Act is a law in all states and the District of Columbia. Most hospitals can give you information, including the particulars of the law, so that you may make the desired arrangements. These designations must be made in advance and the proper identifying cards must be immediately available.
2. *Your body.* Do you wish to be embalmed or not? Do you wish to be cremated? Do you wish your body donated for research? This information must be planned in advance and must be immediately available.
3. *Preferences.* What is your preferred hospital and/or doctor for terminal care? Do you have a Living Will? (See Bibliography.) Do you have a preference of funeral arrangement company? Place of interment?
4. *Who should be notified?* You need, on your person, the names and phone numbers of family, friends, doctor, hospital, attorney, executor, and principal business associate(s) who should be notified in case of accident or sudden death.
5. *Locations.* Where is your original will? (Your lawyer's safety deposit box is the best place.) Where are copies of your will? Where is your safety deposit box and what is the number? Who has signature power? Where are the keys? Do you have a safe or strong box? Where is it? What is the combination? Who knows the combination?

6. *Personal papers*. You should keep updated lists of insurance policies, numbers and agent; mortgages, deeds and leases, with locations, names, and phone numbers of contacts; personal credit cards and numbers with contact phone numbers; investments, their locations, your broker's name, and phone number; registrations of automobiles, boats, other vehicles.

7. *Valuables*. Although your will states all the specifics of the distribution of your estate and valuables, it is sometimes important to keep a list with your other instructions regarding certain items. Be sure they are held and don't "walk away" until the will is probated; conversely, if certain things are excluded from the will, the list may designate their early disposition. Be careful that such designated items do not fall into the category of "residual estate."

8. *Final wishes*. Your survivors should not be left to improvise or guess at what sort of final rites you would prefer. You do everyone a favor by being very specific, in advance. Indicate what sort of service (if any) you desire; where and who you would like to participate and in what manner; what military and/or fraternal organizations should be included; your preference regarding flowers and/or donations, texts, music, material for the obituary, paid notices, interment arrangements, including place and expenses, plus deeds of plots, etc.

9. *Memberships/Subscriptions*. A list of clubs and organizations to which you belong, with addresses and tenure, as well as a list of subscriptions, will greatly aid your executor(s).

Summary

If all this sound tedious and depressing, think again. The preparation of this material (and its constant update) can help preserve the continuity of your company, while aiding your family and friends at their time of greatest stress. If each of these lists is assembled, it is probably best to keep one in your home (where someone else will know how to find the file quickly) and another copy kept with a close and reliable friend (or attorney or accountant).

Our incapacity or death is enough of a blow to those who care for us, without leaving them with a lack of current and complete information with which to execute our wishes.

Chapter 12

Maximizing the Profits from Your Business

You are in business to make a profit. While that may sound obvious and trite, it is worth repeating to yourself throughout the planning and operation process. Not only should your company make a profit; your *profit* should make a profit; and with careful analysis and planning there is no reason why it will not.

Your company profit should do at least three things. It should:

1. Provide you with a nice salary and a comfortable life-style.
2. Provide for your future through adequate pension and/or profit sharing.
3. Help your company grow by providing additional capitalization and operational funds as needed.

This chapter will address the third point.

Under the new tax laws, corporations pay a higher rate of income taxes than do individuals (those variations are addressed in detail in Chapter 3), but there are significant advantages in investing those after-tax profit dollars in a wise and preplanned way.

If your business is a sole proprietorship, a partnership, or an "S" corporation, all profits pass through to you (see Chapter 3) and are taxable as ordinary income. Your investment and loan strategy should be quite specific in order to preserve as much of that income as possible and to provide sufficient funds to keep your business aggressive and financially viable.

If you are a "C" corporation, certain other rules apply. A "C" corporation is allowed to deduct 80 percent of the dividends it receives from a domestic corporation. There is a provision generally limiting the deduction to 80 percent of taxable income (computed with certain modifications). Dividends received from small business investment companies and from certain corporate affiliates are eligible for a 100 percent deduction. (As always, consult your tax advisor for specific details as they relate to you.)

Unless it is your profession, this is not an admonition for you to "play" lawyer, accountant, or broker. However, it is a plea to know your own goals and to ask a lot of questions (see Chapter 9). Be assured that the advice you get is right for you and not some "boiler plate" or "computer program" report that is distributed to most clients.

What Do You Ask a Financial Planner?

There is an old saying: "If you fail to plan, then you are planning for failure." If anybody makes money or expects to make money, they need financial planning, because almost everybody has goals; they have dreams. If they don't plan, they might as well plan to fail.

You should engage a financial planner with the same care as you would a doctor, dentist, or lawyer. The Better Business Bureau recommends that you ask a number of direct questions (and get answers that satisfy you) before deciding absolutely on a financial planner. They are:

1. What is your professional background?
2. How long have you been a financial planner?
3. Will you provide references from clients you have counseled for the past two years?
4. Will I be dealing with you or an associate?
5. To what financial planning trade associations do you belong?

Remember, your broker, your banker, and your financial advisor all have a vested interest to consider; they all have something to sell. You and you alone must decide the financial route you will take. Only you can do it. You must, ultimately, become your own investment advisor . . . your own economist . . . your own financial planner.

If you need proof of that, let me recount a memorable article I found in some of my research reading. In November, 1986, *U.S.*

News and World Report did a year-end wrapup of financial happenings and asked for projections for the next year. John Mendelson of Dean Witter Reynolds "believed that, for now, *cash* is the best investment." John Connolly of Dean Witter Reynolds said, "the reasons to buy stocks seem more compelling than the reasons to sell." Those guys worked for the same company and were asked the same question, the same week! Yet, their recommendations were, at the very least, opposite.

How do you become your own financial planner? By reading, asking questions, following and making note of trends, and setting your own goals.

One way to definitely not manage your money is by trying to short-cut your taxes. The IRS has finally gotten its act and its computer program together and is definitely out to crack down on tax cheats. (The estimate was a collection of at least $2 billion from 300,000 nonfilers and other evaders in 1987 alone.) Good. The Treasury needs the money, You will read a lot about tax codes and tax opportunities in this book, but nowhere will you read a recommendation to cheat. The tax code exists to raise revenue needed to run the business of government and, in many instances, shape the economic and investment behavior of its citizens. I recommend that you know as much about taxes as you need to know in order to shape their requirements to your ends.

What Do You Ask Yourself?

When considering personal investing (particularly if you are a sole proprietorship, partnership, or "S" corporation), there are several questions that will help you determine the strategies that are right for you:

1. What is your financial status? Are you "living on the brink?" "Hocked to your eyebrows?" "Sitting on a little extra cash?" Comfortable with your net worth? Meeting your monthly personal and business payments easily? The answers to these questions will help determine how much you should put into an investment program and the type of investments you should make (preservation, growth, easy access, high income, etc.)
2. What is your annual income? Have you structured your income to stay within a reasonable personal tax limit? What is reasonable to

you? Twenty percent of adjusted gross income? More? Less? Do you need to increase that income through tax-free investing?

3. What is the stability of your annual income? Is it predictable? Do you need a "cushion" for slow times in your company? Tax free or taxable? Readily accessible?

4. What is your age and who depends on you? Is building money for the kids' education important now? Or are they on their own and you are building for a third career or a comfortable retirement?

5. What are your cash reserves? If your business stops for one month, six months, one year, can you cover your costs? Is there insurance in case of disability? Do you have a "fall-back" plan, a "crisis" plan for a drop-off of business?

6. What is the total dollar value of your investment program? Has it grown every year? Do you know? Does it have a variety of components? Is that variety based on any formula? Your needs? Outside advice? Do you have targets for each segment and do you switch as the economic climate swings?

7. What is your personality? Are you a risk taker or a conservative? Does your personality fit your goals? If it doesn't do you allow someone else to manage your money?

8. How much time do you spend studying the market and economic realities? Do you have the time? Is there someone you can trust, who has no vested interest, who can advise you of changes you should be making?

Scale the Pyramid of Investment Growth

There is risk in all investing. (There is a legend that the only safe investing was done by the French farmer who put some gold coins in a sock under his mattress and waited for postwar inflation. We cannot all count on that.) Depending on your answers to all the previous questions, you can decide the level of risk with which you are comfortable. As your cushion of protection grows and your confidence in your understanding of the nation's economy increases, you can become a higher "risk taker." In the meantime, here is a simple rule-of-thumb of levels of risk, the first being the lowest:

Level 1: Cash, savings accounts, series EE savings bonds, money market accounts, mutual funds, CDs, treasury bills.
Level 2: Highest-rated taxable, tax-free, or government bonds.
Level 3: Blue chip stocks.

224

Level 4: Growth stocks, tax-free municipals, tax shelters, real estate.
Level 5: Emerging growth stocks in untried industries, options, commodities.

What Questions Do You Ask If You Are a "C" corporation?

In Chapter 3, you were given an idea of how to use the corporate structure to run your business, pay yourself adequately, and establish a number of employee benefits, including insurance and retirement planning.

Now . . . what do you do with the profit? You want it to make a profit, so that you will have resources to continue running the company in hard times, to capitalize expansion or new products or services when necessary, and to build a reservoir of "retained earnings" (avoiding the "holding company" trap, discussed earlier). You want to determine your corporation's needs and risk potential with the same care that you have exercised on your personal investing plan. Here are some questions:

1. If 80 percent of my dividend earnings are tax free to my corporation, assuming that they do not exceed 80 percent of my declared profit in each calendar year, can't I investigate high-income stocks and funds with the assurance that I will retain a lot of the earnings?
2. Will I be needing "instant access" to some of the funds? All of the funds? Should it, therefore, be readily available, and not "tied up" in CDs or other long-term instruments?
3. Can I divide my investments? A portion for short-term needs (money market funds), midterm "unexpecteds" (CDs, high-performance stocks, or stock funds), and long-term growth or new ventures (treasury bills, municipal bonds)?
4. Can I invest in other small companies and take advantage of the full deductions? (The local food market, a small commercial real estate venture, a friend's new business?)
5. If I loaned my company money to myself to begin or expand, can I simply pay back the loan (tax free to me personally), thereby reducing my corporate profits some more?
6. What are the high-risk, medium-risk, and low-risk investments recommended for this year? Have I talked to my broker? Have I read the advisories listed in this book? Am I prepared to switch my investments within a one- to five-day period?

225

What are Your Needs? Set a Strategy.

Once you have defined your needs and answered the questions posed, you can begin to take advantage of a series of strategies that accomplish a multiple of goals.

Strategy 1: Purchase investment-grade corporate bonds, CDs, or Ginnie Maes for higher after-tax returns and safety or principal and interest. (This is good for the sole proprietorship, partnership, "S" corporation, and individual.)

Strategy 2: Consider preferred stocks for higher after-tax income at lower unit prices. (This is particularly good for "C" corporations.)

Strategy 3: For high income from a large, diversified portfolio, choose from a variety of mutual funds, unit trusts, or limited partnerships. (This is good for the individual or the "C" corporation.)

Strategy 4: Buy municipal bonds for tax-free income and preservation of capital. (This is good for all but the "C" corporation, since it can keep 80 percent of its earnings anyway.)

Strategy 5: For diversification along with tax-free income, purchase a tax-exempt mutual fund or unit trust. (The "C" corporation probably will not need it, but it is good for all other entities, when additional income is required on a regular basis.)

Review your Options

The one thing that seems certain in the foreseeable future is that you will have more and more opportunities for investment, and more and more places in which to do that investing. When I was a child, Sears Roebuck & Company was a mail-order catalog company. Now, I can buy real estate, make investments, buy insurance, and learn how to run my computer there. Lord knows what they will offer in the future!

I am not suggesting that versatility of family services and the broadening of competition in the investing business is a bad thing. Quite the contrary. (However, we can hope that controls on "insider trading" and the requirement of a minimum net worth at banks will become fashionable again!) The real point is that you will probably continue to have a wide variety of investment options in the future, and "keeping up" will require some effort on your part. The above guidelines, applied to your needs, will give you (in concert with

226

your financial planner and accountant) the basis for good decision making for a long time to come.

The Old Reliables

There are some investment ploys that are worth restating, particularly under the new tax code. Given the goals you set for yourself, some of them will be worth your consideration.

Funds and Fund Families

If you are busy running your business, you cannot follow "the market" every hour of every day, but there are some very successful people and funds who can do it for you. Further, if you buy into a "family of funds," you can do telephone switching and keep your money in the area that can provide the most growth, dividends, security, appreciation, and spread your risk among many companies.

The Lipper Analytical Service provides analysis of these funds on a regular basis. You, as an individual, cannot buy the information, but you can read it regularly in most of the major publications in the world, including *USA Today*, and you can ask your broker to let you read his or her copy. They subscribe, I'm sure!

The most successful fund families in 1986 were:

- American Capital Funds
- Capital Research and Management
- Dreyfus Corporation
- Fidelity Management and Research
- Franklin Group
- IDS Financial Services
- Putnam Financial Services
- T. Rowe Price Associates
- Vanguard Group of Investment Companies

Real Estate

There are at least two kinds: the second home you own as a vacation home/rental/investment and the real estate limited partnerships that are still viable under the new tax law.

In terms of that "vacation home," you must decide whether to begin using the home as a second residence, so you can deduct the mortgage interest, or whether to rent it, so that you can claim a loss on a business venture.

Renting to others may result in hefty write-offs, but you must use the house yourself (fourteen days or 10 percent of the rental time) to deduct the mortgage interest. For the time being, most taxpayers would be better off limiting their personal use and operating their vacation homes as a business. As the tax law phases in (by 1990), you should investigate again all these implications with your tax advisor.

In the matter of real estate investment partnerships the tax law still makes this a viable investment; indeed, it encourages (with somewhat less fervor than before) the renovation of older buildings, particularly those that qualify as historical sites (put into operation before 1935) and low-income housing. In these ventures, you may be eligible for tax credits and passive losses, but you can also find small ventures with other partners that will produce positive cash flow (that is, income), and this can become very attractive, particularly to a "C" corporation.

Brokerage Accounts

We have discussed keeping your account at a discount brokerage house, simply because you save a lot of money that way. You tell them what you want to do and they do it. Full-service brokerage houses charge more; and remember, they make money on how much they sell, not on how much you earn.

The real point to make in this chapter, however, is that you can trade cheaper in a discount house, but you can also borrow on your portfolio from any brokerage house. The rate is generally less than any bank rate. You can borrow up to 50 percent of the value of your stocks and up to 70 percent of the value of your bonds. Remember, it is a sitting asset waiting to be tapped. The stocks and bonds continue to make money, while you use your short-term loan for necessities, at a lesser rate than you might pay elsewhere. In your investment planning, the inclusion of a brokerage account has more than one advantage. You make money, but you can also borrow money.

Bonds

Under the new tax law, bonds are still a very good investment. The interest exclusion for bonds whose proceeds are used by governmental units remains intact for both regular and alternative minimum tax purposes. (Other state and local government-issued obligations, referred to as "private activity bonds," are generally fully taxable.) Shop for a good yield, and, if you are not a risk taker, look at the grade of the bond. (Don't go to Bs!) You can sometimes buy into a bond when it is nearing maturity and do very well. More often than not, however, you will want to buy at issue and hold for a number of years. If you don't want to tie up your money, but would like the yield and tax advantages, go with a bond fund. Again, the Lipper Service can steer you to the long-term successes.

Loans

Depending on your company's success and your personal needs, there are opportunities to loan money back and forth. Your company may loan you money (with the necessary agreements, interest, and pay-back arrangements) or you may loan your company money and take certain advantages both ways. One person I know started a business, formed a corporation, and bought one thousand shares at $1 a share. She loaned the corporation the rest of its start-up money and started work. As the business progressed (income began coming in immediately and a little "operating profit" less salary was the result), she paid herself a "draw" against projected salary. She also began paying back the loan in small increments the first month. The corporation deducted the loan pay-back as a business expense, but she did not have to declare it as income personally. As the business grew, the "draw" got larger and she paid personal income taxes on it; but the loan payments also increased, and were beneficial to both the corporation and the owner.

Small Company Investment

As a one-person business, investment is sometimes advantageous in your own community, especially in other small businesses. The opportunities to retain the dividends, tax free, are obvious, and there may be other advantages, which are not quantitative, in committing your profit dollars to your own community. You can also buy enough stock in a small company to have a say in its operation (on the board or as one of the major shareholders.)

229

Ginnie Maes

One of the safest, and, for some time, one of the highest-yielding investments around is the Ginnie Mae. There are funds that specialize in investing in Ginnie Maes and U.S. Treasury obligations (AARP has one, for instance), if you are looking for safe, regular income. However, heed the advice of some good brokers. The yield is high, because, if necessary, the dividends come from the principal. That may not be what you want. This is the kind of investment you would want if you need absolute security—a steady, predictable income, and a risk of principal over the long haul, because the short haul is more important. (They are particularly valuable for retired or nearly retired persons with other income or more interest in income than in building principal.)

Leverage

We read a lot about that term these days, and usually, it is in reference to a new acquisition of a larger company by a smaller company (or individual) who puts up the assets of the acquired company in order to gain enough capital to buy it. It conjurs up the image of the flea devouring the elephant, but it is happening every week to corporations all across America. It makes money for the people who are lucky enough to own the stock of one of the two companies before they go "into play," but its benefit to the country and to the economy is very much in doubt. It makes some people richer and increases the balance sheet of the combined companies, but it puts the new entity into debt just to pay off the loans for the acquisition, instead of using that capital to expand the business, create new jobs, develop new industries.

The "leverage" we are talking about here is the kind that you as an individual investor can engage in to increase your earnings. It is generally much more risky than many of the other investment actions we have discussed; but you should consider some of the possibilities in order to maximize your profits on your profits. The investment instruments are options, margin trading, convertible securities, warrants, low-priced stocks, and rights.

Following is a brief definition of each of these activities, which will help you decide whether or not any of them are right for you.

Definitions of Leverage

Options. Contracts that entitle the purchaser (holder) either to sell or buy a given number of shares within a specified time period to or from the seller (writer) of the contract at a price fixed by the contract. Options available are Puts, Calls, Straddles, Spreads, Strips, and Straps.

Margin trading. If you borrow money to buy stocks and the stocks go up, you have made a profit that you could not have otherwise made. By the same token, if the stock you bought goes down, you have lost more money than if you had invested less. The money comes from your brokerage firm, and, if you are in a loss situation, they "call" the money, which makes up the difference between what you had and what you lost , . . if that is the case.

Convertible securities. A bond or preferred stock that grants the owner the privilege of exchanging (converting) his or her security for a specified number of shares of common stock of the issuing company within a stated time period.

Warrants. An option to buy a given stock within a stated time period at a designated price. It is an instrument that is issued by the company, as opposed to the option contract, which is written by a shareholder in the company. Warrants have a much longer life than puts and calls, and some of them may last indefinitely.

Low-priced stocks. These are generally conceded to be stocks at $10 or less. The leverage is in the price of the stock. If a $10 stock goes up $2.00 that is a 20 percent increase on the stock; presumably, you own a substantial number of shares so that the increase is impressive both in percentages and in real dollars. A $2.00 rise on IBM would be relatively meaningless, in comparison.

Rights. Shareholders generally have the preemptive right to maintain their proportionate ownership in a corporation. Therefore, when corporations plan to issue additional equity instruments, they issue "rights" to their shareholders. A right entitles the owner to buy shares of the stock at a price (subscription price) cheaper than the market price of the stock on the record date of issue of the rights.

Coins/Collectibles/Gems

This is for the risk taker or the wary, depending on your point of view, and you should never enter into this form of investing, unless you are prepared to lose the money, or, at the very least, wait a while for it to appreciate in value.

Recognize the drawbacks of this kind of collecting. It takes capital with no guarantee of reward (a series EE savings bond will double in value in ten years!) It is risky. It requires study and attention, which you may not be able to spare. If it "ain't fun," don't do it.

I mention it only because investing in coins, collectibles, and such is becoming one of the "options" that many advisors discuss. Don't expect to get rich, but don't negate it completely; it offers the possibility of a long-range profitability with a good deal of fun, new friends, and research/knowledge along the way. It has become a subculture of high appeal.

Summary

Make your money work harder than you do. If you earn 10 percent profit on your endeavors, make your money earn 20 percent. Set your goals. Set your parameters of risk. Plan your allocations of funds. Remember always that you are in charge and should call the shots on the way your money earns money. The tax laws are written to encourage us to do so. Let's do it!

Chapter 13

Things to Consider Before You Sell, Merge, or Expand

No business is static. Each business takes on a life of its own and flows with the energies of both the internal and external stimuli. On the face of it, the one-person business seems to live on the needs and expectations of the principal; but financing, marketing, the competition, and the changing environment can have an effect on it just as they can on larger, more fully-staffed businesses.

Sooner or later, influences you have caused, as well as those over which you have no control, will compel you to take stock and decide whether your business will continue in its current form or fashion or whether the entire nature of the business must change.

That decision—whether or not to change—is just as important as the initial decision to start the business, and, while this chapter cannot begin to answer all your questions, it will help you set up "warning flags" and give some facts and criteria to consider when you reach that juncture.

What are the Warning Flags?

What are the things that can happen in your business that tell you that you have reached a "turning point?" "A decision time?"

Too Much Business

While it is easy to speculate that too much business would be a problem you would like to address, the fact is that too much business can swamp a one-person operation just like a wave on a row-boat.

In my experience with young companies, the usual response to too much business is panic. While it is understandable, it is not productive. What are some of the other options?

- Hire help, which we have discussed in other chapters.
- Form loose or actual partnerships with other businesses/suppliers.
- Merge with another company to form a larger and more all-encompassing company.
- Acquire another company to do the things you cannot do.
- Think about franchising your business to other people.
- Sell your business to a larger company that can take on the service to your clients.
- Cut back on your business and retrench to those things that you want to do.

Not Enough Business

This is a nightmare of all businesses and a particularly frightening one for the one-person business. You set your goals, both personal and professional, and plan and market accordingly. When your business does not reach your expectations, you are confronted with a different set of options:

- Sell out, if you can find a buyer.
- Abandon, but there are some pitfalls to avoid.
- Bankruptcy, as a last resort; and we will discuss the ramifications.
- Cut back on overhead and "coast through" until the tide turns.

The Business Matures or You Wish to Retire

If you wish the business to continue after you cease running it, you have several alternatives to consider.

- Sell out to another person or company.
- Merge with another person or company.
- Transfer to the next generation.
- Abandon the business with the good feeling of a job well done.

We will explore a number of these options and the things you should consider before you choose one of them.

Expanding Your Business

There are a number of reasons to expand a business, and several ways to do it. Here are some tips and suggestions for your consideration when you reach that time.

Acquisitions

About 50 percent of all acquisitions fail to reach their expectations, according to some informed sources. If you hope to expand your business by acquiring another company (probably a competitor), there are a number of questions you need to ask yourself.

First, are you doing it because you see your competition doing it? "Monkey see, monkey do" is not a good reason to make any business decision. Is it simply a reaction to a recommendation from your banker? Your broker? Your lawyer? A friend? What is in it for them? Do you have an outside advisor or an inside manager who could help you identify problems you have not seen? Will the acquisition make you a market leader? Give you a hefty proportion of the market? Will you still face one or two heavy market leaders? Will you be the American Motors fighting GM, Ford and Chrysler? (Look what happened to them!) Are you straying from home; that is, are you buying a company that requires management skills, development talent, sales knowledge that you don't have? Would you keep the old management? Would they be loyal?

There are some "rule of thumb" guides for acquisitions:

- Look for after-tax return of capital at over 12 percent (preferably 15 percent).
- Is the market for that product/service growing by at least 10 percent per year?
- Is it a well-known and respected firm in its market or geographical area?
- Would you need to build/rebuild a reputation?
- Is it dependent on a single supplier, customer, or product?
- Does it have a unique patent or royalty position?

Cash deals are subject to capital gains tax, but are best if there is a question of the buyer's solvency. Minimize the tax by treating it as an installment sale. For the buyer, paying cash is more expensive than issuing treasury stock or new preferred. For the seller, taking stock is attractive only when the stock of the company is attractive in itself. As always, consult your legal and tax advisors for devising the best way of making an acquisition for your own financial and tax position.

If you're making an acquisition for the customer list, ask yourself if you wouldn't be better off hiring the best salesperson to go out and acquire some or most of those customers for you. You never know if they will remain loyal anyway.

If you are interested in a firm that has had a good spurt in profits, ask yourself, why. Was it made by slicing a budget? Operating efficiencies? Real growth in sales? Extraordinary income that will never be repeated?

Franchising

If you are in a business in which your major competitors are franchises, you cannot help but wonder whether or not you should become a franchise, too. *U.S. News and World Report* has found that fewer than 5 percent of franchises go bust. That is a remarkable record, and is very tempting to the serious business person.

Don't attempt to franchise, unless you are really doing too much business and have the capital necessary for the franchise. Remember, most businesses fail due to lack of planning and lack of adequate capital.

Look for a franchise system that has training, sales promotion, and computer systems. Franchising a business is no different than starting one from scratch. If you expand too fast, with too little money, with no careful planning and no support systems, you will fail.

Be wary, however. In franchising, the appearance of independence is deceiving. The franchisor fully indoctrinates each owner with the corporation's way of doing business—how to keep the books, handle the payroll, decorate the store, maintain inventories, gain clients, and run an advertising campaign. If your independence is important to you, franchising may not be the answer to your need for growth.

Growth in a franchise can be just as dangerous as in any other business. Don't let your business get out of hand and grow too fast. You are growing faster than you can afford, if you must continually scramble to increase your debt-to-equity ratio, sell stock, liquidate assets, or take more drastic measure to finance your growth.

Franchises can go from safe to speculative; the higher you climb, the higher the risks. In other words, the more growth in your business, the higher the risks. Everyone should have some money invested at the foundation level, where the goal is safety of principal with as little risk as possible.

Chosen properly, a franchise can bring you the best of both worlds: entrepreneurial independence coupled with a successful business record and some hand-holding when needed.

What should you look for? The market and the organization. Is the product or service likely to endure (fast food or auto repair) or is it of transient, fad nature? Is its style right for your neighborhood or customers? What is the image and reputation of the franchisor? Is the organization tried and true? Are there other franchises that you can interview? If it is a new franchisor, do they have a track record in another business that you can examine?

What can you expect to pay? A one-time "franchise fee" that lets you join the club? The costs of the structure and equipment for the place of operation (you will have to build to *their* specifications, even if you are in the same business yourself)? A percentage of your gross sales, which covers your share of national advertising costs?

In franchising, "cheaper" is not necessarily better. If the franchisor is not capitalized well, they cannot bail you out when you get into trouble, or they themselves might fail when other franchises get into trouble.

What can you expect the franchisor to reveal? Seller's past business experience, bankruptcy, and litigation record, prior year's certified balance sheet, a list of all fees that have to be paid to run the franchise, limits on rights to resell, a list of ten closest franchises in the same chain—are all things you should request.

Add to Your Own Business

If business is booming, you can form another corporation and divide up the business. You retain all the stock of the first company, but transfer more than 20 percent of the stock of the new company to a family member, a valued employee, an outside investor. The two corporations are taxed as separate companies and can pay the low corporate rate up to $50,000 earnings each.

Going Public

If business is really booming, consider going public and allowing it to grow as a publicly traded stock. Security Exchange Commission (SEC) regulations have been simplified so that it is easier and cheaper than it used to be. Regulation A can be used for filings up to $1.5 million; Form S-18 can be used for filings up to $5 million. You will have cheaper legal and accounting fees; the filings take from one to three months and require only a narrative discussion, plus accounting forms prepared under the rules of good accounting principles. You can file with regional SEC offices as well as in Washington.

Mergers

The logical result of a good merger should be that the emerging company should be stronger than the two were alone; the new company should be "stronger than the sum of its parts."

The major reasons for a merger seem to fall into one of the following categories:

- Financial: The combined companies are improved financially, either by sales, profits, assets, working capital, or all of the above.
- Product and marketing: By joining forces, the two companies enhance their product lines or their marketing reach.
- Research, development, and engineering: The merger strengthens the R&D capability of the new company. This could be particularly important for a small company with big ideas (or a big patent).
- Manufacturing: Ideally, a merger would extend the utilization of manufacturing assets. If you are tooled up for metal work, a new product that also uses your tooling would be an asset.
- Personnel: While the often stated reason for merging is to strengthen the personnel of a company, more often than not, a merger allows for the cutting of personnel and the streamlining of a staff.
- Community relations: A merger can sometimes "buy" an image that one company needs and another one has.
- Corporate image: The same idea as above.

You should probably consider a merger with the same care as you would consider a marriage. The two companies (and principals) should be complementary to each other; "the same, only different."

238

You should have the same goals and standards and values, but your personalities and company strengths should be harmonious together.

Selling Your Company

If you decide to sell, you will have to clean up the company, financially and organizationally. Eliminate assets that are not business related. Stop nonproductive expenses. Clean up your liabilities.

Review all agreements—suppliers, customers, contractors—and bring them up to date. Have at least three years of your financial statements certified.

Don't go to friends for advice. Go to an expert professional broker (check out references with other clients!) and get advice on setting the price, making the offering, negotiating the deal. Again, "cheaper" is not necessarily better.

Decide whether to get backup management to take your place or ask the broker whether the buyer should be in on that decision. Be prepared to share details of internal procedures, controls, five-year forecasts, inventory, etc.

Don't set an unrealistically high price. The buyers will know it and wonder if they can do business with you. Expect to have to justify the price you set. Don't ramble; be prepared with good accounting and good reasoning.

Also be prepared to get cold feet when the deal gets close. It is your baby; you will be reluctant to sell it.

Avoid Tax Traps

There are tax consequences for selling "good will," which is the amount of the sale price that exceeds the net fair market value of the tangible business assets. The IRS does not recognize good will as a deductible business expense.

If the excess on the sale price can be termed part of "a covenant not to compete," it is completely deductible (to be amortized over the period of the agreement). The seller will have the amount taxed as income. It behooves the buyer and seller, therefore, to arrive at an agreeable compromise on the amount of the covenant not to compete; the after tax benefits to both parties should probably be equal to make for a happy "deal."

Accumulated Earnings

While most small business owners would prefer to pass through the dividends on accumulated earnings to avoid the "tax trap" and pay the 28 percent personal taxes on the amount, an owner who is contemplating selling the company might let those earnings "ride" until the business is sold. Remember, only 20 percent of those earnings are taxable at the corporate rate, and you are allowed to accumulate up to $50,000 in earnings before you pay more than the 15 percent corporate tax. When you sell the company, the proceeds will be taxed as capital gains (now ordinary income) at a maximum of the 28 percent personal rate.

Transfer of the Company to the Next Generation

Just transferring stock in your company to your children and family could have large tax implications, if the value of the stock to each of them is in excess of the $10,000 tax-free gift rule. Yet, you may want to set up an orderly transfer of the company to one or more of your family members.

Work with your lawyer to affect the following change. You recapitalize your company with X shares of preferred stock and X shares of new common exchanged for your original common shares. Then give the new common stock to your children and/or grandchildren. The common stock has a much smaller value and can probably escape the gift tax, especially if you do it over several years. Your exchange of your old common stock for new preferred is tax free. The cost basis of the new preferred (for future tax purposes) is the same as it was for the common.

The new preferred should be callable (redeemable) by the company at par or face value. Its face value will be fixed. As the company continues to grow, all the increased value will benefit the people who own the new common stock. The preferred stock should have a realistic dividend (say 8 percent) to ensure that it is interpreted as having its face value. Provide that the dividends are noncumulative—paid when the company does well, withheld when things are not so good. The preferred stock would have voting rights to ensure that *you* continue to control the company. The common would have voting rights also, but must set up the formula to ensure that the voting rests in the hands you wish during this process.

Get the IRS to rule on the transaction in advance, but not on the value of the preferred stock.

Another variation: you could buy a large insurance policy and give it to the generation you wish to inherit the business. (You may have to pay a gift tax on the present value of the policy, depending on how many people participate and how much it is valued.) Upon your death, they receive the insurance, tax free, and buy the preferred stock from your estate.

Abandon Your Business

A business can be abandoned, either in good times or bad, when you are tired of it or it has "petered out." The best course is to file a formal dissolution with your state. This allows you to sell your assets, close up your doors, and go out of business.

Why not just walk away? Because if you have not filed a formal dissolution and announced the closing of your business, claims can be filed against you personally in the future. And they have a good chance of winning! You can be presumed to still be in business if you have not gone through the process.

Bankruptcy

We all know someone who has gone bankrupt. It is not a pleasant experience and can be very damaging to the person's ego and reputation. However, it can be done with honor, if certain things are understood.

There are two purposes of the Bankruptcy Act: to give creditors an equal opportunity to share in the debtor's property, and to give honest debtors an opportunity to make a new start in life (this is sometimes the option that should be taken when your business is in disastrous financial trouble).

Sometimes the best settlement when a business is in financial trouble is to file a petition in a bankruptcy court asking to be declared bankrupt. Sometimes admitting in writing your inability to pay your debts can be the best thing for the future life of your business. Remember, you must owe $1,000 and be unable to pay it to be placed in bankruptcy.

However, you can never assume or use bankruptcy as an excuse. A person is not bankrupt unless declared so by a court.

If your financial trouble is short term and you anticipate being able to catch up in a few months, being placed in bankruptcy by a court can allow you to preserve your credit. The secret is not that you are placed into bankruptcy but that you arrange to pay off your creditors in a reasonable amount of time and at a reasonable amount of cents on the dollar. (Many people in bankruptcy use the "breathing room" to pay off *every* cent they owe, thus preserving their reputations and credit for the future.)

In recent years an overhaul of bankruptcy laws have consolidated Chapter X, XI, and XII rehabilitation proceedings into one form of business reorganization and puts pressure on financially troubled companies and their creditors to work out arrangements with less court supervision. There are substantial changes in the proceedings, which affect small businesses, either as the business in distress or as a creditor to a company in distress.

Make no assumptions about bankruptcy. If you must seek that course, deal with an attorney who is up-to-date on the procedures. If you find yourself a creditor of a distressed company, use good counsel. Although the bankruptcy committee can now be structured of the seven largest creditors, only three creditors with a total of $5,000 in outstanding debt may force a company to seek relief.

Summary

No business is static. You will arrive at one or more of these "turning points" during the life of your venture. There are no easy answers and the constantly changing tax laws and regulation codes would tax the most intrepid manager to keep up. The best advice is to be prepared to question a variety of professional advisors, as you find yourself in a changing environment, remembering always that your personal needs, goals, and expectations have a great bearing on how you will react to the challenge. You are not just *any* business; you are *your* business, and you are *unique*. You are not above the laws or regulations, and you cannot escape the various plateaus to which every business arrives. *How* you react to it and the decisions that you make are more uniquely yours than in any other venture . . . because *you* are your business. There is no one else involved (with the possible exception of your family), and what may be the "right" choice for businesses owned by many or run by several or encompassing a number of individuals simply does not apply to you. Apply your own criteria, use good common sense, and arrive at decisions that best meet your unique personal goals.

Appendix

Assembling an Appendix for a book such as this is a very personal matter. I assume that you have knowledge of and access to the major newspapers and periodicals, as well as a good bookstore and review material of current business books.

One-person business owners sometimes need other references than those found in general publications, either because the material is more directly related to their special needs or it is less expensive than that available to larger companies; it is sometimes considered "esoteric" in the great run of business enterprise.

This is then a very personal Appendix. It is my way of "accessing" you to a variety of information, some or none of which may be valuable to you. Some of it, I assure you, can give you information that your competitors may not have. Some of it is a restatement of things you already know. Some of it may spark an idea that will be of value to you. Most of it will cost you the price of a postal card to check it out for yourself.

The Appendix is divided into the following general headings:

Advertising
A Business Tax Calendar
Catalogs
Computer Software Information
Credit Card Information—for Lower Interest Rates
Discount Shopping
Information and Publications of Special Interest
Seminars
Services
Special Business Publications
Wire Services, Syndicators, and News Services

You will be able to add to the Appendix simply because you know your business and its opportunities better than anyone else. This Appendix is offered purely in the spirit of sharing. You will add to it as we go along.

Appendix

Advertising

National Mail Order Classified
P.O. Box 5
Sarasota, FL 33578

This company can arrange advertising in a variety of specialty publications at substantial discount offering the one-person business a wide reach for a modest investment.

A Business Tax Calendar

January 15: Farmers must pay estimated tax for the previous year. The final return is due April 15, but, if the estimated payment has not been made, then the final return is due March 2.

February 2: Send Form 1099 statements to recipients of dividends, interest, nonemployee compensation, and other payments during prior year. Brokers and barter exchanges also must send reports on previous year transactions to clients. Information on the 1099 statements must be reported to the IRS by March 2.

March 16: Corporate previous year tax returns, including those for "S" corporations, which are taxed like partnerships, are due. A six-month extension to September 15 is available by filing Form 7004.

April 15: Partnerships must file previous year tax returns. Corporations must pay first installment of estimated tax for current year. Remaining installments are due June 15, September 15, and December 15.

July 31: Self-employed people who have Keogh retirement plans must file previous year returns for the plans. A new, simple 5500EZ form can be used for Keoghs that cover only you or you and your spouse.

Note: If your fiscal reporting is not on a calendar-year basis, you must adjust some of the deadlines. Consult your tax advisor or read the IRS publication # 509.

Catalogs

For Business Supplies and Equipment

NEBS (New England Business Service, Inc.
500 Main St.
Groton, MA 01471
1-800-225-6380

The Reliable Corporation
1001 West Van Buren St.
Chicago, IL 60607
1-800-621-4344

Viking
2120 Valley View Lane
P.O. Box 819064
Dallas, TX 75381
1-800-421-1222

For Promotional Merchandise

Sales Guides, Inc.
10510 North Port Washington Rd.
Mequon, WI 53092-9986
1-800-352-9899

Computer Software Information

Easy Sabre
Reservations for airlines, autos, hotels, through American Airlines.
1-800-638-9636

"One-Write Plus"
17 different journals and reports for IBM-PC or compatibles, 256 K
with dual drive or two floppy discs.

Great American Software, Inc.
P.O. Box 910
Amherst, NH 03031-0910
1-800-528-5015

Credit Card Information: Call for particulars and application.
For Lower Rates
or No Fees*

Security Bank and Trust,
Southgate, MI

First National Bank,
Lincolnshire, IL

First National Bank,
Wilmington, DE

Simmons First National,
Pine Buff, AR

Connecticut Bank and Trust,
Hartford, CT

Home Plan Savings,
Des Moines, IA

First Federal,
Lincoln, NB

First Security National Bank,
Lexington, KY

Goldome Bank,
Buffalo, NY

Union National Bank,
Little Rock, AR

*Source: Jane Bryant Quinn, *Newsweek,* July 21, 1986

Discount Shopping

Consumer Buy-Phone (Requires buying a membership. Call for particulars.)

For appliances (TV, refrigerators, video, air conditioners, washers, dryers, microwave ovens, audio equipment), furniture, jewelry, carpeting, typewriters, pianos, organs, auto tires, and car buying.

Information/Publications of Special Interest

How to Analyze the Competition
American Management Association Extension Institute
P.O. Box 1026
Saranac Lake, NY 12983-9986

250 New Ways to Make Money
American Entrepreneurs Association
2311 Pontius Ave.
Los Angeles, CA 90064
1-800-421-2300

Barter News
Box 3024
Mission Viejo, CA 92690
(The newsletter for barter members.)

Boardroom Classics
P.O. Box 1026
Millburn, NJ 07041
New Tax Opportunities for Owners of Closely Held Companies
Book of Tax Loopholes
The Book of Inside Information
How to Make Money in Real Estate
(and many others)

Business Kit for Starting and Existing Businesses
(for each state)

Enterprise Publishing, Inc.
725 Market St.
Wilmington, DE 19801
1-900-533-2665
(A large range of forms and information for the small business)

Executive Book Summaries
5 Main St.
Bristol, VT 05443-9990
(A monthly summary of business best-sellers.)

Incorporation Kits (without a lawyer)
(for each state)
American Entrepreneurs Association
2311 Pontius St.
Los Angeles, CA 90064

The Living Will Registry
Concern for Dying
250 W. 57th St.
Room 831
New York, NY 10107
1-212-246-6962

Personal Investing
161 Devonshire St.
P.O. Box 832
Boston, MA 02103
(A monthly advisory newsletter.)

Simon & Schuster, Inc.
1230 Ave. of the Americas
New York, NY 10020

Profit Building Strategies
81 Montgomery St.
Scarsdale, NY 10583

How Much is a Business Really Worth?
The Business Owner
383 S. Broadway
Hicksville, NY 11801
1-516-681-1211

Small Business Report
203 Calle Del Oaks
Monterey, CA 93940
(Profit strategies for small businesses.)

Consumer Reports
Subscription Dept.
Boulder, CO 80322

Tax Update for Business Owners
81 Montgomery St.
Scarsdale, NY 10583

Seminars

Write or call for particulars.

"Executive Time Management"
Management Development Group
201 Beacon Pkwy W.
Birmingham, AL 35209
1-205-945-9846

CareerTrack Seminars
1800 38th St.
Boulder, CO 80301
1-303-447-2300
(A wide variety of management topics; ask for catalog.)

Office of Professional Development
Clemson University
P.O. Drawer 912
Clemson, SC 29633
1-803-656-2200
(Nationwide seminars on various uses of computer software; ask for catalog.)

"How to Write a Winning Business Plan"
Creative Planning & Communications
3008-1 13th Ave. S.
Birmingham, AL 35205
(Rates available upon request.)

"Managing Multiple Priorities"
Dun and Bradstreet Business Education Services
P.O. Box 803
Church St. Station
New York, NY 10008
1-212-312-6880

National Seminars
6901 W. 63rd St.
Suite 317
Overland Park, KS 66202
(A wide variety of management topics; ask for catalog.)

Padgett-Thompson
P.O. Box 8297
Overland Park, KS 66208
(A wide variety of management topics; ask for catalog.)

Fred Pryor Seminars
2000 Johnson Dr.
P.O. Box 2951
Shawnee Mission, KS 66201
1-913-384-6400

Services

Write for particulars.

"How to Get Free Publicity"
Visibility/N
450 West End Ave.
15-B
New York, NY 10024

"How to Write a Winning Business Plan"
Creative Planning & Communications
3008-1 13th Ave. S.
Birmingham, AL 35205

Special Business Publications

Write or call for lists.

Inc. Business Products
38 Commercial Wharf
Boston, MA 02110-3883
1-800-372-0018

National Association for Female Executives, Inc.
1041 Third Ave.
New York, NY 10021
1-212-371-0745

Wire Services, Feature Syndicates and News Services

See Chapter 6 for recommendations of use.

AP Newsfeatures
50 Rockefeller Plaza
New York, NY 10020

Jewish Telegraphic Agency, Inc.
165 W. 46th St.
New York, NY 10036

Army Times Syndicate
475 School St. SW
Washington, DC 20024

King Features Syndicate
235 E. 45th St.
New York, NY 10017

Buddy Basch Feature Syndicate
771 West End Ave.
New York, NY 10025

Chicago Tribune
220 E. 42nd St.
Room 2708
New York, NY 10017

Chronicle Features
870 Market St.
San Francisco, CA 94102

Christian Science Monitor
220 E. 42nd St.
Suite 3006
New York, NY 10017

Columbia Features, Inc.
36 W. 44th St.
New York, NY 10036

Gannett Newspapers
535 Madison Ave.
New York, NY 10022

Congressional Quarterly Service
1414 22nd St. NW
Washington, DC 20037

Hollywood Reporter
1501 Broadway
New York, NY 10036

Copley News Service
P.O. Box 190
San Diego, CA 92112

Editorial Research Reports
1414 22nd St. NW
Washington, DC 20037

Entertainment News Syndicate
310 E. 44 St.
New York, NY 10017

Fairchild Syndicate
7 E. 12th St.
New York, NY 10003

Field Newspaper Syndicate
1370 Ave. of the Americas
New York, NY 10019

Gannett News Service
P.O. 7858
Washington, DC 20044

Hearst Feature Service
235 E. 45th St.
New York, NY 10017

Independent News Alliance
200 Park Ave.
New York, NY 10166

Los Angeles Times Syndicate
Times-Mirror Square
Los Angeles, CA 90053

McNaught Syndicate
537 Steamboat Rd
Greenwich, CT 06830

Metro Info Pac Publicity Services
33 W. 34th St.
New York, NY 10001

Philadelphia Inquirer
180 Riverside Dr.
New York, NY 10024

United Feature Syndicate
200 Park Ave.
New York, NY 10166

Universal Press Syndicate
1271 Ave. of the Americas
Suite 3717
New York, NY 10020

Bibliography

Chapter 1

Cummings, Tommie G. *How to Develop a Business Plan*. (Birmingham, AL: Birmingham Area Chamber of Commerce, 1985).

Howell, Robert A. *How to Write A Business Plan*. (New York: American Management Association, 1982).

Parson, Mary Jean. *Back to Basics: Planning*. (New York: Facts on File Publications, 1985).

Chapter 2

American Entrepreneurs Association. *AEA Business Manual No. X1254*. (Los Angeles: American Entrepreneurs Association, 1984).

Lipper, Arthur III, with Ryan, George. *Guide to Investing in Private Companies*. (Homewood, IL: Dow Jones–Irwin, 1984).

Chapter 3

Boardroom Books. *Business Confidential*. (New York: Boardroom Reports, Inc. 1985).

Goldstein, Arnold S. *Basic Book of Business Agreements*. (Wilmington, DE: Enterprise Publishing, Inc., 1983).

Loeb, Marshall. *Money Guide, 1986*. (Boston: Little, Brown & Company, 1985).

McQuown, Judith H. *How to Profit After You INC Yourself*. (New York: Warner Books, Inc., 1985).

Nichols, Ted. *How to Form Your Own Corporation Without a Lawyer for Under $50*. (Wilmington, DE: Enterprise Publishing, Inc., 1979).

——— *Cash: How to Get it Into and Out of Your Corporation*. (Wilmington, DE: Enterprise Publishing, Inc., 1980).

——— *Income Portfolio*. (Wilmington, DE: Enterprise Publishing, Inc., 1977).

——— *The Complete Book of Corporate Forms*. (Wilmington, DE: Enterprise Publishing, Inc., 1980).

Parson, Mary Jean. *The Single Solution*. (New York: Facts on File Publications, 1987).

Porter, Sylvia. *New Money Book for the 80s*. (Garden City, NY: Doubleday & Company, 1979).

Chapter 4

Beinhorn, Courtenay. "A Plan for Prosperity," *Savvy*. June, 1984: 34–35.

Brown, Sonja. "Making it From Scratch," *Savvy*. December, 1985: 16–17.

Card, Emily. "The Business Plan," *Ms*. November, 1985: 80–83.

Cummings, Tommie G. *How to Develop a Business Plan*. *Birmingham Area Chamber of Commerce, Birmingham, AL 1985*.

Cunningham, Robert S. "Ten Questions to Ask Before You Sign a Lease," *Small Business Success*. Birmingham Area Chamber of Commerce, Birmingham, AL. 1982.

Dahl, Jonathan. "Opening The Financial Door," *The Wall Street Journal*. Monday, May 19, 1986: 1.

Dunnan, Nancy. "Good News," *Savvy*. December, 1983: 30–31.

Gould, Carole. "For Richer or Poorer," *Savvy*. June, 1985: 18–19.

———— "Low Antes for High Stakes," *Savvy*. October, 1985: 8.

———— "Money Action: Home is Where the Cash is," *Savvy*. March, 1986: 8–9.

Gumpert, David E. "Where Business Plans Go Wrong," *Working Woman*. December 1983: 119–120.

Jaroslawicz, Isaac M. "Getting a Good Start in Investing," *The Learning Annex*. July, 1985.

Ketcham, Diane. "Small Entrepreneurs Join to Buy a Shopping Center," *The New York Times*. Sunday, July 15, 1985.

Lampert, Hope. "Just Tell Us What You Want," *Savvy*. November, 1984: 69–72.

Larkin, Marilynn."How I Financed My Business" *Sylvia Porter's Personal Finance*. November, 1986: 62–67.

LeFan, Mike. "Your Money and the News" *Modern Maturity*. August/September, 1986: 79.

Lipper, Arther III. *Investing in Private Companies*. (Homewood, IL: Dow Jones–Irwin, 1984).

Neimark, Jill. "Matching the Wealthy With the Worthy," *Ms*. November, 1984: 100–105.

Nicholas, Ted. *Cash: How To Get it Into and Out of Your Corporation*. (Wilmington, DE: Enterprise Publishing, 1980).

Posner, Bruce G. "Real Entrepreneurs Don't Plan," *Inc*. November, 1985: 129–135.

Roy, Susan. "Between Friends," *Savvy*. February, 1984: 28.

Sasseen, Jane. "Ledger Domain," *Savvy*. May, 1984: 23–24.

Scollard, Jeannette R. *The Self-Employed Woman*. (New York: Simon & Schuster, Inc. 1985).

Shell, Roberta. "Hands On," *Inc*. December, 1985: 153.

Sills-Levy, Ellen. "Fifteen Facts of Entrepreneurial Life," *We*. Winter, 1984: 44–45.

Siverd, Bonnie. "Fixing Your Money Problems," *Working Woman*. December, 1984: 52–58.

———— "The 1984 Working Woman Report on Money Management," *Working Woman*. November, 1984: 119–122.

Wiener, Leonard. "Writing Off Your Relatives," *U.S. News and World Report*. November, 10, 1986: 74.

Wiltsee, Joseph. "Investing in Your Future," *Business Week's Guide To Careers*. February/March, 1985: 53–56.

"The Best Places to Invest," *Working Woman*. April, 1984: 101–102.

The Birmingham Area Chamber of Commerce. *Small Business Guide*. Birmingham Area Chamber of Commerce, 1982.

Chapter 5

Boardroom Books. *Business Confidential*. (New York: Boardroom Reports, Inc., 1985).

Edwards, Paul and Edwards, Sarah. *Working at Home: Everything You Need to Know About Living and Working Under the Same Roof*. (San Francisco: Jeremy P. Tarcher, 1986).

Home Office Magazine. New York: Time, Inc. Nov. 1986.

Parson, Mary Jean. *The Single Solution*. (New York: Facts on File Publications, 1987).

Chapter 6

Boardroom Books *Business Confidential*. (New York: Boardroom Books, 1985).

Culligan, Matthew J. and Greene, Dolph. *Getting Back to the Basics of Public Relations and Publicity*. (New York: Crown Publishers, Inc., 1982).

Culligan, Matthew J. *Getting Back to the Basics of Selling*. (New York: Crown Publishers, Inc., 1981).

"Getting Ready for Showtime." *Inc*. August, 1986: 87.

Kurtz, David L. and Boone, Louis E. *Marketing*. (New York: The Dryden Press, 1981).

"Mining for Gold in Yellow Pages," *U.S. News and World Report*, October 13, 1986: 53.

Parson, Mary Jean. *Back to Basics: Planning*. (New York: Facts on File Publications, 1985).

Ries, Al and Trout, Jack. *Positioning: The Battle for your Mind*. New York: McGraw-Hill Book Company, 1981).

Zikmund, William G. *Exploring Marketing Research. (New York: CBS Publishing, 1982)*.

Chapter 7

"Do It Yourself Publishing," *Inc*. June, 1986: 134.

Goodloe, Alfred; Bensahel, Jane; and Keely, John. *Managing Yourself*. (New York: Alexander Hamilton Institute, Inc., 1984).

"How to Publish Yourself" *U.S. News and World Report*. September 15, 1986: 58.

Lorayne, Harry and Lucan, Jerry. *The Memory Book*. (New York: Stein and Day Publishers, 1975).

Love, Sidney F. *Mastery and Management of Time*. (Englewood Cliffs, NJ: Prentice Hall, Inc., 1978).

"Taking A Good Look at the Clones," *The New York Times*. December 28, 1986: 14F.

"The CompuBug." *The Birmingham News*. December 8, 1986: 12D.

"Tricks for Saving on Toll Calls," *U.S. News and World Report*. August 25, 1986: 45.

"Turning Out the Write Stuff," *U.S. News and World Report*. October 27, 1986: 53.

Wild, Ray. *How to Manage*. (New York: Facts on File Publications, 1985).

Chapter 8

Alihan, Milla, Ph.D. *Corporate Etiquette*. (New York: Weybright and Talley, Inc., 1974).

Boardroom Books. *Business Confidential*. (New York: Boardroom Reports, Inc., 1985).

Christie, Linda Gail. *Human Resources*. (Englewood Cliffs, NJ: Prentice Hall, Inc., 1983).

Goldstein, Arnold S., Esq. *Basic Book of Business Agreements*. (Wilmington, DE: Enterprise Publishing, Inc., 1983).

Horn, Jack. *Manager's Factomatic*. (Englewood Cliffs, NJ: Prentice Hall, Inc., 1978).

Job Analysis. (Philadelphia: Hay and Associates, 1975).

Lorentzen, John F. *The Manager's Personnel Problem Solver*. (Englewood Cliffs, NJ: Prentice Hall, Inc., 1980).

Parson, Mary Jean. *An Executive's Coaching Handbook*. (New York: Facts on File Publications, 1986).

Verification of Previous Employment. Chicago, IL: MKM Consultants, Inc., 1980).

Chapter 9

Boardroom Books. *Business Confidential*. (New York: Boardroom Reports, Inc., 1985).

Parson, Mary Jean. *The Single Solution*. (New York: Facts on File Publications, Inc., 1987).

Scollard, Jeannette R. *The Self-Employed Woman*. (New York: Simon & Schuster, Inc., 1985).

Chapter 11

A Living Will
Concern for Dying
250 W. 57th St.
New York, NY 10107

A Checklist for Dying
Bisson Century, Inc.
3008-1 13th Ave. S.
Birmingham, AL 35205

How to Avoid Probate Kit
Homestead Publishing Company
4455 Torrance Blvd. #220
Torrance, CA 90503

Chapter 12

"Changing Course," *U.S. News and World Report*. October 6, 1986: 46–51.

Cuff, Daniel F. "Exploring Strategies That Work," *Personal Investing:* 43.

Currier, Chet. "Some Firms Buy, Sell Limited Partnerships," *The Birmingham News*. Monday, September 15, 1986: 11D.

H & R Block. *1987 Tax-Saver System*. (New York: Macmillan Publishing Company, 1986).

Kindred, Ingrid. "Financial Planning Industry Newly Spawned by Complex World of Taxes and Investments," *The Birmingham News*. Monday, October 27, 1986: 8D.

——— "What Are You Worth?" *The Birmingham News*. Monday, January 19, 1987: 11D.

Schiffres, Manuel. "Money," *U.S. News and World Report*. November 24, 1986: 56–58.

Silverman, Evelyn. *How to Invest Wisely*. (New York: Bantam Books, 1968).

Vreeland, Leslie N. "A Guide to the 10 Biggest Fund Families," *Money*. November, 1986: 215–29.

"The Dean Witter Tax Reform Guide," Dean, Witter, Reynolds, Inc. New York City. 1986 2–9.

"What is a Ginnie Mae?" *AARP News Bulletin*. January, 1987: 7.

"Where and How to Invest Now," *Sylvia Porter's Personal Finance*. October, 1986: 34–40.

Chapter 13

Antilla, Susan. "Get Rich Quick," *Savvy*. September, 1986: 45–51.

Card, Emily. "How to Survive a Money Crisis," *Ms*. April, 1984: 15–18.

Fraser, Jill A. "Is This Your Kind of Place?" *Savvy*. July, 1984: 46–51.

"IRA's on a Tightrope in Congress," *U.S. News and World Report*. July 28, 1986: 38.

Kling, Samuel G. *Your Legal Advisor*. (New York: Permabook, 1955).

Kreisman, Richard. "How Start-Up Franchisors Fail" *Inc*. September, 1986: 106–8.

Kyd, Charles W. "How Fast Is Too Fast" *Inc*. December, 1986: 123–126.

Lee, Barbara. "Scaling the Pyramid," *Savvy*. September, 1983: 47.

Siverd, Bonnie. "Money," *Working Woman*. July, 1983: 43–44.

Woods, Cynthia O. "Financial Counselor," *The Executive Female*. March/April, 1984: 58.

"Wanted," *Mature Outlook*. January/February, 1986.

"What Will They Do in Retirement? Young Professionals Can't Imagine," *The Wall Street Journal*. Thursday, December 12, 1985.

"Who Owns Corporate America?" *U.S. News and World Report*. July 21, 1986: 36–44.

Index